Belinda Alexandra's bestselling books have been published around the world, in the United States, Spain, France, Germany, the United Kingdom, Turkey, Hungary and Poland. She is the daughter of a Russian mother and an Australian father, and has been fascinated by world culture and travel since her youth. She lives in Sydney with her three black cats and a garden full of interesting wildlife. Her hobbies include dancing, piano and foreign languages. A lover of all creatures, Belinda volunteers with several animal charities.

Website: belinda-alexandra.com
Instagram: @belinda_alexandra_author
Facebook: @BelindaAlexandraAuthor

ALSO BY BELINDA ALEXANDRA

**Fiction**
*White Gardenia*
*Wild Lavender*
*Silver Wattle*
*Tuscan Rose*
*Golden Earrings*
*Sapphire Skies*
*Southern Ruby*
*The Invitation*
*The Mystery Woman*
*The French Agent*

**Non-Fiction**
*The Divine Feline: A Chic Cat Lady's Guide to Woman's Best Friend*

# EMBOLDENED

## BELINDA ALEXANDRA

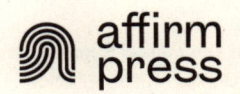

affirm press

**affirm press**

First published by Affirm Press in 2023
Boon Wurrung Country
28 Thistlethwaite Street
South Melbourne VIC 3205
affirmpress.com.au
10 9 8 7 6 5 4 3 2 1

Text copyright © Belinda Alexandra, 2023

All rights reserved. No part of this publication may be reproduced without prior written permission from the publisher.

Every effort has been made to trace copyright holders and to obtain their permission for the use of copyright material. The publisher apologises for any errors or omissions and would be grateful if notified of any corrections that should be incorporated into future editions and reprints of this book.

While this is a work of non-fiction, the names and identifying details of some people have been changed to protect their privacy.

A catalogue record for this book is available from the National Library of Australia

ISBN: 9781922848376 (paperback)

Cover design by Andy Warren
Typeset in Garamond Premier Pro by J&M Typesetting
Proudly printed in Australia by McPherson's Printing Group

MIX
Paper | Supporting responsible forestry
FSC® C001695

Extract on page 224 is taken from *The Tales of Snugglepot and Cuddlepie* by May Gibbs, 1918 © The Northcott Society and the Cerebral Palsy Alliance

*For Kelly, Catherine and Maggie*

## A NOTE ON RUSSIAN NAMES

There are a number of transliteration systems for romanising Russian names from the Cyrillic alphabet into the Latin alphabet. I decided to use the way my family members had written their own names in English, which then created inconsistencies with the most common transliteration of the names of some Russian public figures. For the sake of clarity and ease of use for English speakers, the transliteration system employed in *Emboldened* is a mixed one.

**EMBOLDEN:** to impart boldness or courage; to instil with boldness, courage, or resolution enough to overcome timidity or misgiving.

*Merriam-Webster Dictionary*

# CONTENTS

| | |
|---|---|
| Introduction | 1 |
| Resilience | 7 |
| Purpose | 89 |
| Passion | 191 |
| Connection | 219 |
| Final Words | 265 |
| Acknowledgements | 271 |
| Bibliography | 273 |

# INTRODUCTION

Several years ago, I went through a disastrous experience that affected every area of my life. It felt as if I was falling down the side of a mountain. I tumbled, my feet sliding in the gravel as I tried to grab at rocky outcrops and clumps of grass to stop my momentum. At one point I was left dangling by my fingertips on a metaphoric cliff and I thought, somewhat optimistically, *Well, at least I still have my health.* But then that went too and over the edge I toppled, arms and legs flailing.

Because this story involves other living people, and the laws of Australia are what they are, I can't tell you exactly what happened to me: only that one cold winter's night I fled my home in fear for my life, after having gotten my pets and a few sentimental items out the day before. I had only my wallet, my phone and my latest manuscript on a USB stick. I left an entire life behind.

I had to begin again, sitting on a cardboard box in my father's spare room. I was shattered and traumatised. I didn't even know if it was possible for me to rebuild my life or whether I was going to be broken forever. So, I gave myself an image.

'You are a supernova,' I told my crushed spirit.

A supernova is a star that has exploded and splintered into millions of pieces. Although that star is destroyed forever, the material that is projected out into space from it can be recycled to form another star, or perhaps even another planet or new life forms. The destruction is loaded with positive potential.

By giving myself this metaphor, I was telling myself a powerful story. Not one of a victim, but one of infinite possibilities – even if all I was at that point was a nebula, a giant cloud of dust moving through space.

The other, more elaborate story I gave myself was that I named that spare room 'Belinda HQ'. From my love of history, I thought of those valiant people who had fought in the French Resistance in the Second World War. The German invasion of France in 1940 hit the country like a lightning strike. Most of the citizens accepted the occupation and many actively collaborated with the Nazis. Only a brave few risked torture and death to hide out in barns, farmhouses and forests to resist. I tried to instil myself with their courage. I wasn't fighting anyone. The damage had been done, and there was no point avenging the past. I was summoning up the strength to get up on my own two feet again and to slay my fears that I wouldn't succeed. What had happened to me wasn't considered a crime in Australia at that time. It was poorly understood and it didn't even have a proper name. Therefore, I didn't know who to turn to in the aftermath of triggers and terrifying nightmares, and the hypervigilance that would see me pacing up and down that spare room for hours, trying to calm my nervous system. Nobody gets PTSD from something that doesn't exist.

I look back on myself as I was then with compassion, but also with a sense of awe. Because I *did* get up. I *did* create a new life – a happy and thriving one. I was doing the very best I could with all the knowledge I had at that time, and nobody can ask more of themselves than that.

Nevertheless, a year after the event, in the midst of this new life, my physical health deteriorated from all the stress. It was only then that I sought help from a psychologist, who looked me in the eye and said:

## Introduction

'What you have been through is the same level of trauma a hostage experiences in a siege situation. I'm amazed you are still standing at all.'

I knew I was still standing because I had emboldened myself, and I had done it by telling myself true stories of courage and resilience.

~

My mother was a tremendous storyteller. As a child she enthralled me with stories of my ancestors, people of the vast Russian Empire – Russians, Ukrainians, Poles, Latvians, Estonians, Lithuanians, as well as some Finns and Swedes. Their stories were epic and often tragic, but the message was always clear: life knocks you down, you get up; it knocks you down again, you get up again. When I fell off that metaphorical cliff, my heart and mind were smashed. I was sure every bone in my body was broken. I didn't see how I could possibly stand up. When I did eventually raise myself, tottering on shaking legs, I dusted myself off and lurched forward, not certain of my direction, but moving nonetheless.

It wasn't pretty, and it wasn't particularly heroic or graceful, but I felt I was doing what humans are naturally designed to do and what our ancestors have always done. We get up, move forward and try to learn from whatever has happened to us.

That was how life was presented to me. That was the *story* I had always been told. My parents demonstrated that narrative to me in their own lives. My mother reinforced it with the coming-of-age stories she gave me to read – *Black Beauty*, *Little Women*, *Great Expectations*. I reinforced it in myself with my addiction to reading biographies – the life stories of entertainers, artists, writers, human-rights activists and environmentalists, as well as the stories of ordinary people who had overcome some adversity and had gone on to become extraordinary: they became emboldened.

Biographies gave me a certain point of view about life. It seems that many of us have some significant event that occurs in our childhood or youth, some sort of life-changing adversity, and the rest of our life is spent resolving, understanding and overcoming it, and eventually making peace with it. In some sad cases, if the event isn't dealt with, it usually destroys the person involved. It's as if we are all given a divine assignment and the choice is ours about how to complete it.

Most writers are familiar with 'the hero's journey'. But if you haven't heard of it, you will recognise the concept. George Lucas, the creator of *Star Wars*, said he followed this story structure to create one of the most successful movie sagas of all time. Across Hollywood, screenwriters use it to write everything from romantic comedies to horror movies.

In 1949, an American mythologist named Joseph Campbell compared several classical myths and developed the theory that they shared a common structure that he believed came from deep within the human subconscious. A hero or heroine will be given a quest that will require them to leave their ordinary world and overcome various trials and temptations, as well as find a mentor and gather like-minded companions on their journey. They will go through a series of trials and endure many dark nights of the soul. These will cause the hero or heroine to draw upon the strength they need for the final supreme ordeal when they must face their nemesis, whether it be a beast or a mortal enemy. After overcoming these obstacles and being victorious, the hero or heroine is profoundly changed. They may return to their ordinary world, but they are now more effective and happier in it.

There is power in stories, and the storyteller traditionally played an important role in ancient societies. Their job was to create a virtual reality, in which their listeners could try on the courage of heroes and heroines for themselves and also be reminded that, in the darkest of times, the sun will always shine again.

# Introduction

~

There is so much power in the stories we tell ourselves and each other, and in the meaning we decide to assign to certain events. The stories we choose can either frighten us or strengthen our resolve. In emboldening myself, I told my soul stories of resilience, purpose, passion and connection. I was not interested in stories of revenge or anger or being a victim. They would have only made me bitter and unable to transform my supernova dust cloud into a new star or planet.

It is my hope that I can take on the role of the storyteller for you, and that I will embolden you with the stories that helped me find my courage in one of the darkest and most challenging times of my life.

~

Before we begin, I want to be clear that this book is in no way prescriptive. I won't be telling you what you *should* do to be emboldened. I'll be sharing some incredible stories with you and my own responses to them. I hope that you will use your own critical faculties to decide which aspects of these stories may work for you on your journey. It is certainly not a self-help book, or a motivational or philosophical treatise. While I think that self-help books are wonderful on many levels, I also find them overly simplistic when I try to apply their advice to my own life. The subjects of the 'real-life' examples in them *appear* to go in straight lines from A to B to C. They start with a problem, find a solution and end up living a perfect life. I don't believe our human existence is like that. I think we go from A to T, then back to J, before lurching forward on to M or N. Then we catch a quick glimpse of Z, before reversing over W and finding ourselves back at G again.

Life is a bumpy ride. The struggles are real and sometimes relentless.

But the journey can ultimately be a beautiful and rich one. And overcoming the struggles are what will make it worthwhile. You already have everything inside you that you need to live life courageously and boldly. I hope that is exactly what this book inspires you to do.

# RESILIENCE

# 1

If you had to flee your home urgently, and most likely forever, what would you take with you besides your family and your pets? For many it is only a theoretical question, something to muse over, but as I write this thousands of Australians have recently lost everything in floods and bushfires. Many people have lost their homes to a financial or health crisis, and we now know that the leading cause of homelessness for women in this country is domestic violence. Those of us who have lost a home will all tell ourselves a similar thing: 'My family and pets are alive, and that's what's important.' And that's absolutely true. But there are moments when the loss of things you treasured, collected or preserved with care pains you. And I believe you must mourn them. There are times, too, when the realisation that you have lost something of a more practical nature triggers you: like when a friend invites you swimming and you remember why you no longer have a costume; you open the cupboard expecting to find a certain baking dish and you recall that it went with your former life; or someone asks to see a picture of you in your youthful backpacking days and you are reminded that all those photographs are gone too.

You might think that we would all take the same items when we flee our homes, but I've learned that to be far from the truth. What is true is those things we regard as precious say everything about us and what we consider to be of value.

Many years before I ran from my home, I had a taste of what that emergency decision-making process might look like.

In January 2002, I was minding my parents' home in a bushland suburb of Sydney while they were away on holiday. I had recently returned from living in New York and was in the process of putting roots down in Sydney again. After ten years of nothing but rejections for my writing, I had just signed a two-book deal and was now a full-time writer. Although I had loved travelling, I had grown tired of the rambling life and having mainly fellow travellers and expats for friends. My plan was to settle down and, as proof of it, I had acquired two kittens, Gardenia and Lilac. The Christmas that had just passed had been particularly hot, with daily temperatures in the high thirties. The yellowed, parched lawn crunched when I walked across it. The trees had taken on that limp, grey look of a dry summer. There was talk of water restrictions.

But inside my parents' house it was cool and peaceful. I was busy working on the edits for my first book, *White Gardenia*, to be published later that year. The kittens were playing with their toys around my feet. They were more like miniature mountain lions than cats. When they went quiet, I never had to look under beds or chairs to find them. They were usually perched precariously at the top of a door or clinging to a light fitting. Since they'd come into my life, there was never a painting that hung straight in the house.

But I had learned to work without letting their mayhem distract me. In fact, I had reached such levels of focus that, as the afternoon wore on, I didn't even notice the thrum of helicopters circling the sky or the wail of fire engine sirens. I had come from New York and those noises were the soundtrack to the city. I was so used to hearing them that they only existed on the periphery of my attention, although they were foreign sounds in the tranquil, leafy suburb where my parents lived.

Then the telephone rang. It was a friend of mine, Felicia.

'I'm calling because I know you don't pay attention to anything when you are working,' she told me. 'Have you turned the television on?'

'No.'

'Well, you had better. There is a massive bushfire heading your way.'

I turned the television on as she was talking. The images on it were confronting. Helicopters were dropping water on 60-foot flames and residents were filling up buckets from their swimming pools to try to defend their homes. Strong winds were blowing down from the drought-ridden, parched interior, making the spread of the fire particularly fast.

'They are saying you must stay put and that it's too dangerous for a mass evacuation,' Felicia said. 'You can pack your car and be ready to go if you are told to. But you should also decide on the most essential things to take – the things you can carry – in case you have to run.'

That sounded ominous. I took Felicia at her word because she'd once been a volunteer with the New South Wales Fire Brigades. Such strong gusts of wind could make a fire that seemed contained turn ferocious in minutes. At the same time, I wasn't panicked. I had grown up in the area and the fire warnings of my childhood had consisted of the fathers of the neighbourhood sitting on the roofs of their houses holding hoses and listening to transistor radios while the mothers manned the taps. The children played about in their gardens, unconcerned. Usually, the day would turn out to be a non-event and we'd all go back inside and have dinner.

For most people, though, that lax attitude had changed after the horror of the 1994 eastern seaboard fires. I had been away at the time, studying at the University of California. My roommates had to comfort me as I watched the horror unfolding on the television. Sydney was in flames, many of the fires having been deliberately lit during windy conditions. Thousands of homes were lost, national parks were decimated, and the fires came close to the CBD. My mother was forced to evacuate with my nephew, who was a toddler at the time, driving through the smoke to safety. My father was away at work, and I'd wished I'd been there to help her.

So, while I wasn't particularly scared, I wasn't complacent either.

I saved my work to a floppy disk (remember them?), emailed a copy to a friend, put the cat carrier next to me, and packed my wallet and toothbrush in a small backpack. That was me done, but what about my parents? This was their home, and it contained a lifetime of memories. Where did I even begin? I went to my mother's glass bookcase and took out a photograph album containing pictures of her side of the family, all of them long since dead. It was embossed leather with a picture of a sampan on the cover. It had come all the way from China and had survived many disasters – both natural and man-made. Whatever happened, my mother could not lose it. I put it in my backpack along with other items that I knew to be precious to her: a ring that had been formed by melding together the wedding bands of my grandparents and then set with a stone of amethyst, a favourite Russian gem; a silver icon; and a silver and crystal tankard mug.

I went out into the back garden. The sky was smoky with a foreboding tinge of red. My father was good about regularly clearing out the gutters, raking up dead leaves, and not leaving rubbish lying about, but weren't there other things I was supposed to be doing to protect my parents' house? My mind ran over what I had been taught at school. I began moving the garden furniture into the garage and removing the doormats. I remembered something about hosing the garden and the house, but then hesitated. What if I affected the water pressure from other places in the suburb that needed it more urgently?

The telephone rang and I went back inside. It was my mother on the line.

'Go speak to Ian at Number 10,' she told me. 'He'll help you. He's an ex-army captain and will know what to do. He ought to know that you are at the house alone anyway.'

She hung up before I could ask her which items she wanted me to take. I looked back to the television, but I couldn't tell if things were getting better or worse, so I went in search of Ian. He was a new neighbour who had moved in while I had been away, and I liked the idea of someone who would know 'what to do'. I probably judge myself too harshly – I have extricated myself from tricky situations while travelling with quick thinking – but I've never thought of myself as a particularly practical person. If you need someone for emotional support, a short story or an interpretive dance, I'm your woman, but as for what to do in an emergency situation, I felt I was in unchartered territory.

Ian had a sign on his letterbox to let the fire service know he had a backyard swimming pool, and I glimpsed a figure disappearing around the side of his house wearing a protective suit and guessed it was him. Both were indications that Ian was the right person to help me. But when I stepped into his back garden, I found him grey in the face and trembling. After a strong start, my would-be hero seemed to be floundering. He was trying to take the frame off a large painting. I glanced at his car and saw it was packed so tightly with artwork that the driver wouldn't be able to see out of the back window.

'I can't get the thing off,' Ian said, aware that I was standing next to him but not particularly bothered that he didn't know me. 'I'm not leaving this behind no matter what.'

A twist of my gut told me that Ian may not be the hero I was hoping for, and if we did have to evacuate it might be me saving him. I left Ian to his artwork and went to see my former piano teacher who lived next door to my parents.

Over the years, Vivienne and her husband had transformed a small cottage into an English-style house with a garden worthy of Gertrude Jekyll: sprawling trees, statues, ponds and thickly planted garden beds. But now that the sky was turning blood red and ash was starting to fall, everything had taken on a strange Gothic atmosphere. I knocked on the door and Vivienne quickly ushered me inside.

'I was wondering if I should be doing something to protect my parents' home,' I said. 'Am I supposed to be filling the gutters with water?'

Vivienne shook her head sadly. 'When it gets like this there is little you can do except go.'

We both looked in the direction of her grand piano. It had been a gift from her parents when she entered the Sydney Conservatorium of Music. How many hours had she sat at it, perfecting her Chopin and Brahms? On jasmine-scented summer evenings when I was a child and Vivienne was practising for a recording or a concert, my mother used to turn the television off and we would listen to the beautiful music together: our own neighbourhood concert.

For a worrying moment, I thought Vivienne might have given way to fatalism, and was going to face the bushfire playing her piano the way the stoic musicians on the *Titanic* carried on playing as the ship sank. It would have been easier if Vivienne had mastered the flute or the violin. But everything in Vivienne's life was big – her house, her garden, even her musical instrument.

We went outside, and she pulled a pair of secateurs from her pocket and took a couple of plant cuttings. 'I grew these from cuttings taken from my mother's garden,' she told me. 'Perhaps I will be able to grow them again.'

It occurred to me that if we did have to evacuate we would make a funny little procession: me with my kittens and stash of family heirlooms, Ian and his oversized artworks, and Vivienne and her plants.

I returned to my house and rang a friend who had been living in the south of Sydney when the 1994 fires had been at their worst. From what I'd seen on television, not everyone had driven out in their cars in an orderly fashion. Some people had fled for their lives on foot.

'What did you take?' I asked her.

'I packed clean underwear and deodorant.'

It seemed to me those things could be bought on a credit card and I would rather take something irreplaceable. I asked her what her husband Bob had packed.

'All his receipts for the tax year,' she answered. 'He was expecting a big return that year and wasn't going to miss out on it.'

That sounded exactly like Bob. He has a pathological resentment of the taxation department.

After an anxious night's wait, the valiant efforts of the firefighters and community volunteers combined with the wind easing meant that the danger had been averted. I could continue editing my book with my kittens batting pens off my desk, Vivienne could carry on playing beautiful music and watering her garden, and Ian could spend the next week reframing and rehanging his paintings.

But when I took the photograph album and other items from my backpack to put back in my mother's glass bookcase, I remembered that fleeing from their homes in terror, or being dragged out of them, had been a reality for nearly everyone whose picture was in that album. I had never met any of them and yet I knew them all intimately. They had been kept alive by my mother's stories about them, and by the objects they had taken from their homes before they ran from them.

## 2

My family must have a penchant for choosing sentimental things over practical ones when they are about to take flight from danger. In our possession we have a silver and crystal tankard mug that has travelled vast distances over continents and battlefields. It has survived not only wars and revolutions but also hurricanes and corrupt customs officials. Carved on its body is the double-headed eagle, the symbol of Imperial Russia, a grand empire that looked to both the east and west. The shield on it depicts St Michael slaying the dragon. It was presented to my maternal grandfather, Pavel Puntakoff, by the last Tsar of Russia, Nicholas II.

Although Pavel died when my mother was four years old, my grandmother, Alexandra, kept him alive in her daughter's imagination – as my mother would do later for me. For, while I have never heard his voice, I feel close to the man in my mother's photograph album. We have the same dark eyes and the same high cheekbones. He represents a passionate, adventurous and heroic ancestry that I often remind myself of when I am feeling faint-hearted, discouraged and rather ordinary. He was a Russian with heritage linked to the Finnish Vikings who settled in Russia in the mid-9th century. He was a strong yet gentle man. He read poetry, and his favourite poet was Alexander Pushkin.

The occasion of Pavel receiving the mug was his graduation as an officer in the Russian Imperial Army in the last days of the First World War. Things were not going well for the Russians – nor the Tsar. There had been a surge of nationalism at the beginning of the war, but that was now fading with economic and social unrest, and outrage at the increasing influence that a debauched monk named Rasputin was holding over the Imperial Family. Nearly three hundred years of Romanov rule was at risk of coming to an ignoble end. Nonetheless, Pavel put aside his university studies to join the military in those fraught last days. The son of a family of merchants and intellectuals, Pavel may have wished that the Tsar would modernise, as the British monarchy had and as the Tsar's advisers were telling him to do, but he would have also supported the traditional values of Mother Russia and the Orthodox Church.

I imagine Pavel on the day of his graduation, cleanly shaven, with his uniform meticulously pressed and his boots polished to a high shine, waiting for his turn to be acknowledged by the Tsar. Afterwards, when things were relaxed, he would have slapped the backs of his fellow officer graduates and offered his congratulations, particularly to his best friend from his home town of Ufa, a young Russian Tatar named Azat. The Tatars are an ethnic group of Turkish origins who were famous for their horsemanship.

While Russians toast with vodka, the celebratory drink of the Russian Court and the higher ranks of the army was Russian Imperial stout – hence the presentation of a tankard beer mug. It was a tradition set by Peter the Great, who enjoyed strong, dark English beers and had them specially shipped to St Petersburg.

But things would change rapidly in Russia after Pavel's graduation. He did not fight against the Germans as he had anticipated, but against his own countrymen. The Tsar to whom he had sworn his loyalty was forced to abdicate, and was then butchered, along with the Tsarina and their children, by the Bolsheviks in the basement of a house in Yekaterinburg.

After the collapse of the monarchy, my grandfather joined the White Army, which had been formed by Imperial generals loyal to Mother Russia. The Civil War was a bitter battle that lasted for five years. Pavel was promoted to colonel in his cavalry unit, the cavalry working like shock troops in battle. You may have heard the saying, 'Send in the cavalry'? It was the cavalry's role to see weaknesses in the opposing army's defences, and then ride in for surprise flanking attacks.

It was during the final days of the war and a particularly fierce battle when Pavel was shot several times and slashed with a sword. He fell from his horse – the worst possible scenario. The horse bolted to freedom, and he was left on the battlefield as his battalion retreated. All around was the acrid smell of gunpowder and the moans of the dying. He must have looked up at the clear blue sky and thought that he was done for. Did he think of his beloved mother and father at home? Or about his two pretty red-haired sisters who always loved to tease their older brother? He would never see them married now. He was barely twenty-three years old, and he would neither marry nor have a family himself. But he had fought bravely and would have to be satisfied with that.

> I've lived to bury my desires,
> And see my dreams corrode with rust;
> Now all that's left are fruitless fires
> That burn my empty heart to dust.
>
> Struck by the clouds of cruel Fate
> My crown of summer bloom is sere;
> Alone and sad I watch and wait
> And wonder if the end is near.

> As conquered by the last cold air,
> When winter whistles in the wind,
> Alone upon a branch that's bare
> A trembling leaf is left behind.
>
> Alexander Pushkin

As his eyes closed, and the sounds of fighting and the dying began to fade, he heard another sound. A voice calling out to him by the familiar form of his name.

'Pasha! Pasha!'

It was the deep, sonorous voice of Azat, his second-in-command. Although Azat had been told Pavel had fallen, he would not leave his commander and best friend for dead. He rode back into the heat of the battle and searched among the mutilated dead for my grandfather. Pavel squinted at the face of his friend, backlit by the sun, then felt himself lifted by strong arms onto Azat's horse. The two young men were not out of danger yet, and Azat had to navigate away from enemy fire. To reach the military hospital, he had to ride across a flowing river. As the icy water reached the horse's neck, Pavel wondered if they would make it to the other side. But Azat was an expert horseman, and the animal was surefooted under his direction. With no penicillin, and with morphine in short supply, my grandfather must have been strong to survive his injuries. Thanks to his friend's loyalty, he would get the chance to marry and have a child. When my mother was born years later in Harbin, China, Pavel, a deeply devoted member of the Russian Orthodox Church, asked Azat, an equally devoted Muslim, to be her godfather.

~

In the first years of the Civil War, the White Army was successful in winning back territory from the Red Army. They had the help of the Allies, who were keen to keep Russia involved in the war against Germany. But the White Army did not have the support of the peasantry, which made up the majority of the population and did not want a return of the Tsar. This, coupled with the fact that the Bolsheviks had control of the major munitions factories within the country, made it a war that the White Army couldn't win and they were driven back further into Siberia. Eventually, the remnants of the defeated White Army crossed the border into Manchuria, China, and headed for the northern city of Harbin. In their wake came thousands of others fleeing from the Red Army and persecution by the communists – people of the aristocratic and bourgeois classes, intellectuals, artists, writers, ballet dancers and priests, as well as a number of Cossacks.

For the Russians pouring into China after the Civil War, Harbin was a home away from home. In the late 1800s, many Russians had come to work on the Chinese Eastern Railway, an extension of the Trans-Siberian Railway and a joint venture between Russia and China. Harbin, on the Songhua River, was where many of the administrators, engineers and workers had settled with their families. It was a city of onion-domed Orthodox churches, as well as the Russified version of Art Nouveau buildings, garnished with floral motifs, ornate windows and embellished balconies. With its Russian street names, wide cobblestoned boulevards and grand parks, Harbin was often referred to as the 'Moscow of the Orient'. There was a substantial Chinese population as well, but it was Russian that was most widely spoken. The Russian residents called themselves *Harbinsky*, and the cultural life was rich, with a Russian symphony orchestra as well as ballet and opera companies. Bookshops and literary salons abounded.

After five years of fighting for Mother Russia and its values, military defeat must have been a crushing blow for my grandfather. But if he had any consolation, it was meeting my grandmother, Alexandra Pohelin.

~

Born in Moscow to a Latvian father and a mother from a mix of ethnicities, including Polish and Ukrainian, my grandmother came to Harbin as a young child when her father, Mikhail, was employed as an engineer on the Chinese Eastern Railway. Alexandra was a vivacious woman with sparkling eyes and a full mouth, who laughed uproariously at almost anything. She was kind and made friends easily, and she never let life get her down for long. In fact, anyone I have ever met who knew my grandmother said words to this effect: 'She had a knack for making the best of whatever situation life handed her.'

~

Although I never had the chance to meet Grandmother Alexandra, that description of her has always stayed in my heart. What a beautiful characteristic to have people remember you by. What a statement of resilience. There is so much that happens to us that we have no control over, and as you will see when I continue the story of my grandmother, she had to endure some devastating events. She could have played the victim. She could have given up. But she was like those cooks who open the cupboard to find they have only three ingredients and, instead of going into meltdown, somehow manage to produce a delicious meal. That was how she approached life. There was no use crying over spilt milk, or lamenting over what could not be changed. This was life, and if life only gave you three ingredients, then you would have to find a way to make it work, to make it worth living and to make it beautiful. In that way she understood the art of life better than those of us with a tendency to make mountains out of molehills.

My grandparents were introduced by one of Harbin's matchmakers. The officers who had escaped from Russia were introduced to suitable young ladies from the local community over elegant afternoon teas. For Russians, tea is not simply a beverage – it is something that warms you, wakes you up and is a lubricant for social interaction.

Traditionally, Russians use a samovar – a metal urn that boils water – to make tea. I still have the decorative one that my grandmother bought off a friend when she came to Australia.

Although my own mother always drank her tea black with a slice of lemon, I remember in my childhood being quite fascinated by one of her friend's husbands, who would place a sugar cube between his teeth and sip his tea through it, assuring me that was how most Russian men prefer to drink tea, although I can't imagine it was any good for his teeth. When I travelled through Russia myself, and I visited someone in their home, I was always served tea with a small plate of delicious strawberry or blackberry jam but no bread or crackers to spread it over. It took me a while to work out that you were supposed to put the jam in your tea to sweeten it.

I can't say how my grandparents drank their tea on the day that they met, but if there is one thing I can surmise about Grandfather Pavel, it is that he wasn't an overthinker. He was obviously an intelligent man – he had been a university student and he liked poetry, so he wasn't all animal instinct. But to lead a cavalry charge he couldn't afford to focus on the chance of being hurt or killed, although they were very real – and somewhat likely – possibilities.

It seems that when he spotted Alexandra across the room, sharing a joke with friends, he knew what he wanted and wasn't timid or hesitant about it. He asked her to dance a foxtrot to the jazz tune being played on the gramophone, and it appears that his mind was quickly made up. He wasn't going to lose her to the competition. They were engaged soon afterwards and married a year later.

~

Alexandra's optimism and kindness must have made her an uplifting partner for Pavel, who had left behind his beloved country and family in such turbulent circumstances. Although he had married happily, he still faced much heartbreak. When the leader of the Russian Revolution, Vladimir Lenin, died in 1924, he was replaced by the ruthless Joseph Stalin. To consolidate his power, Stalin was determined to get rid of anyone he considered a threat to his position. He instigated a series of show trials, where the evidence was faked and confessions were obtained under torture. Soon the purges spread from the political sphere into the Red Army. So many of the high command were sent to gulags that when Germany attacked the Soviet Union in 1941, the country was woefully short of experienced military leaders.

Soon it was ordinary citizens who were bearing the brunt of Stalin's paranoia. Anyone considered an 'enemy of the state' could be picked up in the middle of the night by the secret police and either executed or sent to a gulag. Those belonging to the former aristocratic or merchant classes were the most common targets. Things became especially dangerous when people began denouncing each other to the secret police to avoid being denounced themselves. Shortages of materials and components were rife at factories, due to the regime's inefficient systems of production and distribution. Yet any factory manager who failed to meet Stalin's unrealistic quotas could find themselves accused of being a 'wrecker'. Such was the spread of terror, almost everyone kept an emergency travel bag packed with necessities in case they should suddenly be arrested. Nobody kept journals. Anything written down could be turned into fake evidence. Eventually, the situation became so ridiculous that, as in the words of Valentin Orlov from my novel *Sapphire Skies*, 'Everyday, people were arrested and shot for nothing more than accidentally bumping a portrait of Stalin or wiping their backsides with a piece of newspaper with his image on it.'

It was in these circumstances that Pavel's younger brother met a terrible fate. Foolish and full of bravado as any sixteen-year-old boy can be, he drew a caricature of Stalin in his schoolbook and was denounced by his teacher. He was taken away by the secret police and shot. Pavel's parents were sent to a gulag, where they were worked to death, and his two sisters had to quickly marry commissars – members of the Communist Party whose job it was to indoctrinate people with political ideas and instruct them on correct behaviour – in order to avoid the same fate. All ties they had with my grandfather were severed. To Pavel, it must have felt as if a tsunami had passed through his life, sweeping away all that he had loved and treasured in a devastating assault of madness.

~

My grandfather's hatred for Stalin has run right down my family line. Once when I was very young, still at home with my mother, a picture of Stalin flashed on the television screen and she pointed at it and said with intense bitterness: 'There is the man who killed your great-uncle!' To this day, I cannot look at a picture of Stalin, with his brushed-back hair and walrus moustache, without my gut twisting. He appears in several scenes in *Sapphire Skies*, and when writing about him I found all over again that the duplicity he displayed towards people who trusted him gave me chills. I would have to take long breaks after putting him down on paper, as if to shake his evil off me.

Later, the millions of innocent people who were killed during Stalin's purges would be declared 'rehabilitated' by an order issued by Soviet President Mikhail Gorbachev in 1990. I don't know what consolation that is, because to me it just emphasises the shocking waste of life for no good reason.

~

Even in China, Pavel wasn't safe from Stalin's clutches. The Soviet Union sent out assassins to kill anyone who might be a threat to Stalin's regime, including those who had held prominent positions in the White Army. When his friend, a fellow White Army colonel, was assassinated, my grandfather knew that even Harbin was not a refuge for him. He organised a passage to Brazil for himself and Alexandra, but at the last moment her beloved sister, Irina, fell gravely ill. It was decided that Alexandra would remain with her until she was better, and would follow my grandfather later.

The trip to Brazil took three months by sea. On the ship, Pavel studied Portuguese from a textbook and practised with the Portuguese crew, so that by the time he reached Brazil he was able to speak the language well. He initially worked on a banana plantation outside of São Paulo, and then later went to Rio de Janeiro where he found a position as a motorcycle policeman. He sent back a photograph of himself to my grandmother, sitting on a park bench and looking dapper in a white suit and Panama hat. He was a handsome man with chiselled features, a trim moustache and deep-set, soulful eyes.

~

When I began travelling myself, I often thought of my grandfather. I journeyed through Asia and Europe. I went to university in California and worked in New York. I had an insatiable desire to see things and understand other cultures; my journeys were about growth and self-fulfilment. My grandfather had been obliged to travel to create a new life for himself out of the rubble of his old one. I learned foreign languages out of interest; he out of necessity. It must have been an honour when he was accepted into university in Russia before the war. I can imagine the pride that it would have brought his parents, who had hoped for a bright future for their son. But his life was turning out differently to the one he had planned. At thirty, he was sailing away from everything familiar: his family and homeland were gone, and his young wife was far away in China.

I especially thought of him when I travelled to Moscow to research *White Gardenia*. Ten years earlier, on 25 December 1991, the Soviet hammer-and-sickle flag had been lowered for the last time over the Kremlin. Russia was no longer a communist country but an independent state. Pavel had lived for that moment, but never got to see it.

A remarkable event happened when I was walking along Arbat Street, in the historical centre of Moscow. It was early January, and I was rugged up in a thick coat and snow boots. I stopped in front of the Tiffany-blue apartment building, where the Romantic poet and novelist Alexander Pushkin had lived with his wife Natalia after they were first married. Pushkin was the great-grandson of an African slave boy named Gannibal who had been kidnapped by the Ottomans and later presented as a 'gift' to Peter the Great. The Tsar was so impressed by the boy's intelligence, he adopted him as his godson, and Gannibal went on to become an important member of the Imperial Court. His great-grandson Alexander would become revered as the father of modern Russian literature. That day on Arbat Street, I was thinking about my grandfather's love of Pushkin's poetry when I was suddenly overcome by such a strong feeling of joy that it took my breath away. The world shimmered vividly around me, and I had an urge to sing and dance all at once. Some spark seemed to have ignited in me. It was one of those moments when you feel in the presence of something larger than yourself, lifting you up higher and higher, so that for a moment you feel that you have a bird's-eye view of the world.

Then the sensation vanished almost as quickly as it had come, and once again I was simply another person standing on a snowy street in Moscow. I have no idea what happened that day, but I like to think that perhaps it was a sublime moment of genetic memory, and that maybe in some magical way I had taken Grandfather Pavel back to his beloved Russia. Perhaps he had hitchhiked on my DNA.

~

Rio de Janeiro, that seaside metropolis and melting pot of cultures, agreed with Pavel. His letters to Alexandra were full of enthusiasm for the warm weather and hot-blooded people. He wrote of the scenic promenades – something that would have appealed to the Russian love of strolling in your best clothes to see and be seen – and the golden sand of Copacabana Beach, with the jungle-clad mountains as its backdrop. He described the elegant cafes and tearooms where one could sit for hours with friends, enjoying the splendour of the mirrored surfaces, the marble counters and the skylights. He tried to persuade her to join him and make the city their new home. And as part of his campaign, he sent her that picture of himself sitting in the Botanical Garden, looking tanned and sophisticated in his white suit and Panama hat.

But Alexandra did not want to be separated from the Russian community in Harbin, and Irina and her husband Boris did not want to live in South America, which was prone to political upheavals and revolutions of its own. Alexandra would not go anywhere without her sister, so Pavel decided to return to Harbin. Circumstances had changed in Manchuria, and the Soviets were no longer an ever-present threat to the White Russian community. However, a new danger was to come from another direction entirely.

~

The Japanese had always had their eyes on Manchuria. It was rich in natural resources and, like the Germans at the time, the Japanese saw themselves as a superior race with the right to invade neighbouring countries. Directly across the ocean from Japan, Manchuria offered the Japanese much-needed living space for their burgeoning population, as well as a sizeable market for their goods. In 1931, the Japanese army stormed the region and annexed it, declaring it an independent state by the name of 'Manchukuo'. Initially, the Japanese did not interfere with the foreigners living in China, but their attitude towards the Chinese population was brutal.

Then, in 1937, they invaded the whole of China at the cost of twenty million Chinese lives and inflicted some of the worst atrocities in modern world history. The most famous of these was the 'Rape of Nanking'. In December 1937, the Japanese army stormed the city and went on a debased killing spree during which women and children were raped, tortured and murdered, and unarmed citizens were used for bayonet practice and decapitating competitions. Many victims were thrown into ditches where they had gasoline poured over them and were burned alive. The death toll of the massacre has been estimated at 350,000 victims – more than the combined number of Japanese people killed by the atomic bombs dropped on Hiroshima and Nagasaki in 1945.

The Chinese army was practically annihilated, but resistance continued in the form of partisan warfare and underground movements.

In Harbin, the brutality was not so openly displayed, but Chinese citizens were treated poorly and humiliated. Alexandra's stomach turned when she saw that her Chinese friends were forced to stop their cars at Japanese checkpoints and bow to the Japanese soldiers who manned them.

In 1935, the Japanese bought the lease for the Chinese Eastern Railway, and this had a profound effect on the Russians in Harbin. Those who held Soviet passports were invited to repatriate to the Soviet Union. Many took up the offer, including a number of Alexandra's relatives and friends. Initially, things seemed to go well for those who returned to the Soviet Union, but when the purges got into full swing a few years later, anyone with foreign contacts fell under suspicion of being a 'wrecker'. In 1937, 48,000 *Harbinsky* were arrested as traitors. Of this number, 31,000 were executed and the rest were sent to gulags.

It was a curious thing for me, growing up in the peace and safety of Sydney, when my mother showed me the photograph album she had brought from China. It was full of sepia pictures of exotic people with sultry eyes who had met terrible fates – firing squads, assassinations, killed in air raids, worked to death in Siberia, or who had simply 'vanished'.

~

Although the Japanese occupation made finding work difficult for Pavel, the birth of my mother, Tania, brought my grandparents enormous joy. My mother's memories of the father she only had for a short while were implicit. She would recall him when she saw sunflowers or heard the deep, sonorous sounds of a man singing while working in the garden. From the photographs of them together, it is clear how much Pavel adored her. He is always lifting her up or clutching her hand. In some of them he is a playing practical joke on her: hiding behind a tree or a fence, ready to surprise her. It was just as well Alexandra owned a camera and documented the pair together, because Pavel would only be around for the first four years of Tania's life. The injuries that he had sustained in battle years earlier had damaged his heart.

One day, while Alexandra was cutting flowers and Pavel and Tania were playing in the garden, he collapsed. By the time Alexandra realised that her daughter had ceased giggling and was now kneeling next to the prone figure of Pavel, her beloved husband was already gone.

For Tania, the loss was tormenting. The Russian custom of the time was for the deceased to be laid out in the front room before burial. The curtains were drawn and the mirrors were covered with black cloth. The house was filled with the sounds of weeping of mourners and the dirge-like prayers of the Orthodox priest. The rituals were more frightening than comforting for a little girl. She was told to say goodbye to her father before the coffin was finally closed.

She crept closer to the coffin and was lifted by her uncle Boris, so that she might give her father one last kiss. His face was waxen, and his flesh was cold when she touched his hand.

'Papa. Papa,' she whispered, desperately trying to talk to him. 'Papa. Papa.'

But she received no answer.

~

My grandfather, Pavel Puntakoff, died just shy of his fortieth birthday. For my grandmother and mother it was tragic, but I can see that Pavel also lived by my grandmother's creed of always making the best of whatever life handed him. It seems that whenever his life took a twist, he met it with an equal degree of courage, and reinvented himself if necessary. He always did what needed to be done.

As someone who tends to overthink things, often to the point of overwhelming myself, I take strength in his example. I imagine him riding into battle, or confidently crossing a room to ask Alexandra to dance with him, or sailing in a leaky ship and studying Portuguese to make a living in Brazil. His life was hard, but I think a good one – even if it was cut short.

So many of us hesitate and waste time. In a way it's the luxury of our age and affluence to overthink things. These days we live longer, safer lives, but we don't always live them fully. None of us knows how much time we have and yet we are always putting things off. Life does not reward timidity; it rewards boldness.

I have a friend who uses the Nike slogan when she needs to remind herself that life is short and to stop procrastinating. 'Just do it!' she tells herself.

For me, I draw on my family history. When I find myself wondering if I'm good enough or capable enough, or whether this is the right thing for me to be doing, I tell myself:

'Pavel Puntakoff it!'

# 3

Life was hard for Alexandra as a young widow with a small child. Initially, the White Russians who worked as engineers and administrators on the railway had been prosperous. But since the revolution, those who refused to take Soviet citizenship became stateless people with no country to protect them, and had limited opportunities for employment. While Alexandra could have used family connections to get herself a job in administration for the Chinese Eastern Railway, as the requirement of such a position was a Soviet passport she instead made a meagre living sewing clothes and selling what produce she could from her little market garden.

Her sister Irina helped where she could. But Irina's husband Boris was also finding his prospects limited by the Japanese administration, which used every bureaucratic difficulty it could conjure up to drive the White Russians out of Harbin so as to destabilise the region.

'Sometimes I miss Pavel more than I think I can bear,' Alexandra confided in Irina. 'But if I can just get myself through this difficult patch, I know things will get better.'

On Alexandra's side was her gregarious, optimistic nature, which meant people naturally liked her and sent work her way.

One afternoon, Tania was playing in the garden when a well-dressed man appeared at the gate holding a bouquet of white roses. She recognised him as Sergei Morosoff who owned a clothing and leather-goods factory in the city. His wife had died a few years earlier, and although Sergei was handsome, with a well-built physique and chiselled features, he had avoided romance after his wife's premature death and had devoted himself to his work. That is, until a chance meeting with the vivacious Alexandra at a friend's house gave him the idea that he might like to get married again.

Sergei courted Alexandra slowly and respectfully. As was the Russian custom, the colour of the roses he brought with him on each visit deepened from white to pink to red, to reflect his growing feelings for her. Like Alexandra, he had a confident, easy manner, but it was the way he treated Tania, always listening attentively to her stories and showing concern for her welfare, that won Alexandra's heart.

After they were married in 1941, Sergei adopted Tania as his own daughter and moved the two new women in his life to his house in the city. Many friends and business colleagues came to visit. Alexandra was a good cook and loved to entertain. Tania was always welcome to converse with the adults. Sergei thought it was imperative for her to mix with and have empathy for people from a variety of backgrounds.

'To be happy and successful in life, it's important to get along with everybody,' he told her. 'Never bear anyone a grudge.'

~

Sergei's words obviously made an impression on Tania. Whenever anybody talks about my mother, they always remark on how kind she was to others. She seemed to have a special gift for lifting the spirits of the despondent. It was certainly a characteristic she nurtured in me. She didn't believe in only associating yourself with the 'in-crowd' but instead in seeing the potential in everybody. When she would drop me off at preschool she would say, 'See that little boy all alone on the swings, Belinda? Why don't you go and play with him?'

My mother believed that treasures could be found in the hearts of the shy and lonely that might not be discovered in the charismatic and wildly popular.

But although her kindness was treasured by everyone close to her, my mother was a sensitive soul and she often got hurt by people, and sometimes exhausted herself trying to meet all their emotional and physical demands while neglecting her own.

I would love to have met Sergei. He seems to have had the kind of personality that I admire: dynamic and yet sensitive at the same time. But surely as a successful businessman he must have had some experiences of people who tried to cheat him or offer him dubious products? Is it really possible to get along with everybody all the time?

Emboldened people have a connected, strong energy and a clear sense of direction. The wonderful thing about becoming emboldened is that we usually attract similar people – high-vibing friends who cheer us on to succeed, as they anticipate we will cheer for them. But the bright energy emitted will very likely attract difficult personalities too: either people who are too lazy to conjure up their own power sources so they want to plug into ours, or worse: people who, due to their own perverse and disordered psychology, will delight in seeing us fail and may even actively work towards our demise.

So, a question I often find myself asking is: how can I stay both open to life and people while at the same time protecting myself from those who might not be as sincere as they make themselves out to be?

The catchcry of the present day seems to be 'healthy boundaries'. Initially, 'personal boundaries' was a concept coined to help co-dependent people know where they ended and another person began.

However, in pop psychology the term has taken on a meaning more akin to having a kind of emotional garden fence with a locked gate to keep others out. Theoretically, the boundary demonstrates the limits a person can expect in a relationship with us. Trespassers will be prosecuted.

But I see a problem with the concept and how it is applied. Setting a boundary is often an act of defence to protect the vulnerable person living within it, and for that reason while a boundary may work for limiting the access of an annoying relative who offers unsolicited advice, or a friend who borrows our things without permission, it won't protect us from the far more dangerous types of personalities – the master manipulators – who can truly derail our lives and our dreams. To illustrate this, let me tell you about one of the greatest boundary fails in history: the Maginot Line.

~

After the catastrophe France suffered in the First World War, the French government and the military were certainly not going to let Germany invade the country again. They decided to create an impenetrable boundary along the entire French–German border. It was named the Maginot Line, after the French minister of war André Maginot, and consisted of state-of-the-art concrete fortifications, obstacles, and weapons installations, as well as underground bunkers and railways. So impressive was the structure that it was considered the best fortification in the history of humankind. Dignitaries from around the world came to study it, accompanied by marching bands and other fanfare. The boundary was coined a 'work of genius' by the press, and the French population had so much faith in it that they were still buying yo-yos and haute couture with confidence right up to the eve of the Second World War. But in the Blitzkrieg of 1940, the German army simply went around the Maginot Line, effectively trapping the Allied forces from behind and forcing them to hastily evacuate at Dunkirk, and leaving the troops in the south with no effective defence. A boundary that would have cost $9 billion in today's currency resulted in the death of 360,000 soldiers and nearly two million more being taken prisoner. Mighty France fell to Germany in a mere six weeks. The morale of the French people was shattered, so much so that many of them simply ended up cooperating with their occupiers.

~

Manipulators and truly toxic people are rarely deterred by our boundaries. In fact, they may even appear to initially respect and honour them. These dangerous types glide into our lives on the scent of our insecurities and wounds the same way mosquitos follow a trail of exhaled carbon dioxide.

It's easy to tell what our insecurities are because they are the aspects of our lives or selves where we seek outside validation and assurance. Wounds are the painful aspects of our past that show up in places where we haven't been able to process and move on from abuse, neglect and abandonment, and we fear that similar situations could happen to us again.

Therefore, it seems to me that instead of spending time and energy trying to control the behaviour of others through boundaries, we'd be better off addressing our insecurities and wounds. It's hard work and takes longer than simply building fences. But the rewards are greater because we can feel whole and good about ourselves, no matter how others are behaving. It also means that we can move more fluidly about our lives and deal with situations from a position of strength as they arise. It's a much better option than having to erect a clunky boundary fence with everyone we meet.

I wonder what Sergei would think of this theory and the lessons I've had to learn about 'getting on with people' in my effort to live an emboldened life? One thing we would certainly have agreed on was to not bear grudges.

I don't like to hold on to anger because it makes me feel stuck in the past. Going over and over what someone did is like deciding I didn't like a certain movie and yet paying for a cinema ticket to watch it over and over again. Nevertheless, I've seen people harbour grudges so fiercely that they destroy themselves in the process. A person might have a hundred things to be happy and grateful for in their life, but they focus on their resentment towards one person like their survival depends on it.

Neuroscience tells us that anger is addictive. When we think angry thoughts, we produce adrenaline in our body which heightens all our senses. It makes us feel alert, like a shot of espresso, so we can develop a dependency on it. The sun might be shining, we might have just secured a job promotion and met the person of our dreams, but sooner or later our minds will return to focusing on our grudge simply because it makes us feel alive.

An emboldened life cannot be sustained by anger. Living boldly requires us to cultivate elevated emotions, like courage, excitement and passion. Imagine what our lives would be like if we were addicted to those sorts of emotions!

But for all their positivity and gregariousness, Alexandra and Sergei were going to have their skills of diplomacy tested only a few months into their marriage, when the enemy arrived on their doorstep.

~

One afternoon, Alexandra and Tania were making *pryaniki*, a traditional Russian glazed biscuit that is usually served with tea. They don't look like much, and I don't recommend the store-bought variety, but when you bite into a homemade one, the dough is rich with the flavours of coffee, honey, vanilla, nutmeg and anise.

There was a knock at the front door. Expecting that some guests had come to visit, Tania rushed to answer it. But instead of friendly and familiar faces, she found herself standing opposite a Japanese colonel and two officers. Her eye fell to the long swords in the scabbards at their sides.

'Tania, who is it?' Alexandra called from the kitchen.

When Tania didn't answer, my grandmother took off her apron and came to the door herself. She stopped in her tracks when she saw the Japanese military men, and a chill ran down her spine. She had heard the rumours that the Japanese army was commandeering the houses of citizens to accommodate their high command. She'd only learned that morning that the Zhang family, including three small children and infirm grandparents, had been thrown out of their house with nowhere to go. With Sergei away on business, Alexandra could only hope that this visit was about something else.

'Madame Morosoff,' the colonel said, 'I must speak to you about a matter of importance.'

He spoke in perfect Russian, and his tone was cultured and polite. Alexandra knew she had no choice but to let the men inside. The colonel complimented the fine Turkmen rug and the antique Mongolian sideboard that Alexandra's father had brought with him from Russia. The officers went up to the second storey and made careful note of the views from the windows.

The colonel turned to Alexandra and told her in a tone that was more apologetic than threatening that her house was being requisitioned by the Japanese army. Alexandra stared at her feet and held back a sob. My six-year-old mother, on the other hand, looked the colonel straight in the face. He had eyes that bulged and a slow blink that, to her, resembled an enormous frog. Tania had always loved frogs. Not understanding what a terrible thing was being done to her family, she beamed a smile at him.

Having issued his order, the colonel was about to leave again. But then he hesitated, thinking something over. He turned back to Alexandra and said, 'My family and I will only occupy the top floors. Your family may continue to live in the rooms downstairs.'

It was a kindness unheard of from the occupying forces, but it worried Alexandra. If she refused to hand over the house at all, she and Tania would be thrown out anyway and perhaps even be deported to the Soviet Union for her insolence. But how would living with a member of the occupying army look in the eyes of the Morosoffs' many Chinese friends?

In the end, Alexandra felt she had no choice but to accept. Only time would tell if her decision was a wise one.

~

When Sergei returned to discover half of the house had been taken over by the colonel and his elegant, kimono-wearing Japanese wife Natsumi, he was shocked. But he agreed with Alexandra's decision – they didn't have a choice. Luckily, his Chinese clients understood his dilemma and continued to do business with him. Even Alexandra's Chinese friends and neighbours were sympathetic, but they stayed away from her, believing that one of the reasons the Japanese were moving into the city houses rather than staying in barracks was to spy on any local resistance movements. If they kept in contact with Alexandra, the colonel might force her to spy on them. So, sadly, Alexandra found her ties cut with many of her Chinese friends.

In fact, it seemed the colonel had another motive for allowing the Morosoffs to remain in their home. Along with his wife, he had brought his five-year-old son Takuya with him to China. As the child of a Japanese colonel, Takuya was a prime target for Chinese 'terrorists': those who were actively resisting the occupation of their country. In my gentle, polite and friendly mother, the colonel had seen an ideal playmate for his boy.

Each afternoon, Tania and Takuya were accompanied by two young Japanese officers in the colonel's car to one of Harbin's beautiful leafy parks. There, under the guard of soldiers with machine guns, Tania and Takuya would play together, sharing jokes and pulling funny faces at each other. Takuya did not speak Russian, so Tania's Japanese greatly improved during their games of make-believe. Takuya would imitate the dignified gait of a Samurai soldier, and Tania would tease him by playing the part of a haughty Russian snow queen.

When the Japanese occupied Manchuria, the study of the Japanese language had become compulsory in the schools in Harbin. Teachers were brought out from Japan, and they were harsh disciplinarians compared to the Catholic nuns whom Tania was used to being taught by. If a child got a kanji character wrong, the teacher would cane them. But worse for Tania were the forced cross-country runs. Those who came first were not given any praise, but the pupil who came last was severely beaten. Tania, who was tiny for her age, could not keep up with the other children. One day, she returned home with such vicious welts on her body that Alexandra complained to the colonel. He issued a stern reprimand to the teachers and instructed them that they were not to lay a hand on Tania in the future. To the amazement – and envy – of the other children, Tania was never punished for anything ever again, and was thereafter exempt from the torture of the cross-country run.

~

From my mother's description of the colonel, he was an intellectual and an artist who deeply regretted being involved in the war. The officers who took Tania and Takuya to the park each day were university students who had been conscripted into the army. They constantly complained about being kept away from their studies. This seems a far cry from the brutality that was going on elsewhere. The fear Alexandra had initially felt towards the colonel diminished over time. Indeed, she and his wife, Natsumi, became friends. When Natsumi had to return to Japan on family business, the colonel took a mistress. Alexandra was so incensed that he would cheat on lovely Natsumi that she wrote a letter to her informing her of the situation. Natsumi returned from Japan earlier than expected. She chased the mistress out of the house and gave her husband such a tongue-lashing that he was from then ever after trying to make up for his transgression by buying her beautiful clothing and taking her anywhere she wanted to go. He once lamented to Alexandra that he had no idea how his wife had ever found out about his affair.

When my mother would tell me these stories as an adult, I was always intrigued. From my university studies in Asian history and culture, I knew that the Japanese occupation of China had been bloodthirsty and brutal. The impression I had always been given of the Japanese military was that they were crazed fanatics on a suicide mission. My grandmother's relationship with the colonel and his wife seemed at odds with that image.

My mother would remind me that human nature is not black and white but grey.

Although she had witnessed extraordinary things in her life, I never heard my mother say anything racist about anyone. From a young age she'd seen the complexities of life. She saw a culture where Japanese women were laden like packhorses while their husbands strode on ahead of them unhampered. And yet, the colonel treated his articulate and well-educated wife with respect. As Sergei often had to travel for his work, the colonel told Tania that he saw himself as a substitute father to her. Some evenings he would sit down with her and teach her calligraphy. He told her that Japan had an elevated and ancient culture, that the language had fifty words to describe different types of rain, and that onomatopoeia was used to evoke the sounds of nature. Light rain was conjured up in the imagination as *para-para* and hot, humid weather was described exactly as it felt: *mushi-mushi*. One natural phenomenon that always inspired a deep sense of beauty in Tania was the sight of dappled sunlight shining through the leaves of the trees and making intricate, wave-like patterns. But while Russian, or English for that matter, requires a whole sentence to describe it, the Japanese need just one word: *komorebi*.

Across the city from where the Japanese colonel was teaching Tania to appreciate Japanese culture, a horror was taking place that would only be revealed after the war. It was known as Unit 731: a covert biological and chemical warfare research facility where live subjects were injected with typhoid and other diseases, and then vivisected to see the effects on their living, breathing bodies. Others had limbs amputated and reattached to different parts of their body. Some of the victims were prisoners, others were captured Allied servicemen, and others were ordinary men, women and children from nearby villages. There were even some Russians among the victims. The men who inflicted these horrors were some of Japan's best doctors and scientists. The facility developed 'plague bombs', and nearly half a million people across China died as a result.

When I would burn with anger at the injustice and horror of what had been done by the Japanese army in China, my mother would remind me that not one of the doctors or scientists who were captured by the American forces was punished as a war criminal.

'Do you know why?' she asked. 'They received immunity in return for giving their research to *American* scientists so they could use it in developing their own biological weapons programs. The Japanese are both good and bad, as the Americans are both good and bad. Just as we all are.'

~

Like my mother, I believe that the human race is both beautiful and monstrous. Which characteristics we exhibit in our lives comes down to which ones we choose to cultivate. We are all very much like gardens: we can decide to grow beautiful flowers, or we can allow ourselves to become overrun by weeds.

In my Australian education, I was always told that people were essentially good and wanted to do the right thing. My mother disagreed with that. She believed that most people were simply average. She didn't see that going to work, doing your job and not breaking the law was enough to declare yourself a 'good person'. Doing only those things merely made you a law-abiding person following societal norms.

In her mind, true goodness was something seen in people like Mahatma Gandhi, Martin Luther King Jr, and Mother Teresa. It takes a certain amount of discipline, allegiance to a higher ideal and sacrifice to cultivate true goodness. It often means walking against the crowd if you have to and exercising self-control. Otherwise, when war – the worst expression of collective human evil – breaks out, there aren't enough truly good people to oppose it. The conflict will then go on a trajectory of horror and carnage before resources are depleted and the resolve to keep fighting peters out. Her solution for world peace was for more of us to be cultivating a high level of goodness *before* such catastrophes happened. For that reason, she believed we should all be studying history to avoid repeating the mistakes of the past.

So much has my mother's viewpoint affected me, that I voiced a version of it through my character Rosa in my novel *Tuscan Rose*:

> ... she had come to the conclusion that while most Italians – and probably many Germans – had not wanted war, they had chosen a path of greed and pride and the result had been war. For where else did violence begin but within each individual human heart? It started with violence of thought and action, jealousy of others and loathing of oneself. It had its beginnings in the daily choices one made, including the indifference towards the suffering of animals in what one selected to eat and wear, and towards the poor and oppressed. From there it escalated into a collective consciousness of competitiveness, selfishness, pettiness, spite and greed. Violence of even the most seemingly innocuous kind begat more violence. That was the origin of war ... What the Germans had done was an extreme form of what any human being was capable of, if they chose to do so.

In order to be emboldened, we need to stand firm on the idea that we are responsible for who we become. No matter our upbringing or circumstances, we do have free choice. It is in exercising that choice daily that we become strong.

~

After school one day, Tania was playing alone in the front garden of her house when a young, well-spoken Chinese man stopped by the fence. It was a hot afternoon, and he asked Tania if she could bring him some water. She went inside the house and returned with a glass to give to him. But she instantly recoiled when she saw the inflamed, bloody flesh where his fingernails should have been.

'What happened to your hands?' she asked the man.

He lifted them up so Tania would get a closer look. 'The Japanese did this to me,' he said. 'Tell me, why did your parents allow the Japanese colonel to stay with you?'

'They had no choice,' she explained. 'He just turned up.'

The young man was silent for a long time before he handed Tania back the glass along with an ominous warning: 'We Chinese won't forget who helped us ... and who helped *them*.'

~

Danger surrounded Tania's family on all sides. In the end, the colonel would end up saving their lives. In the summer of 1944, the newspapers were full of Japanese victories. To everyone reading the highly censored news, it appeared the Allies were losing. But then, one afternoon, the colonel asked Alexandra to come to the room where he had set up his office. He closed the door behind him.

'Everything you read in the newspaper is nothing but lies,' he told her. 'Japan is losing this war. When they do, the Soviets will storm into Manchuria and you and your family will be sent to the Soviet Union. I can get transit papers for you, but you must leave now.'

Giving such top-secret news to Alexandra put the colonel's own life at risk, and my grandmother did not take his words lightly. She and Sergei quickly set about getting ready to leave Harbin. Sergei would stay behind to sell his factory and house as soon as he could, but Alexandra and Tania, along with Irina and Boris, left with only what they could carry in one suitcase each. All the beautiful furniture Alexandra had collected would have to be left behind. She went to the cemetery to put flowers on Pavel's and her parents' graves, and then it was time to leave. The Morosoffs said goodbye to the colonel and his family, knowing they would never meet again.

But one thing that Alexandra certainly took with her was the silver and crystal tankard mug that my grandfather had been presented with by the Tsar. The mug that had travelled thousands of leagues.

# 4

After the genteel atmosphere of Harbin, the city of Shanghai was a shock to Tania's family. Unlike Manchuria, which had been influenced by the Russians and the railways, Shanghai was an international port city. The British, Americans and French dominated in business and had their own concessions in the city – districts within which they governed themselves and were not subject to Chinese law. The wealthy inhabitants were financiers, businesspeople, mega-rich playboys and playgirls, gangsters, spies, adventurers, movie stars, and opium-dealers. Shanghai had a vibrant jazz scene, with many of the musicians being White Russian émigrés. There were also many Jewish refugees from Europe. Having been refused entry to the Allied nations, the Jewish refugees had come to Shanghai without any visa requirements and thrived there. But it was a city of enormous contrasts. Most of the Chinese population lived in abject poverty. The rich, after a night out dining on caviar and dancing at nightclubs owned by former Russian nobility, would have to make their way home past the corpses of the people who had starved or frozen to death in the street.

The sight of the dead lying in the street filled Tania with horror: their mouths gaped towards the sky; their half-closed eyes that seemed to be watching her as she passed by. And the putrid stench! She could not forget it. Each morning a municipal truck would come around to remove unclaimed bodies. Many infants were left exposed to the elements to die because their parents could not afford to feed them. It was a horror my mother never got used to, and it wasn't something she censored herself from discussing when I was growing up. If I ever complained that my life was hard in any way, my mother would repeat the Chinese proverb: 'I was angry that I had no shoes. Then I met a man who had no feet.'

I know that many children hear similar sentiments from their parents, but I do truly believe that my mother's shaped me. Perhaps it was because they were accompanied by such vivid stories. Even now when things go wrong for me, I'm always quick to remember the good things I have and how fortunate I actually am.

~

In 1944, the Allies were at war with the Japanese, and much of the British and American population in China had been interned in camps. The White Russians, with no allegiance to the Soviet Union and considered stateless, were mostly left alone to carry on with business. Sergei was able to purchase a new factory and a house in the desirable French Concession with its tree-lined streets and Parisian-style buildings. My grandmother employed a manservant named Yao to assist her in the house and a maid named Jing, who, among her other duties, was responsible for walking Tania to and from school. Shanghai was not a safe city for a young girl to wander around in on her own.

Tania went to an international school run by Irish nuns. She now added English and French language skills to her Russian and Japanese. Because some of her classmates came from wealthy Chinese families, she also learned Mandarin and a smattering of the Shanghai dialect. Friday afternoons were devoted to softball matches, where, to the amusement of the girls, the normally demure nuns would become competitive with each other. They would tuck the skirts of their habits into their bloomers and run hell for leather between the bases.

'Tania, have you ever been to the International Settlement?' Tania's friend Mila asked her one day.

'No. Jing and I never leave the French Concession. Whenever I ask "Can we go to the International Settlement?" she pretends she hasn't heard me.'

'So, you've never seen the beautiful English-style park there, with its bandstand and its flowerbeds teaming with roses?' Mila said.

At Mila's suggestion, Tania kept at Jing to take her to one of the parks in the International Concession. Finally, Jing relented, but when they arrived at the park Tania saw the sign indicating that Chinese people, unless they were nannies of babies, were not permitted to enter. Sorry for the humiliation she had caused Jing, Tania took one look at the park and insisted they go home again.

~

Inequality was unbearable to my sensitive mother and Shanghai was not a city built on fairness. One story she often recounted to me was the time she came out of a sweet store holding a paper bag full of candy. She was looking forward to tasting Shanghai's new milky, chewy 'White Rabbit' candies, but before she could even take a few steps towards home, a beggar snatched the sweets from her and put the entire bag in his mouth, waxed paper and all. My mother told me that she hadn't been frightened or angry at the man's actions, but deeply saddened. She understood then how desperate he must have been to do something like that.

There was one thing, though, that the excuse of poverty and

ignorance never allowed her to forget, and that was the cruelty she saw towards animals: donkeys and goats that were nothing more than skin and bones being beaten because they could no longer bear the goods that were piled onto them and had collapsed from exhaustion; the pitiful faces of the dogs and cats crammed into wire cages to be hauled off to meat markets; the screams of the pigs from the slaughterhouse as their throats were slit.

As an adult in Australia, there were two causes my mother was passionate about: disabled and blind children, and preventing cruelty to animals. Just as in the biographies I read, my mother's childhood experiences shaped the woman she would forever become.

It was also in Shanghai that my mother witnessed first-hand an atrocity committed by the Japanese army.

~

If there was one thing Tania particularly liked about her new school, it was the smart uniform of a pleated skirt and crisp, white blouse.

'If you don't stop admiring yourself in the mirror, you are going to be late for school' was something Alexandra had to tell her more than once.

Tania was studious and she loved her school lessons. She was especially proud of her penmanship. But on that awful autumn afternoon of the atrocity, she was unhappy with herself.

'Why the long face?' Jing asked her, when she came to collect her after school.

'I only came second in my English composition.'

'You can't always be first,' Jing told her. 'Someone else has to have a chance sometimes.'

They were walking down Avenue Joffre together, under the plane trees that were turning golden with the colder weather. The street was bustling with people going about their business and shopkeepers hawking their wares. Tania stopped to look at some canaries in cages outside a clothing store. There was a commotion, and a group of Chinese men rushed past her, practically knocking Jing flat as they pushed her out of the way. Most of them were young, but there was an old man with them who struggled to keep up. Japanese soldiers shoved through the crowd in pursuit. In the confusion, Tania and Jing were separated. The younger men escaped down a laneway, but the soldiers captured the older man and made him kneel on the pavement with his hands on his head.

The pedestrians backed away from the soldiers, but Tania found herself trapped between them and the captured man who was trembling. Tania could guess why the soldiers had stopped him and she felt sorry for him. With the shortages caused by the war, all the rice produced was to go to the Japanese army. To save their starving families, some farmers would take the risk of smuggling rice into the city to sell on the black market.

A Japanese officer arrived and questioned the old man. Tania expected he would be taken to prison. But to her horror, the officer drew his sword and drove it straight through the man's torso. The man fell forward in front of Tania. Blood and rice poured from his clothing and gathered around her shoes. She stood on the spot, paralysed by shock.

The officer sneered at the gore on his sword and searched around for something to clean it on. His eyes narrowed on Tania in her crisp school uniform. He moved towards her but the crowd let out a collective gasp of disgust and he changed his mind at the last minute. Instead, he turned and wiped his sword on the suit of a Chinese businessman who could say nothing.

Years later, when my mother related the story to me, she said that when the old man was caught she truly did see the light go from his eyes. But the most chilling thing she experienced that day was the expression on that Japanese officer's face.

'From the time he arrived to the time he killed the old man to the time he moved towards me, the look on his face never changed. It was cold and impassive, like a machine that felt absolutely nothing.'

~

Although the White Russians were left to carry on their businesses, the Japanese occupation soon took a toll on them as well. The Americans had blockaded the city and food was in short supply for everyone. Alexandra and Jing spent hours every day going from shop to shop searching for food, and often paid exorbitant prices for nothing more than crackers, dried noodles and tea. Luckily, they had potatoes and onions stocked in the larder. Many Russian dishes use potatoes but they are often eaten with sour cream and butter. Not having those, a staple meal for the Morosoff family became baked potatoes with chopped chives and onions cooked in water. Sergei would arrive home and declare that he had eaten at the factory and insist that Alexandra and Tania take his portion. He had been a strongly built man when Alexandra met him in Harbin, but now his clothing seemed to hang off him and there was a pallor to his skin. Alexandra guessed that he was only pretending to have eaten so that she and Tania wouldn't feel guilty about eating his share.

Whenever my mother spoke about Sergei, it was with deep feeling. It was clear that she loved her stepfather very much. And I can understand why. In a world where she witnessed such cruelty and uncertainty, he represented not only a strong protector and provider, but also someone who was very kind and stable. Which makes what happened next all the more tragic.

With gasoline in short supply, Sergei had taken to walking to his factory every day. Then one cold January morning in 1945, he kissed Alexandra and Tania goodbye before walking out onto the street, his hands thrust into his pockets and his breath blowing steam into the air. Only a few minutes later, he was crossing the busy intersection of Avenue Joffre and Rue Cardinal Mercier when a Japanese military truck ploughed at high speed through the intersection, sending pedestrians hurrying in all directions. Sergei had no chance to move before he was run down by the truck. Bystanders rushed him to hospital, but he died from his injuries.

~

For a long time, I could never quite get an answer from my mother about how Sergei had died. It was only when I was researching *White Gardenia* that I came across a simple slip of typed paper signed by the head doctors at the hospital where he was taken among some of my mother's documents. It was his death certificate:

> We undersigned certify on 4 January 1945, Mr Sergei Morosoff was brought to Hôspital Sainte Marie, after an accident on Avenue Joffre and Rue Cardinal Mercier; and died in our presence. He was killed by a Japanese military truck. This certificate was given to his widow.

When I asked my mother about the incident, the pain of that day was etched on her face as if it had just happened. I could picture her as a little girl coming out of school and wondering why Jing looked so solemn and could not meet her eyes.

'You must be very brave,' Jing told her. 'You must be strong for your mother.'

Fifty-five years later, it was me comforting my mother. 'It's all right, Mum,' I told her, touching her shoulder. 'We don't have to talk about it if you don't want to.'

She looked at me through her tears.

'They were laughing.'

I shook my head, not understanding. 'What? Who? Who was laughing?'

'The Japanese soldiers,' she said. 'The witnesses said the soldiers were laughing as they ploughed through the intersection. They said they had run down Sergei on purpose.'

How my mother grew up not hating anyone still astounds me.

~

The loss of Sergei was devastating, but despite the grief she felt over the death of her second husband, Alexandra took over the running of the factory while her sister Irina looked after Tania. Irina was glamorous, a Russian Louise Brooks, but also warm-hearted. She and Tania often played dress-ups together. She was a tremendous comfort to Tania, but in a short while, tragedy would strike again.

It was a hot, muggy day and Tania sat in her classroom with the other girls, beads of sweat gathering around their hairlines and dripping down their backs. Tania grimaced as her perspiring hands caused the ink in her neat schoolbook to smudge. Through the open windows, the sky was clear and blue. Then Tania felt it. At first, she thought it was the traffic passing by the school that caused the floor to vibrate beneath her feet. She sat back and glanced at her friend Larissa, who frowned, sensing something unusual too. The schoolteacher noticed and went to the window and peered out at the sky. Everyone was thinking the same thing, but nobody could quite believe it might happen. For weeks they had been told to prepare for the possibility that the Allies might bomb the city. Air-raid shelters had been dug in preparation, but they were woefully inadequate in both number and construction. A mere 7 or 8 feet in depth, they were often nothing more than a mishmash of sandbags. But they were safer than staying in the buildings, which were prone to collapsing even in high winds. They were certainly not built to withstand sustained bombing.

The teacher squinted at the sky then looked at the street below. People were starting to walk faster or pedal more furiously on their bicycles. They were fleeing.

'Get into pairs as we practised!' the teacher told her students.

Tania and Larissa held hands, their eyes wide with both horror and excitement.

~

Meanwhile, at the factory Alexandra had heard the planes approaching too. She instructed her workers to leave quickly. After turning off the power, she followed them to the shelter. It was already crammed with terrified people.

Irina was alone in her house when she heard the American B-52s approach the city. Boris was at work, but he had reinforced the basement with sandbags to turn it into a shelter as the nearest city one was too far away for Irina to run to in an emergency. She went down and sat in the dark basement, holding a silver icon and praying.

~

Tania and Larissa embraced each other in the shelter as the hum of the planes turned into a roar. Then came the horrific whistling sounds as bombs began falling. Later, everyone would learn that the Americans had attempted to bomb strategically. They were aiming for oil refineries and transmitters, not civilians. But the Japanese had purposely placed their important military targets near the most populated parts of the cities to act as a deterrent. That the Americans didn't intend what happened didn't make the result any less heartbreaking.

For what seemed like hours Tania, Alexandra and Irina cowered in their respective hiding places. Tania wondered where her mother and aunt were. The smell of smoke was thick all over the city.

'It wouldn't take much to turn this city into a conflagration,' the factory foreman told Alexandra soberly. 'Shanghai is practically built out of matchsticks.'

When the bombing subsided and sirens sounded the all-clear, people began to emerge like pale ghosts from the shelters. Tania and her friends were ushered back to their classroom by their teacher. Alexandra told her workers to go home and find their families. She went to her office and tried to call Tania's school and then Irina, but the telephone lines were out. Tania was safe, but even if the lines had been working Alexandra would never have reached Irina. She would never hear her beloved sister's voice again.

Irina's house had collapsed in the aftershock of the bombing. A wall had fallen on top of her. It would take workers several hours to retrieve her broken body from under the rubble, still holding the silver icon in her hand.

# 5

I only have to scroll through social media to see how often the word 'trauma' is used. The term was originally applied to situations that were considered catastrophic, involving a direct or very possible threat to one's life. Events that came under that definition included natural disasters, war, sexual assault, horrific accidents, loss of a limb, being taken hostage, and long-term physical or mental torture.

Our brains are designed to keep us alive. When there is some event out of the range of normal that threatens our survival, the brain takes note of it. Often to such a degree that any situation that vaguely resembles the original trauma – the weather, the time of day or year, a certain person's appearance – can irrationally trigger a stress response that is overwhelming.

Many psychologists have expressed concern that the word 'trauma' is now being used too broadly to include events that are more accurately described as 'distressing', 'upsetting' or 'challenging'. On the other hand, there are other psychologists who argue that if any life event makes someone lose their sense of self and security, then it can be validly classified as a trauma.

I would never want to invalidate or minimise anybody's pain or their right to define their own experience. So I say this only in reference to myself: I am inclined to agree that 'trauma' is being used inaccurately in the same way that an anxious desire to control and organise one's environment isn't necessarily OCD. However, just because something isn't technically 'trauma' it doesn't mean that it's not significant or that the impact of it shouldn't be taken as seriously. But it is my belief that misclassifying something may result in the wrong approach to healing, and could make the suffering harder and more prolonged.

'You need to feel it before you can heal it' is good advice for someone who is going through grief. Talking about their experience can be therapeutic, as is finding ways to keep the memory of their loved one alive. It is almost the exact opposite for those who are suffering trauma. They are feeling too much all at once and need to calm their nervous systems down. Talking more than necessary about what happened can make things worse. It's only in recent times that we are coming to understand that the damage done to someone who has suffered trauma is neurological rather than purely psychological. Like the shell-shocked veteran of the First World War, the sufferer's brain was switched on to high-alert mode for too long.

In recounting my mother's stories, I think we could all agree that her experiences, especially at such a young age, could be defined as traumatic: witnessing executions and other horrors; living under occupation and through war; having bombs dropped on her city; and losing adults who represented security to her in tragic circumstances. Yet, my mother never used the word 'trauma'. I don't think she even realised that she was deeply affected by what happened to her. The reason for this, I believe, is because the people around her were also going through similar experiences. The unsafe world she and her friends occupied was normal. My grandmother Alexandra was the very definition of resilience. She kept going no matter what life threw at her, and after the deaths of Sergei and Irina there were more difficulties to come. My mother could not have had a stronger role model, but I'm sure she witnessed Alexandra's grief too.

Untreated and unrecognised trauma has its costs. As well as their resilience, our ancestors sometimes pass on their burdens.

~

Recently, I was sitting in the garden of a fascinating woman I had been introduced to by a friend to help me with some research for one of my books. As we drank tea and breathed in the sweet spring scents of jasmine and lavender, she shared with me how she and her adult daughter battle with chronic anxiety. Angela is probably the last person you would expect to be plagued by a constant sense of mental agitation. She exudes effortless chic, is vivacious and articulate, and surrounds herself with beauty in her garden and in the sculptures she creates. A widow, Angela has a social network of long-time friends, and is always keen to make new ones. She is cheerful and upbeat, reads voraciously, and seeks fresh challenges in the adult education courses she regularly takes. But Angela is also the child of a Holocaust survivor. She is attended by a psychiatrist who specialises in inherited genocide anxiety and who claims it takes at least three generations to resolve itself. Physical scars can't be passed on to future generations, but emotional ones certainly can.

I grew up on the North Shore in Sydney, one of the safest and most conservative areas in the city. The migrants who lived there were mostly of British origin. They were the kind of people who still referred to England as 'home'. Refugees were rare. A mother with a Russian accent, who made *kulich* at Easter and saw visions of angels, was unique. I often went to Chinatown in the city with my mother, the only place she could buy sufficient rice for the Chinese meals she made for my family.

There she would read out the signs in Mandarin for me. I remember thinking, *I don't think my friends' mothers can do that*.

In my mind, my mother was magical.

The photograph albums she and my grandmother had brought with them from China were fascinating, and also very sad. I looked at the pictures of exotic women and dashing men who had all met terrible fates. I knew what a gulag was and that Stalin was an evil man before I even went to school. It was a far cry from what I saw when I went to the barbecues and birthday parties at my friends' houses. They seemed to have more uncles, aunties and cousins than I could count. The conversations were all about cricket and netball. Not one of them could have explained what a 'gulag' was.

I inherited my mother's burden of anxiety. Not a fear of being alone or heights or public speaking. She had me up on stage from an early age, so I didn't develop the almost universal fear of making a fool of myself in front of others. The anxiety certainly wasn't a fear of social situations; my mother was sold on the importance of friends and refused to accept any shyness on my part as an excuse for not approaching people first. Instead, it was a low-grade shadow that lurked in my mind. Rather than anything that manifested itself in stuttering or panic attacks, it was a constant foreboding that no matter how good life felt, everything I held dear could be swept away tragically in an instant. The only way to prepare for it was to never allow myself to be *too* happy, and to never let my guard down completely. Therefore, I often felt like I was standing on tiptoes at the edge of a great precipice. One false move and I could tumble to my demise.

Who could blame my mother for having developed chronic anxiety? She'd witnessed things that no child should ever see. She'd had two fathers who adored her, and both had died prematurely. Her mother had loved her and done her best to protect her, but she had been helpless to defend her child against the crashing waves of world events that had swept over them. While I had looked out the window of my childhood bedroom early in the morning and seen colourful parrots and magnificent trees, my mother had watched the Shanghai municipal truck picking up dead bodies.

It wasn't that my mother was joyless. Far from it. She had the most beautiful laugh, and when she laughed it was the best sound in the world. I liken its lightness and musicality to the bells on a winter sleigh. She loved flowers and animals, and it was from her that I learned a deep appreciation for nature and wildlife. It was also from her that I developed a love of dancing, and I don't think there can be any more passionate and joyful expression of life than dancing.

And let's face it, her fears were not entirely unfounded either. Life is like the ocean – both beautiful and dangerous! Mothers have a biological duty to teach their children what not to do, touch or eat to stay alive. What they fear, we naturally learn to fear too. It happens as if by osmosis.

We all know that there are things that can randomly befall us, no matter how carefully we tread: disease manifesting out of nowhere in a supremely healthy – and young – person; a parent distracted for a fraction of section as their toddler inches towards a wading pool or sees a shiny object lying on the road. Our newspapers are full of stories like that. We don't have to live in war-torn countries run by bloodthirsty tyrants to appreciate the fragility of life. In fact, the knowledge of it can help us to live more fully, more deeply, more boldly. It can make us dismiss a stupid argument faster or be more mindful of how we spend our time. But if there's too much of it, we can't enjoy our lives at all.

~

My mother hadn't transferred her fear to me deliberately, of course, the same way we don't purposely infect our loved ones with influenza. But fear is just as contagious. It might not transfer in droplets of vapour we breathe out of our lungs, but it reaches us almost as imperceptibly – by body language and an aura we emit that is often referred to as a 'vibe'.

My mother never waved goodbye from the couch or grunted absent-mindedly while reading a magazine or watching television when I left for school in the morning. This time of day was always *an occasion*. She would embrace me fiercely then hold me by the shoulders, peering into my face as if trying to memorise my features. It conveyed the feeling that this might be our last moment together, *ever*. I would head off not with excitement, or even a sense of ennui, but with a rock in the pit of my stomach. It was a parting more suited to a fighter pilot about to undertake a dangerous sortie over enemy territory than for a young girl heading off to school. I'd turn when I reached the bottom of the driveway, and my mother would be standing by the house looking after me. We would share one last wave and she would call out, 'Have a nice day at school!' But the tremble in her voice and the apprehension in her eyes belied her cheerful words.

My poor mother. Loved ones leaving the house and not returning had been a traumatic childhood reality for her. But my terror had more to do with the fear that she wouldn't cope if something happened to me. Therefore, at all costs, I had to avoid any activity that could have been considered risky or dangerous. I never did anything even vaguely rebellious as a teenager – I never drank, I never smoked, I never hung out with irresponsible boys. When I was in primary school, I never even somersaulted in case – and my mother had warned me about this – I broke my neck.

~

Because my sense of apprehension never seemed to be related to a particular situation – spiders, the dark, strangers – it was a battle to solve. It was like fighting in the dead of night against an enemy I couldn't see. From a young age I felt that the anxiety that pestered me wasn't quite mine. It belonged to someone else and was more a thing that floated by my side, whispering in my ear, than something that resided in me. I sensed it most strongly in the company of other children, who seemed impossibly carefree as they bounced and skipped through life. I, on the other hand, felt that I was staggering from carrying the weight of the Russian Revolution on my shoulders.

My father did balance things. He didn't – and still doesn't – have time for anxiety. He has always been fuelled by grit and determination. Australian-born of rugged Irish-Scottish stock, and from a family that suffered many difficulties and tragedies of its own, he has never had much sympathy for neurosis or overthinking on my part.

To give an example of the difference between my mother and father in parenting styles, imagine the golden yellow sand of Palm Beach in Sydney. It's a hot day in January and I am seven years old and standing in pristine clear water that reaches below my waist. My mother is next to me, clutching my hand. There are people around us playing and splashing happily while my mother is admonishing me, 'Watch for sharks, Belinda. Watch for sharks.' Later that day, when my mother's attention is on making lunch, my father, a former volunteer lifesaver on Bondi Beach, takes me out past the breakers to where the water is colder and smoother. I can't see the bottom, let alone touch it. My feet are floating freely and my father holds firmly onto me. I'm a little scared to be this far from the shore, but my father tells me I won't be a strong swimmer if I always stay where my feet can touch the sand.

'But what about the sharks?' I ask him, nervously looking around for a menacing fin.

'Oh, don't worry about them,' my father assures me, eyeing a solid-looking man who passes by us doing backstroke, his sunburned paunch protruding above the waterline. 'We'll just swim behind him.'

Teetering between blasé Australian optimism, characterised by our national motto of 'she'll be right, mate', and the Russian penchant for melancholy was not always an easy seesaw to play on.

Many people hold their parents responsible for the struggles in their lives. They spend a lot of time wishing that their parents had been ideals of harmony and sanity. I have chosen to view things differently. Instead of blaming my mother, I appreciated the tremendous gift she gave me in eventually landing herself safely on Australian shores so that I could thrive in a lucky country. In homage to her efforts, I long ago decided to embrace the resilience she implanted in me and at the same time destroy the anxiety that came with it. I was sixteen when I made that decision. My maturity in making such a decision at that age, when most children are criticising their parents, astounds me. I'm not even sure I'm capable of such emotional maturity now.

I believe it was the result of copious reading of coming-of-age stories – *Great Expectations*, *Jane Eyre*, *Rebecca* ... and more. Stories about the gaining of wisdom after taking a journey – physical or emotional – had great appeal for me. They helped me make sense of life. They taught me that as long as I was always open to lessons, I could be the captain of my ship. Later, this would expand into a love of reading biographies and autobiographies. I am a collector of stories. They embolden me.

I realised that I had to do battle with my anxiety and destroy it (or, at least, they were the terms in which I thought of my fears as a teenager). Only I had no idea exactly how to do it. So, initially, my attempts involved doing more reading to find my path by learning about what others did. Then later, on a university friend's recommendation,

I went to see a qualified psychiatrist who specialised in hypnotherapy. Our conscious mind, which only makes up 5 per cent of our brain's capacity, is no match for the subconscious where our deep-seated programs, habits and fears live. Hypnotherapy is a way for us to reach that subconscious part. I was up for it.

Hypnotherapy doesn't work with some patients, the psychiatrist warned me straight up. He did a test where he got me to relax, and then spoke to my hand, telling it that it was a balloon. In response, and with no conscious effort on my part, my hand floated gracefully upwards towards the ceiling (still attached to my arm, of course – he was a hypnotherapist, not a magician!). When he then informed my hand that it wasn't in fact a balloon, it took a while for it to gradually deflate and drift down again. On a scale of 1–10 of responsiveness to hypnotherapy, I was near the top: as easy to hypnotise as a chicken, apparently. I have no embarrassment about this. Being highly responsive to hypnotherapy has everything to do with your ability to concentrate and nothing to do with your level of gullibility or intelligence. In fact, the worst candidates for hypnotherapy are imbeciles, the criminally insane and children under six years of age.

But when we came to the main part of the session, the deep trance, things took an unexpected turn. The standard technique to reach someone's subconscious is to get them into a state of profound relaxation. To this end, the hypnotherapist started by asking me to visualise a tropical beach with warm sand, swaying palm trees and a salty ocean breeze. But instead of an island paradise, I found myself walking through the aftermath of a battle. The acrid smell of gunpowder seared my nostrils and sweat burned my eyes. The mangled bodies of the dead and the moans of the dying were all around me. The image was apocalyptic and terrifying, and I had to call out to the hypnotherapist to get me out of the trance, which he immediately did.

We sat looking at each other, trying to make sense of what had just happened.

'That's not yours,' he told me, firmly. 'That's somebody else's memory.'

It was a frightening experience that made me worry that there was something wrong with me that couldn't be fixed, or that perhaps I possessed some unwelcome psychic ability and I'd been 'channelling' a memory from the grave. No wonder people constantly distract themselves to avoid looking at what is really going on in their mind! But fortunately, the hypnotherapist didn't abandon me or let me walk out of his office distressed. Instead, he was reassuring. He told me that what I'd experienced in hypnotherapy was a heightened version of what I felt in daily life: when life was good and beautiful, my mind sensed that an impending disaster must be looming on the horizon and sent up an image to correspond to it. The picture of the battlefield scene was my own imagination bringing to life what it must have been like for my grandfather when he fought in the Russian Civil War.

My empathy, in that regard, is quite legendary. I hate it when people tell me about their surgeries or their accidents. Whatever body part was damaged or sliced on them, the corresponding part on my body squirms and throbs. I don't only visualise it when someone tells me they fell off their bicycle and broke their arm, like impassively watching a movie on a screen. I experience the whole thing as a virtual reality in my mind: the sky going upside down; the asphalt rising up; the 'crack' as the weight of their body makes contact with the ground; the mind-numbing pain; the voices of the people gathering around saying, 'Are you all right? Did you hit your head?'

'We'll leave hypnotherapy for a while,' the psychiatrist told me. 'But at some future date it could be useful. Why don't you tell me more about yourself and your family?'

He listened with sympathy about the things that had happened to my mother; with interest about the pleasure my university studies gave me and how I felt so alive when I travelled; and with alarm about the dodgy boyfriend I was dating at the time.

'You need to get away from everything familiar,' he said, a serious note in his voice. 'I don't mean for a holiday. You need to go somewhere far away ... *and for quite some time*.'

It seemed I was about to embark on a coming-of-age story of my own. But before I tell you about that, let me return to the lives of my grandmother and mother in Shanghai.

I am going to tell you one epic tale of resilience. And not just of my own family, but a whole community.

# 6

In September 1945, when Japan surrendered after atomic bombs were dropped on Hiroshima and Nagasaki, it seemed like Shanghai might return to the vibrant, decadent city it had been before the war. The British and American internees, thin and weary from their imprisonment, returned to their homes to find them ransacked and their heirlooms for sale at the local Chinese markets. But they were businesspeople who knew how to make money, and it wasn't long before their establishments were back up and running. The American GIs, who were pouring into the city to supervise the takeover from the Japanese, lent a certain carnival atmosphere to the city. My mother remembered their broad smiles and the way they would throw candies to the children when they drove by. They paid the rickshaw drivers generously to take them for rides and sent photographs of their adventures back home to amuse their sweethearts and families. Shanghai nightlife began to buzz again as the GIs filled the restaurants and clubs. Tania was eleven years old when the war ended, and to her the Americans looked like giants in a land of petite people.

But it seemed that no sooner had the Japanese left than tensions between the Chinese Nationalists and communists broke out again. The country quickly slid into a civil war. The United States backed the

Nationalists led by Chiang Kai-shek, while the Soviet Union supported the communists led by Mao Zedong. American money poured into China to arm the Nationalists in their fight. But to the foreigners in Shanghai, what was going on politically in the country didn't concern them. All was well, as long as they could keep their businesses running. In their minds, the Chinese economy needed them, and while they might support the Nationalists in principle, they felt that the communists wouldn't want them to leave and would find a way of working with them. They couldn't have been more wrong: Mao Zedong regarded the decadent foreigners as bloodsucking imperialists.

By 1948, the Americans began to withdraw their support, tired of Chiang Kai-shek's incompetence and corruption.

~

Alexandra read the newspapers every morning before leaving for the factory, searching for the truth between the lines in the heavily censored articles. The pages were full of Paris fashions and dog shows, but there was something clearly wrong. There would be sudden, inexplicable shortages of materials she needed at the factory, and inflation was starting to run rampant.

As her manservant, Yao, drove her to the factory, she would see the crowds of starving, frightened refugees pouring into the city from the countryside, all their worldly goods piled onto carts and bicycles. It was from them, not the newspapers, that she learned of the crushing defeats of the Nationalists in the countryside.

'The United States Consulate has told American companies that their employees must send their wives and children home,' Alexandra's foreman told her one morning, when she arrived at the factory.

Alexandra sat down at her desk and stared out the window. The

Americans were leaving Shanghai like rats abandoning a sinking ship, while the British were being told to stoically stay put. Every foreigner was asking the same question: 'Should I stay or should I go?'

But while the British, Americans and Europeans had countries they could go back to, the White Russians were stateless. Going to the Soviet Union meant certain death. Alexandra closed her eyes and remembered her brother-in-law, Boris.

After the war, with Irina dead he'd insisted that there was nothing left for him in China and accepted repatriation back to the Soviet Union. Nobody had heard of him since. Alexandra couldn't bear to think what his fate may have been.

'What are you going to do?' the foreman asked Alexandra. 'Everyone is relying on you to keep the factory going.'

Alexandra nodded. The responsibility on her shoulders was immense. Her employees were loyal, and she cared for them and their families. But she was also a mother with a daughter to think about. Everyone else was gone: they only had each other. But there was another truth, far more frightening. If she wanted to leave, where could she and Tania go? Having an American sponsor was a requirement for emigrating to the United States, and if she went to Europe she didn't think she'd be safe from deportation to the Soviet Union. Tania spoke English, but she didn't. How would she support her daughter? She thought of her house in the French Concession. Surely she wasn't going to have to flee a home and leave everything behind a second time?

When Nanjing fell to the communists in April 1949 and it was clear that Shanghai would be next, Tania, Larissa and a couple of other Russian girls were the only ones left at their school.

From their classroom they could see the people fleeing the city in droves. They had heard that the airlines were running extra services, but the planes were so crowded they barely cleared obstacles on take-off.

They were also fired on by communist gunners. The poor had to take trains, riding on the roof or clinging for their lives to the sides. For most people, ships were their only option, and even they were not safe. A British ship was fired upon, proving that being a foreigner was no guarantee of safety.

'You must go home,' the headmistress told them one morning. 'The school is being closed down.'

Tania returned home to find Alexandra cutting off the ends of toothpaste tubes and stuffing them with pieces of gold.

'There is a Spanish merchant ship leaving tomorrow, and we are getting on it,' she told Tania.

'We are going with a people-smuggler, a pirate?' Tania asked.

Alexandra nodded. 'There is no other choice.' She looked at her daugher with tears in her eyes. 'I sent Jing back to her family.'

'What?'

'She can't come with us, Tania. They won't take her. I gave her some clothing and other things she might be able to sell.'

Tania bit her lip. She wanted to be brave for her mother, but she wondered if she was ever going to see any of her friends again.

That night, Tania and Alexandra sewed jewellery into the hems of their clothing. My grandmother had managed to secure some American dollars, but not much: Chinese money was worthless due to the rampant inflation. She gave whatever supplies she could to her workers before she let them go. No doubt her factory and house would be taken over by the communists, and it was unlikely she'd be compensated for them. She and Tania were only allowed one small suitcase each on the ship, so all they took were photograph albums and other sentimental items, including Grandfather Pavel's mug. Exhausted and frightened, they climbed into bed together and held each other for comfort. The sound of machine-gun fire was growing closer. They only hoped they could leave the city before it was completely surrounded and escape became impossible.

The following morning, Yao drove my grandmother and mother as far as he could towards the wharf. The city had taken on the atmosphere of an imminent apocalypse. Fear and terror were written on the faces of those attempting to escape the city by any means possible. The streets were choked with horse-carts and wheelbarrows piled high with worldly possessions. When they reached the wharf, the American GIs who had been sent to oversee the orderly dispatch of foreigners out of the city were firing at the Chinese communists and deserting Nationalist soldiers alike. Alexandra and Tania got out of the car.

'Take the car,' Alexandra urged Yao. 'It may be useful to you to earn money for your family.'

Indeed, the car was worth a lot of money, and Yao perhaps could have earned a living as a driver. But he shook his head. The communists were coming, and it would look bad for him to have such a luxurious car. So, the vehicle was left on the wharf.

My grandmother and mother struggled to hold on to each other against the bustling crowd as they made their way to the ship that would be taking them to some unknown destination, but at least out of China.

A soldier in a Nationalist uniform elbowed Alexandra to get past her. Nationalist soldiers were deserting the army in droves. They were dragging foreigners off the Spanish vessel in order to board it themselves. Bullets flew as the GIs warned them off.

Alexandra and Tania found themselves pressed against a shipping container.

'We aren't going to get on,' Tania cried in panic. 'We're going to miss it.'

One of the GIs spotted them. He was a giant of a man and pushed through the crowd like Moses parting the Red Sea to reach them. Then, as Tania described it, he lifted them both by the collars of their coats and got them onto the ship.

Once on board, the unshaven, grubby-fingered captain asked Alexandra what she could pay – he wasn't taking anyone for free. She gave him the gold nuggets she had hidden in the bottom of the toothpaste tubes.

There were so many people on the ship that Alexandra and Tania could only find seats on the exposed bow.

'Sit with your head low,' an elderly man advised them. 'The communists will fire at us for trying to leave.'

As the old and dirty ship departed, Tania turned for one last look at the city that had been her home. China was all she had known.

'We'll be back,' said one confident young man with an accent Tania couldn't quite determine. It was a mix of British and something else. 'The Chinese can't survive without foreign businesses. They'll be begging us to come back soon.'

But Tania didn't believe it and neither did Alexandra. As they clung to each other, they knew the departure was forever. The captain had said he would get them to the Philippines, but beyond that they were on their own.

Although they were on their way out of Shanghai, the ordeal was far from over. The ship had to make its way down the Huangpu River before it reached the larger Yangtze River and could travel towards the ocean. The overloaded vessel sat low in the water and the river had been mined. A few months before, a ship called the *Jiangya* was spiriting away some of Shanghai's wealthiest Chinese citizens to Taiwan when it exploded. An estimated two to three thousand lives were lost: more than had perished on the *Titanic*.

After several tense hours, the ship reached the open sea, and those on board gave a cheer. But the jubilation was short-lived. The ship began to list dangerously to one side. There was a shout from below deck that it was taking on water. The crew tried to find the source of the leak, but it was impossible. The captain sent out a mayday call. There were no lifeboats or lifejackets. If a US Navy ship hadn't been in the vicinity to come to the vessel's aid, all on board would have perished, my grandmother and mother included.

# 7

I cannot tell the story of how my grandmother and mother ended up living on a small, uninhabited island in the Philippines without first introducing a Cossack and a former colonel in the White Army by the name of Gregory Bologoff.

The man is a legend among the White Russians of China, and any mention of him to my mother and her Russian friends would produce a collective cry of admiration at his daring and boldness. For there was little doubt among them that without Bologoff's intervention – and flair for the dramatic gesture – many of them would have perished.

When Shanghai was in danger of falling to the communists, Bologoff was the president of the Russian Emigrants' Association in the city. In late 1948, the situation was looking desperate for the White Russians who had no allegiance to the Soviet Union. They were aware of what had happened to those who had previously been convinced by the Soviet government to repatriate and who perished in the purges.

Bologoff knocked on the doors of the foreign consulates and sent out appeals to the United Nations (UN), pleading for asylum for the six thousand White Russians he represented. What he got in return was sympathy, but no offers of practical help. He turned to the International Refugee Organization (IRO), an agency of the UN that was formed in 1946 to deal with the massive displaced persons problem created by the Second World War. The agency was understaffed and overwhelmed when Bologoff met with their representatives from Geneva. With no countries coming forward to help the Russians, they made an offer to evacuate only five hundred of them.

'Gentlemen, are you playing with me?' Bologoff asked them.

'It is the best we can do,' the representatives told him. 'You'll have to take our offer or leave it.'

On hearing this, Bologoff took a revolver from his pocket. The representatives gasped and begged him to calm down.

'As a sign of my protest,' he told them, 'I will kill myself right here in this office if you do not meet my full request. You must evacuate all the Russians, or none. Their deaths will be on your heads.'

Bologoff's threat had the desired effect. The IRO officials searched their map for possibilities. During the war, the United States had used the Philippines as a base in the Pacific. Some of the islands had some infrastructure in the form of Quonset huts, orderly streets, warehouses, hospitals, churches and sometimes even swimming pools. They had electricity and running water. Such an island would be suitable for a refugee camp. Perhaps they could petition the Philippine government to let them lease one of these islands? Then the IRO could transfer the White Russians there until they could figure out a more permanent solution for them.

The Philippine government agreed that it could offer a tiny island in the archipelago named Tubabao. Unbeknown to the IRO, it was not one of the islands with infrastructure left by the Americans. It was a former leper colony that belonged to a good friend of President Quirino. As the IRO would be paying a per-head rental, there was money to be made for the president's friend.

Trusting that the president would not have offered them an

unsuitable site, the IRO did not send a scout to check it before the first refugee ship, carrying pregnant women, infants and young children, and elderly people set sail from Shanghai. A volunteer working party of Russian engineers and able-bodied men was sent ahead to set up the camp a short while before the ship was due to arrive. They expected that all they would be doing would be cleaning out the camp huts and making sure all the generators were working. What they found on arrival shocked them: the island was a jungle.

The working party's attempts to contact the IRO to stop the SS *Hwa Lien* coming all the way to a deserted island were met with silence, and the party did not have the tools to start clearing the jungle or the material necessary to build a camp. It was a disaster in the making.

But as the saying goes, necessity is the mother of invention.

With no one to translate for them, the working party managed to communicate to the locals living on the nearby island of Samar that they needed spades and other tools. They cleared some of the jungle and dug toilet pits. When they finally managed to make contact with the IRO about the dire situation, the IRO organised for some ex-army tents to be loaded onto the *Hwa Lien* when it docked in Manila.

When the ship arrived, those on board found themselves staring at an idyllic tropical island of white sand and palm trees surrounded by an azure sea. But Tubabao was not a resort. Beyond the beach, the jungle was full of mosquitos, snakes and scorpions. To complicate matters, before leaving Shanghai the refugees had been told that it wasn't necessary to bring practical items such as blankets, dishes or cooking and eating utensils, as those would all be provided. Most people had used their luggage allocation to pack their sentimental items, or things that could not easily be replaced, such as musical instruments, sewing machines, fur coats and evening wear. Many had brought jewellery, hoping to be able to sell it when they got to their permanent place of asylum. All those things would be of little use to them on a tropical island, but they did make the refugees sitting ducks for pirates.

The tents that were provided were left over from the war, and were of different sizes and many had holes in them. Those who came on the *Hwa Lien* found that instead of arriving at an established camp as they had been promised, they were having to stomp down on the long jungle grass and erect their own tents. It was a long way from Shanghai for those who had lived in fine houses, and dined on sturgeon and caviar. But even for those who had lived more modest lives in China, it was a long way from civilisation. It was *Gilligan's Island* for six thousand White Russians. But, initially at least, without the comedy.

~

Taking six thousand White Russians from Shanghai was very much like taking six thousand random people from Sydney, my native city, or any other large modern city and dumping them on an uninhabited island. These were not people used to living rough. Among them were businesspeople, artists, ballerinas, musicians, doctors, engineers, writers, teachers and seamstresses. Many of the families coming out to Tubabao included grandparents as well as young children and babies. Some of the refugees had chronic health conditions. While they were referred to as 'White Russians', they were in fact a mix of ethnicities: Russians, Ukrainians, Latvians, Lithuanians, Tatars and Poles.

Having in recent times emerged from a global pandemic that gave us all a sense of uncertainty, both in terms of our health and economically, we can perhaps sympathise more with the story of the refugees on Tubabao. During the pandemic, 'resilience' became the word of the day, as everyone had to adapt to a situation that was unprecedented for most of us, and one that was constantly changing. For the refugees on Tubabao, their resilience was tested in every way.

Financially they were all crushed, having left their homes and livelihoods behind with no compensation. With no countries offering them asylum, their futures looked bleak. For the sick, or those taking care of elderly parents or young children, the medical facilities on the island were primitive and soon many came down with dengue fever, typhoid and skin diseases.

Instead of nice homes in the French Concession, they were living in tents surrounded by jungle. Some feared that they might be left on the island forever, while others were afraid of being betrayed, as the Russians in Europe had been, and sent to the Soviet Union. It was a situation that could have crushed anyone's spirit and set nerves on edge. Many times, in similar situations, anarchy takes over as people fight for limited resources. Think of the toilet-paper hoarding and the refusal to comply with public health orders during the pandemic, not to mention the riots and the looting that sometimes took place.

It's this that makes what actually happened on Tubabao all the more extraordinary, and says something quite beautiful about the human spirit when people pull together.

~

The initial camp was a chaotic shanty town. With shipments of supplies from Russian societies in America being looted by corrupt customs officials, and help from the IRO being slow in coming, the refugees had to make cups and bowls from coconuts. They carved bits of bamboo into chopsticks, which fortunately most of them knew how to use from their experience of living in China.

There were doctors and nurses among them but no medicines or other supplies. In the hot, humid atmosphere, cuts could quickly turn septic. For the first four months, the only food the refugees had was macaroni, dehydrated vegetables and tins of corned beef hash that had been left over from the war. For fresh food, they had to eat the bananas and coconuts that grew on the island. Their toilets were holes in the ground and there was no privacy.

Initially, the refugees were required to write their letters in English, so they could be censored by the IRO lest news of the conditions of the camp be leaked.

~

It was into this surreal existence that my grandmother and mother arrived, sent there by the US Navy who didn't know what else to do with them. The other latecomers to the island included a dashing pilot who had defected from the Soviet Union by flying his military plane as far it would go before it ran out of fuel, and a seaman who had set out from the Soviet Union on a raft and would have died if he had not been rescued by Japanese fishermen.

'Well, the more hands on deck, the better,' the camp director told my grandmother and mother as he led them towards their tent. 'You're lucky to have come now rather than at the start. The place was a mess. Now we have fourteen orderly districts, each one responsible for its own communal kitchens and sanitary facilities.'

They passed old oil drums that were being used to collect rainwater for showers.

A hospital was set up, along with an asylum for the mentally ill. Later, they would learn that the refugees had traded with the local fishermen to get basic medicines until the IRO was able to provide them.

'Well, here it is,' said the director, indicating a tent with the sides rolled up. Tania's eye roamed over the two camp beds and the mosquito nets. A single 25-watt bulb dangled from one of the tent posts. 'The electricity is switched off at ten o'clock,' he told them, 'except on Saturday night when it stays on until eleven.'

After he left, Alexandra and Tania sat down on the beds and looked at each other. They were hot, bewildered and exhausted. They had been wearing the same clothes for a few weeks. They had thought that the US Navy base where they had stayed after being rescued from the sinking Spanish vessel had been spartan, but it was like the Ritz compared to Tubabao.

'It's a shock at first, but you'll get used to it,' a friendly looking blonde lady in the tent next to them said.

If there was one thing you had to learn to live without on Tubabao, it was any sort of privacy.

'Now the engineers have built a water pump, we don't have to make those dreaded trips to the creek each day. That place is a breeding ground for snakes,' their new neighbour told them.

Alexandra shivered. *Snakes?* But when she saw the look of terror on Tania's face, she pulled herself together. 'Listen, Tania,' she said, sitting next to her and putting her arm around her. 'We are better off here than in Shanghai. We must be thankful that the Philippine government has given us this island. Some of your friends from school will be here. Let's go find and them.'

That was what Alexandra was like. She was a woman who had lost everything and everyone, except her daughter, and yet she could always rally not only herself but those around her. In fact, it seemed that everyone on the island had approached the situation in more or less the same way. It's one thing for an individual to be resilient, but when a whole group of people are resilient together, it is extraordinary what they can achieve.

Despite the uncertainty and primitive conditions under which they were living, the Russians on Tubabao got on with life. They built churches and places of worship from leftover wood – including a Russian Orthodox church with a cupola and bells fashioned from empty gas cylinders that were filled with water at various levels to produce different tones. Weddings were officiated and babies christened. Schools were set up for the younger children and all the adults were given some sort of rostered work to do.

The musicians on the island, of which there were many, were given their own district and eventually formed a symphony orchestra, as well as a brass band and jazz group. An entertainment square with its own stage and dance floor was built in the middle of the camp. It was here that operas, ballets and plays were performed. The local population were invited to the island to participate in these cultural events. Another popular activity was Saturday night dancing to live jazz music.

The refugees who had been lawyers set up an Arbitration Board in case any disputes should arise, and the ex-policemen among them kept order – although the main problem they dealt with was people singing loudly after curfew, due to imbibing too much San Miguel beer.

~

While Alexandra worked with the other women in the district in the communal kitchen, Tania explored the island with her fellow teenagers, including a large contingent of boy scouts, scavenging for every piece of string, nail or bit of metal that had been left by the US Navy when Tubabao was used briefly as a receiving station. But teenagers being teenagers, they goofed off a lot too. They watched Hollywood movies that had been provided by the IRO (my mother would become an expert on the films from the Golden Age of Hollywood, but more on that later), dipped themselves in the pristine sea full of tropical fish under the watchful eye of a swimming instructor (as many of them couldn't swim) and collected shells. Sometimes they disobeyed their parents and hitched a ride with friendly natives on an outrigger to other islands, where they gazed at the beautiful sunsets from the beach.

Tania made some good friends on Tubabao, and they were to remain a tightly knit group after they migrated to Australia. One of them, Valentina, became my godmother.

But it wasn't always paradise. There was one suicide and another attempted one. Even in a near-idyllic natural setting, long-term uncertainty takes a toll on the mind – especially on those who have already been traumatised by previous experiences.

~

Australia had to be practically bribed by the IRO to take some of the refugees from Tubabao. Initially, the Australian government agreed to only accept men under forty-five, women under thirty-five and childless couples – and no matter what their profession had been in Shanghai, they would have to agree to perform manual work for the government for two years. Australia was looking for a workforce for postwar reconstruction, and the limitations imposed must have been disheartening for the older refugees, who perhaps wondered if they would ever practise their former professions again.

It also meant a potential break-up of extended families, when grandparents insisted their children take up the offer to start a new life while they remained behind on the island. After all, Australia had the reputation of a good climate and tolerance towards refugees. Russians who had migrated there earlier gave glowing reports on the country.

The United States, which eventually took most of the refugees, required sponsorship by an American citizen to guarantee employment and accommodation. To further complicate things, Russian children born in China were classified as 'Chinese' and were to be accepted under a different quota system, again resulting in the possibility of families being split up. France did throw a lifeline when it agreed to extend humanitarian aid by taking in those refugees who were suffering chronic illnesses for lifelong care. Such illnesses, including tuberculosis and other diseases contracted on the island, meant automatic rejection by the other countries.

~

The siren installed on Tubabao was the fastest means of communication. One blast was sounded to indicate 12 noon and 18:00 hours. Two blasts called a meeting of the district leaders. Three blasts was a summons for everyone to gather in the square. Four was for fire, a rare occurrence. It was the five blasts that everyone dreaded as the fifth blast signalled a typhoon warning.

With no solid buildings, there were few places to hide from the 140-miles-an-hour winds.

One afternoon, Alexandra and Tania were playing cards together on an upturned crate. The day had been especially hot and humid, and the women were perspiring fiercely, with beads of sweat pooling at the small of their backs.

Their concentration was broken when they heard excited voices. The district supervisor was going from tent to tent, telling people to tie down anything they could and to prepare for a storm. 'The camp director has just received the news. A typhoon is heading this way.'

'They've turned off the electricity to the walk-in refrigerator,' one woman told Alexandra. 'They're going to put the small children inside.'

That made sense to Alexandra. It was about as solid a structure as any on the island. But, she thought, glancing at Tania, what about the rest of us? What about the patients in the hospital? What about the old people?

The afternoon was full of industry. People dug holes to hide in from the winds. But the district supervisor had other ideas for the section of the camp where Tania and Alexandra were staying. He handed everyone ropes and told them to start moving to higher ground. They were going to tie themselves to palm trees, the way the natives did.

'You can't be serious?' Alexandra said.

But from the piercing look he sent her, she knew that he was.

Of all the things she had gone through, Tania thought the night of the typhoon would be her last. It was the sound of the wind she would never forget – howling like demons. The rain lashed at her face along with loose sticks and leaves. The palm tree that she and Alexandra had tied themselves to bent and shook with the strength of the wind. Every so often over the noise of the storm, Tania heard people weeping or calling out to their loved ones. The hospital's roof partially tore off and became a dangerous projectile, but fortunately the rest of the building remained intact.

When daylight broke, a terrible scene of devastation met Alexandra and Tania as they made their way back to the camp. The tents had collapsed. Many of them were torn. Trees had been uprooted. People's belongings were scattered everywhere. Tania rushed to her tent, tears streaming down her face. But although the tent had collapsed, her own and Alexandra's suitcases were undamaged. Apart from some water damage, the photograph albums they had brought with them had survived the storm.

Despite all the difficulties and dangers, the refugees keep their spirits up. They shared clothes with those who had lost them. Once the camp was cleaned up and order restored, they dressed in whatever finery they had and promenaded down the main street of the camp, sharing gossip and checking each other out, the way the Russian aristocrats used to do on the streets of Moscow, St Petersburg and Harbin.

Sometime afterwards, the Tubabao symphony orchestra gave a performance of Tchaikovsky's *1812 Overture*. The piece was written to commemorate the successful Russian defence against Napoleon's army and, rather aptly, had first been performed in a tent. As the overture reached the rousing moment of triumph in which church bells are supposed to ring in victory, the water-filled gas cylinders of the makeshift Russian church rang out instead.

The White Russians were people who had lost everything and whose future was uncertain. Yet, they remained resilient, undaunted, ready to face the future, no matter what it might bring.

~

The refugees were only meant to be on Tubabao for a short while. My grandmother and mother were on the island for five months before they sailed for Australia on 31 October 1949. My grandmother had upped Tania's age by three years to eighteen, so she would be permitted to migrate to Australia as Tania's adult dependent.

As well as the United States, others among the refugees were accepted into Brazil, Dominican Republic, Paraguay and Chile. Those with tuberculosis remained in the island hospital until late 1951. Some refugees waiting for US visas, which had been slow in coming, were also still on Tubabao at this time. It was this last remaining group that was hit by a lethal typhoon on 9 December 1951, the centre of which passed directly over the island. Two people were killed and many others injured. Tubabao was flattened. Afterwards, the remaining refugees were taken to Guiuan on the nearby island of Samar.

With the White Russians gone, the jungle grew back and obliterated all traces of the camp that had once stood there. It was if the six thousand people whose history was forever changed by that island had never been there at all.

# PURPOSE

# 8

With such ancestors as mine, sitting on my derrière too long and feeling sorry for myself when things went wrong for me was never going to be an option. It would be an insult to the memory of Grandfather Pavel riding across the plains of Siberia on his horse, the cup given to him by the last ill-fated Tsar tucked in his satchel and the sounds of battle ringing in his ears. What would Grandmother Alexandra have said of my own broken heart and grief, when she had lost everyone except her daughter, fled two homes and still carried on? Or my own mother, who went from being a privileged schoolgirl to a refugee with an uncertain future?

But isn't what is true for my forebears, true for everybody else's, too? The reason we are all here is because somebody in our ancestral line refused to give up.

And that, I think, should both encourage and humble us all.

The 'Third Generation Curse' refers to the phenomenon of family wealth built up by one generation being entirely lost in succeeding ones, quite often by the third. Surely we don't want to be the generation that squanders the resilience passed down from our parents and grandparents? It is a gift we need to draw on when our struggles threaten to overpower us. We need to remember that they too passed many dark nights of the soul *and survived*.

We are here because of the struggles and sacrifices of the generations before us. Let's make something of it.

~

After leaving Tubabao, the adventure – and the hardship – was not yet over for my grandmother and mother. Their arrival in Sydney in the early hours of the morning was something of a shock. While Shanghai had been all congestion and chaos, Australia's largest city seemed supernaturally quiet and orderly. The passengers gaped at the massive Harbour Bridge as the ship passed under it. It was late spring, and they had heard that Australia was warm, but a cold wind was blowing across the water, bringing the smell of brine with it. The passengers shivered in their thin cotton clothing. Seagulls swooped overhead, squawking and screeching. They were the only familiar thing about the setting.

There was a train waiting on the dock, dirty and grimy.

'It's a goods train,' Tania said to Alexandra.

'I think you are right,' my grandmother replied, taking a thin blanket she had acquired on Tubabao and wrapping it around Tania's shoulders.

Their sparse luggage was unceremoniously unloaded by a crane and deposited in an unruly pile. The passengers had to scramble to retrieve their belongings. After that they went through immigration, before being rounded up like cattle and told to board the train that Tania had thought was for freight. Tania and Alexandra found window seats. They had thought they would be staying in the city, but discovered that everybody was being sent out west to a camp.

~

The sun was beginning to rise, and Tania laid eyes on her new country. The central city was modern, with Art Deco buildings, but soon the train was passing through depressing suburbs with shanty-type housing and broken washing lines. Sydney was in the midst of a housing shortage. People were sleeping in bathtubs or renting out the landings on stairwells. Tania held back her tears for her mother's sake, but once the train began the ascent up to the Blue Mountains, her spirits lifted again. There, the Australian bush worked its magic on her; it was a love affair that would last the rest of her life. The trees were unlike anything she had ever seen before. Tall, majestic. Some of them had white bark. Later she would buy a book that listed all their names – blue gum, stringybark, scribbly gum – but at that moment they were all a fascinating mystery.

It was dusk when they arrived at Kelso train station. Tania looked down at the strange copper-coloured dust that covered her shoes when she walked through it to get to the bus. When they arrived at the camp, she squeezed Alexandra's arm. It was an army barracks. An Australian flag hung limply on a flagpole in the centre of it and there were rabbits hopping everywhere.

~

My mother always spoke of Australia with high regard, and my father tells me that my grandmother was the same. They were so glad to be given asylum that they never criticised the food and shelter they were given. When I was researching *White Gardenia*, I read many stories about the migrants who came from all over Europe to the camp.

The accommodation was unlined, unheated iron sheds or timber barracks. The migrants suffered the heat in summer and froze in winter. But due to the housing shortage, there were many Australians living in similar situations or worse. Tent cities in parks and on the verges of country roads were a common sight, so I don't believe it was discrimination on the part of the government.

The biggest heartbreak for most of the migrants was that families were broken up – and at a time when they needed the support of their loved ones the most. Orders were barked out of loudspeakers – often in German, which was considered a unifying language for many of the Europeans. Often those who had been in concentration camps broke down at the sound of it. Due to the large influx of people to the camp, the toilet blocks were often filthy and overflowing, and blowflies were always swarming around them. Sometimes there were maggots in the meat that was served at dinner.

Tania, sensitive as she was, seems to have survived all of this by exploring nature. The first time she saw a kangaroo near her barracks, she went running to tell the other women. One of the women thought the animal might be dangerous, and tried to shoo it away – unsuccessfully – with a broom. Tania thought the pink and grey galahs were the most beautiful birds she had ever seen.

The only thing that she ever said against camp life concerned a slight she never forgot. When the English migrants arrived, they were given proper tablecloths and vases of flowers, while those from Europe had their tables covered in brown paper.

'At our table were opera singers and ballerinas. Very cultured and educated people,' my mother told me. 'The English migrants were ordinary people, but were treated like kings and queens. I didn't resent them being treated well or made to feel welcome, but it did make the rest of us feel less welcome and of less value as human beings.'

~

My mother placed all people on an equal footing. She didn't like hierarchy that made one person more valuable than another. When Queen Elizabeth II came to Australia in 1954, her boss sent her and the other employees to Farm Cove to see Her Majesty arrive by boat. My mother always commented on how beautiful the Queen's skin was, but she was not a royalist despite her father being a supporter of the last Russian Tsar, who, along with the Tsarina, was a first cousin of King George V of England. She hated colonialism, having witnessed the exploitation of the Chinese people. She didn't like communism either – she thought it corrupt and hypocritical – but she believed China had a right to rule itself without the interference of foreigners.

Like Grandmother Alexandra, my mother made friends with people of all nationalities, and it never occurred to me to not pick a friend based on their race. It took me a long time to realise that hadn't been the case for many of my Australian-born friends. My father was Australian through and through, and yet he was colourblind, too. I can only explain this by the fact that my father was a senior engineer in the NSW Health department for many years. He is highly technical and tends to relate to people at that level rather than noticing appearances and accents. He worked with people of many different nationalities. He was so colourblind that when I was dating a Japanese student at university with a strong accent and the very Japanese name of Hachiro Yamamoto, my father didn't notice he was Japanese until six months later, when Hachiro told him that he had been born in Tokyo. My father shared this exciting discovery with my mother.

'Did you know that Hachiro is Japanese? He's from Tokyo. Isn't that interesting?'

It was all my mother could do to not roll her eyes.

I think a bold life and a rich life are synonymous. I believe to live boldly you have to live broadly – to read widely and to experience different cultures; not from a five-star hotel or a cruise ship, but by forming friendships with people from different parts of the world.

I'm sure if my parents hadn't brought me up that way, I wouldn't be able to write fiction set in different countries that feels authentic even to readers born in those countries.

~

Alexandra and Tania were in the migrant camp at Bathurst for three months before accommodation could be found for them in Sydney. Initially, they shared a bedroom in a house with an Italian family in North Sydney. Tania's English was fluent, and she was able to go to secretarial school and eventually gain employment with a timber merchant. Alexandra had done her best to learn English at the classes that had been offered in the camp, but she found it difficult to grasp the Australian accent. She found work cooking and cleaning for an elderly couple, and did sewing work when she could get it. She and Tania scrimped and saved enough money to buy a modest block of land in Port Stephens as a future investment. They also moved into a small apartment of their own. At fifty-one years of age, and having lived through so many tumultuous events, Alexandra was still her buoyant, cheerful self, but Tania noticed that she tired more easily and sometimes had trouble breathing.

'You must go to the doctor,' Tania told her one afternoon, when Alexandra was wheezing as she climbed the steps to their apartment.

Her mother shook her head. 'What for, Tania? I'm fine. Doctors cost money.'

But still Tania was worried.

Their life in Australia was not without incident. Alexandra was used to cooking dishes based on rice, but the grain was difficult to find in Sydney in any decent quantity. She and Tania would go to Chinatown and buy a large sack of rice, and then cart it home together on the bus. One day, as they were carrying a sack into the apartment, a nosy neighbour spotted them and reported them to the police as 'communist spies'. They were interrogated at the police station, both terrified that they were going to be deported to the Soviet Union. When they learned that the reason they had been suspected of shaky loyalties to their adopted country was because they ate large quantities of rice, they switched to cooking with macaroni. For all Australia's parochialism, tuna and macaroni bake was a popular staple in the 1950s, and spaghetti bolognaise had taken off as an exotic dish served in five-star restaurants such as Romano's.

'Let's hope they don't arrest us as Italian fascists for eating pasta,' Alexandra quipped.

~

If it wasn't for postwar migration from countries other than Britain, I hate to imagine what we would still be eating in Australia. Even the beach staple, the Chiko Roll, was inspired by Chinese spring rolls. Glancing through a few 1950s women's magazines gives me a clue as to what a nightly dinner without ethnic influences might have looked like: pea and ham soup, fish fingers and mashed potato, carrot gelatine salad, all finished off with a slice of chiffon pie. Nevertheless, the 'New Australians' were encouraged to assimilate as quickly as possible. It had been a hard sell for the Chifley government to convince the Australian people that an influx of foreigners would be a good thing for the country. Therefore, the migrants were encouraged to only speak English in public and take up Australian cultural pastimes so that the locals could perhaps overlook the fact that Luigi, Wolfgang, Zsófia and Jadwiga hadn't been born here.

My mother's first name was 'Tatiana', most often shortened to the

Russian diminutive 'Tania'. But even that was too exotic-sounding for her colleagues at the timber merchants, so her boss suggested she call herself 'Deanna' instead. My father would later turn this into 'Diane', while others got confused between 'Deanna' and 'Deanne', or 'Diana' or 'Diane', and my mother politely never corrected anybody. When I was a little girl, it seemed to me my mother had so many different names, depending on who she was talking to, that I was relieved I only had to call her 'Mum'.

Alexandra kept her diagnosis of heart failure from her daughter. The doctor she had secretly seen had given her some tablets, which she hid in her sewing basket. She disguised her need to sit down when her heart started racing as a sudden interest in detective novels, a pile of which she kept next to the sofa. The doctor had given her five to ten years at the most. Her greatest goal became to see Tania happily married. She sewed her a lovely dress of white silk with a beaded, strapless bodice and full skirt to go dancing at the Trocadero, a large Art Deco dance hall on George Street that featured big band orchestras.

'You must go out dancing with young people,' she told Tania. 'You must make lots of friends in Australia. Don't be shy. Friends are the best gifts you can have in life.'

At the Trocadero, Tania met an outgoing young Polish woman with Grace Kelly good looks. Her name was Victoria and she would become one of Tania's lifelong friends. She would also change the course of Tania's destiny one summer, when she invited her to join her on a YMCA camp on the picturesque Grose River.

Tania had begun dating a young man named Peter, whom she had met at the Trocadero, who was at the camp too. She wanted him to take her rowing on the river, as she'd heard that there were koalas in the bushlands and she was keen to see them. Peter wasn't particularly athletic, and after taking the boat around in circles for a while, they set off down the river. A handsome young man with jet-black hair and green eyes named Stanley was rowing on the river that day too. A volunteer lifesaver, he had strong biceps and a six-pack. He had trained in rough surf conditions, so he found the river easy to navigate. He saw Peter struggling and approached him to offer some helpful advice.

'Use your legs first, then your body, then your arms. And don't put your blades in too deep. You'll find it easier that way.'

Stanley, who would one day become my father, then smiled at the pretty, slim young woman sitting in the boat, who would one day be my mother. He'd seen her at the camp, always surrounded by friends. She was good at shuttlecock, he'd noticed.

'Maybe you could take Deanna on a tour of the river?' Peter said. 'I'm beat.'

'It would be my pleasure,' Stanley said, trying to not look as keen as he felt.

Having swapped places with Peter, my future father rowed my future mother down the river.

The Grose Valley is scenic with towering forests of eucalypt trees. It teems with wildlife. As Stanley rowed Deanna along the quiet, pristine river, they would have heard the iconic song of the eastern whipbirds. The male bird makes a call that sounds like a long whistle which finishes with a whipcrack, and the female answers him with a few sweet melodic notes.

My parents fell in love on that boat trip along the Grose. Although Peter would constantly rib my father that he had stolen his girl, he took it with good humour, as it was clear to everyone that my parents were a love match.

'Your mother always treated people well,' my father told me recently when he was reminiscing about that camp. 'That's what I liked most about her. Good looks come and go, but a kind heart is forever.'

~

My parents got married in 1957, but it would be a long time before they would think about having a family. They wanted the security of a home of their own first. My father was working as a draftsman during the day and studying to be a mechanical engineer at night. My mother had been required to give up her job at the timber merchant upon getting married, but she managed to find private secretarial work. They found an apartment in North Sydney and Alexandra lived in the apartment next door. She did the shopping, cooking and cleaning. She loved my father and spoiled him often with his favourite dessert of rice pudding.

One hot February evening in 1962, my mother went to Alexandra's apartment after work. My grandmother looked unusually tired.

'Sit down, Mama,' my mother told her. 'You've been working too hard in this heat. I'll make dinner tonight.'

'All right,' Alexandra reluctantly agreed. 'I must be getting old.'

'Nonsense, you're only sixty. You're still a young woman.'

My mother went to the kitchen and started on the meal, peeling the potatoes and shelling the peas. As she worked, she told Alexandra about her day, only noticing after a few minutes that her mother had stopped talking.

'Mama?'

My mother walked out into the lounge room. Alexandra was lying on the sofa. At first, my mother thought she must have nodded off to sleep. But then she stepped closer and saw that her mother was deathly pale and completely still.

'Mama!'

But Alexandra was gone. Her heart had given out as the doctor had warned her it would. I don't think my mother ever got over the loss.

# 9

That I never got to meet Grandmother Alexandra is something I have always regretted. My mother would often tell me how similar we were in our personalities.

'You laugh like she did,' she'd say. 'And both of you are strong-willed.'

My mother's heart was broken by her mother's death. Her friend Victoria told me that she was very quiet for a year after Alexandra died, and hardly said a word to anybody. When, years later, I eventually came along, she was delighted because she believed she and I would have the same close bond she'd had with her mother.

I adored my mother, but unlike her and my grandmother, we were from two different cultures. Even our first languages were different. I would have loved to have grown up bilingual, but unfortunately one xenophobic and ignorant man put an end to that.

Although my mother had become an Australian citizen, and she grew to love this country passionately, she and many other Russians living here had a deep-seated fear of being sent to the Soviet Union, where they would be executed. Therefore, they were always on their 'best behaviour' around Australians. But my mother also loved her Russian heritage. One day, when I was four years old, we were standing at a set of traffic lights waiting to cross the road. We had just been shopping together and were laughing and enjoying ourselves. My mother was speaking to me in Russian and then suddenly, seemingly out of nowhere, a man appeared and screamed right into her face, 'Speak in English! Bloody communist!'

I was scared because I had no idea why the man was angry. But my mother was so terrified that she never spoke to me in Russian again. Ever! I have often wondered what it was like for her to have to speak to her children in her second language, not her first – her heart language. What a great loss for her and for me.

~

I struggled to understand my mother sometimes – especially her fears, because it seemed to me that life was quite safe and lovely. But then, I was growing up in Australia where life *was* generally safe and lovely compared to the experiences that she had gone through. When I was at university it became clear that my beloved and adored mother, my best friend, was a significant contributor to my illogical anxiety. That was a hard pill to swallow. My older brothers resisted being wrapped in cottonwool: the eldest drove in car rallies, and the other brother took up high-risk activities like skydiving and scuba diving with sharks. Later, as a federal agent, he accepted assignments to dangerous parts of the world and went undercover. My brothers and I reacted to our mother's overprotectiveness in opposite ways, and as a result their worlds expanded while mine shrank.

But when I met the hypnotherapist, I knew that what he said was right. I was going to have go away and spread my wings if I was ever to be free of my mother's anxiety. Perhaps I would even discover an anxiety that was uniquely my own.

It was difficult for my mother when I told her I was going to finish my degree at the University of California, and that I'd received a scholarship and funding to do so. It was as if I had betrayed the sacred mother–daughter bond. She and my grandmother had been two peas in a pod. They had been through everything together. They would never have dreamed of separating from each other. Yet, and I will always be thankful for this, my mother accepted my need to fly, even if she didn't quite understand it. My father was also supportive, reassuring her that it was a wonderful opportunity and the result of all my diligent study.

The day I was leaving for Los Angeles, two friends of mine from university came along to the airport, not so much to farewell me but to support my mother. I remember how flushed her cheeks were as she tried her best not to cry.

'She'll be back before you know it,' my father kept telling her. 'And what an amazing adventure she'll have.'

When it was time for me to go, my mother held me fiercely by the shoulders and peered into my face as she always had when I was younger and leaving for school in the morning. But then her grip softened.

'You'll have a wonderful time,' she told me. 'I'm so proud of you. Make the most of every minute.'

I felt relieved that she wasn't picturing me as the victim of a college shooter or a serial killer, and it lifted my spirits. But as I walked towards the gate and turned back once more to my parents and friends, I saw my mother lift her hand to wave, but then turn and sob into my father's shoulder. I left Australia, not feeling like a university student going on an adventure, but like the worst and most ungrateful daughter on the planet.

~

As it turned out, going to study in California was a transformative experience. Not only did I come fully into my own, but my relationship with my mother blossomed from that of two terrified human beings clinging to each other, to a healthy adult mother-and-daughter alliance. Left to my own devices and fending entirely for myself, I discovered that I was quite good at looking after myself. I found a wonderful place to live on Balboa Island, just off Newport Beach, with another student. I made lots of friends. Together we studied, we travelled, we threw parties. I fell in and out of love with ease. I was on a grand adventure and felt for the first time that I was defining myself and living as I wished to live. Not because I was away from my mother, but because I was away from Sydney and what in many ways was a stifling atmosphere for anybody who didn't fit a certain mould.

After Sydney hosted the Olympics in 2000, it transformed into a truly international, vibrant metropolis. Since then, it has grown more elegant and confident, and developed a sense of style. Now it is a city friendly to artists, funky fashion, dreamers, spiritual seekers and women in a way it never was before. These days I feel very at home here and not lacking for anything. Although I sometimes toy with the idea of living in Paris, it is a whim that has no sense of urgency about it. But back in the mid-90s, I found Sydney a dull place, with such a conservative mindset that living in it felt like walking in too-tight shoes. Although its natural setting is one of the most spectacular in the world, I never related to its masculine, brawny energy or its crude humour, or to a lifestyle that was so focused on sport and pub life that people who didn't relate to those things were immediately regarded with suspicion. It wasn't a hub of creativity, and even though I went to its most prestigious university, student life was rather staid. Any sort of originality was immediately shot down.

I think, in the end, my mother saw that and sometimes felt it too, and that's why she knew I had to go.

California in the mid-90s had a conservative puritanism of its own.

Sometimes it could be downright cheesy. But those things produced a counterculture on campus that was irreverent and exciting. It was also highly theatrical. The proximity to Hollywood meant nearly every party was an elaborate costume affair. All of this thrilled the Russian part of me. Russians dress up for life. They dress up to go to the supermarket. Russian women have been known to wear high heels to go to the gym or jogging. It had always been a sad disappointment to go to a student party in Sydney and find everyone wearing the same jeans and the same Doc Martens. Since I was a child, I've always craved glamour and pizzazz (a fantasy no doubt fed by all the old Hollywood movies I watched with my mother). Until California, I only ever found it in ballet pantomimes.

The university offered courses in fiction as well as summer writing camps. Revered Australian writer Thomas Keneally was visiting professor for the university's graduate writing program at the time. Although as an undergraduate I didn't have access to his classes, the fact that everybody on campus knew him and spoke about him with reverence showed that writing and writers were taken seriously.

I hadn't gone there to study writing – my undergraduate degree was in Asian studies – but I had dreamed of being a writer ever since I could hold a pencil. My mother had fostered that dream by buying me notebooks and encouraging me to write my stories down as soon as I was old enough to string five words together. But nobody apart from her thought of it seriously as a profession. I once told my school's careers adviser that I wanted to be a writer, and he replied that I needed to think about a 'real job'. He sent me for work experience to a metropolitan newspaper, where hardened journalists with alcohol issues told me that a cadetship would involve reporting on car accidents or else putting together the television guide. It wasn't the sort of writing I'd had in mind.

I kept my desire to write novels secret for years, only later daring to mention it once to my dodgy boyfriend (whom I had left behind in Australia). His supportive comment was, 'You? A writer? But you haven't got anything interesting to say.'

In California, when I dared to reveal my secret desire, my fellow students were fully behind it. 'You've got to go for your dream!'

That statement could perhaps be the life motto for Californians. I was in the land of big dreams. It didn't matter if they were studying medicine, they still believed in their dream of being a champion surfer. Or if they were studying to be a teacher, they wanted to be the kind of teacher who transformed the lives of disadvantaged children. In the mind of my Californian peers, a life without big dreams wasn't a life worth living. And if, after giving it your all, you should die on the sword of your unrealised desire, so what? At least you tried, instead of forever wondering what might have been.

I was in the right place at the right time and with the right people around me.

Surrounded by such energy and verve, my creativity exploded. The campus I attended was popular with European students and, all being far from home, we gravitated towards each other. I realised that I naturally connected to European ways of viewing the world. Like me, many of the students had families who had been uprooted by the Second World War and its aftermath. Some were the offspring of orphaned parents, others had grandparents who had been part of resistance networks, and there was one who bore the guilt of having a grandfather who had been an active member of the Nazi SS. His grandfather felt no shame, but my friend felt it keenly on his behalf. Their sensitivities and viewpoints were very close to my own. We shared similar senses of aesthetics and humour. I had loved American writers for years – John Irving, Kurt Vonnegut, Edith Wharton – but now my European friends encouraged me by giving me novels by their favourite European writers: Hermann Hesse, Marguerite Duras, Italo Calvino and more.

Many were writers I had heard of, and some I had already read, but now I had people who wanted to discuss these books with me in cafes, over a bottle of wine, even on the beach as we watched tanned *Baywatch*-worthy beauties strut through the sand in gold bikinis and high heels.

For somebody embarking on a dream, a crowd of people who cheer you on and take your quest seriously is a gift indeed.

~

As I came into my own in California, my mother blossomed too. Email was not a thing then and calling overseas from Australia was expensive. As Skype and Zoom were still far off in the future, our main communication was by letter. It sounds so Jane Austen when I say it now, but that is how it was. As it turns out, it was rather lovely because my mother kept my letters and I re-read them recently when I was helping my father declutter his home. In the words on the page, I could feel the warmth of our exchanges. I was happy to discover I was not a self-absorbed young woman, and that my letters were kind and encouraging. It comforted me because there was a time after my mother died when I wondered if I had appreciated her enough. The evidence that I did was there in writing. Those exchanges would have been lost if we had been texting.

Without me constantly in sight to worry about, and with the lags resulting from the vagaries of the postal service between the United States and Australia, my mother simply had to trust that I was all right, and that no news meant I was busy with life – not that something terrible had befallen me. She took up her own interests: tai chi, Japanese conversation skills, modern history. She made new friends, as well as keeping up with her old ones, and took better care of herself and her own needs. My brother Paul and his wife had their first child, too, and so my mother looked after my first nephew a few times a week while her daughter-in-law was working. It's amazing, when you leave home, how quickly your parents find a new use for your room. Mine became a shrine to Baby James and his fascination with Thomas the Tank Engine.

# 10

After I finished my studies in California, I wasn't ready to return to Sydney. Instead, I went to visit my European friends in their home countries. It was an expansive cultural experience. Many of them were undertaking their graduate studies, so I stayed in their student dorms with them, often going back on weekends with them to visit their parents. I got to experience life as a student in several different cities – Berlin, Heidelberg, Vienna, Rome, Bologna, Venice, Prague and Paris. I went to their student parties, sat in on some classes, ate in university canteens (the food at Ca' Foscari University in Venice was five-star!), and got around on a bicycle. While I was travelling, a friend in California sent me information about a postgraduate course in creative writing that the University of Melbourne was offering for the first time. So, after returning to Australia and staying with my parents for a month, I was off to Melbourne. My mother was happy because the city was only an hour away from Sydney by plane, in the same time zone, and phone calls within Australia were inexpensive.

I lived in a cute Art Deco apartment in Carlton North with an interesting woman from Zimbabwe and her smart and personable niece. Every Sunday evening, the furniture in the lounge room would be moved out of the way and other members of the African community in Melbourne would come round for a dance-a-thon. It was a fun cultural education.

Melbourne was a city with an old-school grandeur. Despite its bitingly cold winter, I liked its vibe and Gothic atmosphere. Unfortunately, at that time, the University of Melbourne was rife with sexual harassment, bullying and nepotism, and 'old-school' quickly lost its appeal. In the end, I was glad to get away from it after finishing my course and return to Sydney, where I undertook a master's degree in creative writing at the University of Technology. The head of school at my new university was the revered and adored author Glenda Adams a winner of the Miles-Franklin Award.

~

My dream of becoming a writer did not eventuate quickly. I studied part-time while working in publicity for a book publishing company and lived in a tiny studio apartment in Potts Point, near Sydney's Kings Cross. It was a happy life with interesting work colleagues who supported my dream, and through my work I met plenty of professional writers who also offered their encouragement.

Yet, despite all my sincere efforts, everything I wrote was rejected. Everything! A novel; a non-fiction book; numerous short stories; and hundreds of magazine and newspaper articles. It was discouraging because I spent nearly all my free time working on my writing, but I kept writing nonetheless. Part of the problem was that my subject matter and style was out of step with the kind of Australian fiction that was being published at that time. It was the era of 'grunge lit': books about inner-city recreational drug use – raw, explicit and vulgar. The stories involved copious amounts of body fluid – vomit, urine and blood – as well as pointless violence. I couldn't think of anything that interested me less. I wanted to write coming-of-age stories and books that celebrated human dignity and courage. I wanted to write about European and Asian history. Although I was surrounded by great people, I was in the wrong place at the wrong time.

Despite the difficulties, it was a special time for my relationship with my mother. We had grown into good friends. She had accepted that I was not going to be the daughter she had envisioned, one that stayed close to home and provided her with a multitude of grandchildren. But that adjustment in her expectations in no way diminished her love for me. When I felt discouraged by all the rejection I was receiving for my writing, she buoyed my spirits with her unwavering faith.

~

Over many cups of tea, my mother began telling me the story of her childhood again, only now she was relating it to another adult, not a child. She could share the more difficult parts of her life without needing to censor them. It was clear that she was still very much affected by what had happened to her, and she would start to cry when she spoke about Pavel or Sergei. For my master's degree, I was required to write a full-length novel in place of a thesis, and it would be assessed by two published authors. My mother's story became the inspiration for that novel.

Then, an opportunity that I had only dreamed of seemed to manifest out of nowhere: a chance to work in New York. The city shone in my mind as a place for artistic and literary inspiration equalled only by Paris. It had been home to the Chelsea Hotel, where Simone de Beauvoir, Mark Twain, William S. Burroughs and other literary luminaries had stayed and written their masterpieces, attracted by the cheap rent, the Queen Anne rosewood-trimmed rooms and the vibe. The 3-foot-thick walls would have been a bonus for writers as well, as the hotel was also used by music legends such as Bob Dylan and Janis Joplin. At the time, I was enamoured of Anaïs Nin's minimalist yet rich writing, and what she wrote about New York to her lover and fellow writer Henry Miller, that the city was beautiful and magic 'like drinking from a Venetian glass'. To Nin, the city was 'made for great swoops of daring' and was 'full of hope.'

My mother sighed when I told her I was leaving the country again, but this time she was confident in my ability to take care of myself and said, 'You need to go. Your soul is a restless one.'

She bought me a laptop, which was still something of a novelty in the late 90s. She also gave me a special gift. When Pavel died, my grandmother had his and her wedding rings melded together and set with a stone of amethyst, her favourite gem. 'Wear it when you write,' my mother told me. 'Your ancestors will help you.'

~

The New York I found was not the New York I had expected. The bohemian cafes where I had hoped to listen to poetry had been taken over by Starbucks. Greenwich Village was occupied by bankers. The novelists and playwrights had been replaced by screenwriters. But it was still a rich experience. A very *rich* experience. The company that I worked for ran financial conferences and our clients were the likes of Goldman Sachs, Morgan Stanley, Deutsche Bank and Moody's. I got to travel around the USA, Europe and the Caribbean and stay in some of their most luxurious hotels. Then, when the conference was over, I would return to the shabby, draft-ridden apartment that I shared with five British girls.

My bedroom came directly off the kitchen, a common layout in

New York apartments where that room is referred to as 'the maid's room'. The telephone for the apartment (mobile phones were still a novelty – even Carrie from *Sex and the City* was using payphones in 2000) was right outside my door, so I initially tried to write *White Gardenia* and its Russian characters with the voices of English, Scottish and Welsh young women speaking to their boyfriends in my head. As that proved unworkable, I started getting up at four or five o'clock in the morning to write. I'd light a scented candle and put on the ring my mother had given me and work until seven o'clock when my roommates got up. The central heating in that apartment was unreliable and the seals on the window in my room were broken. One January morning, I woke up to find a pile of snow along the inside of my windowsill and on my rug. After that, I was terrified I might freeze to death in my sleep like the Little Match Girl, so I moved to a large and well-heated brownstone in Brooklyn with an American woman and her two cats. My new home was so quiet and cosy that, after having acclimatised to the chaos of my previous apartment, for the first month I found it almost impossible to write.

~

People often tell me: 'I would love to write a book, if only I could find the time.' I assure them that when I wrote *White Gardenia,* I also did not have the time. When I wasn't in the office from eight in the morning until six in the evening, I was in airports, on aeroplanes or in hotel rooms. I spent my days making sure some of the most important people from the most important financial companies in New York had enough pens and squeeze balls. I had to remind some of the most important people from the most important financial companies in New York that they needed to take their passport when they were going to a foreign country – there was no special exception to the rules, even for them. Late at night, I was often helping the most important people from the most important financial companies in New York find their way back to their rooms. It was exhausting.

But what I did have was a tremendous desire to tell the story I was writing. I was consumed by passion, something that I say more about when I share the story of Carmen Amaya. A lot of the time, writing will be associated with terms like 'self-discipline', or even get broken down into something that involves time management and a certain number of words per day. You don't need any of that if you are consumed by passion. If you have a clear picture of what you want to create and the strong urge to create it, that is enough to push you through any difficulties. Even people with the perfect conditions – a romantic farmhouse in the Tuscan countryside, along with a maid to serve them meals and a butler to stand at the door and shush anyone making too much noise – won't be able to write more than a first chapter, maybe not even a first page, if they aren't driven by desire. I liken it to world leaders and CEOs and other extremely busy people managing to have illicit affairs. How do they maintain a double life when the rest of us are struggling to fit work, exercise and sleep into the same twenty-four hours allotted to us all? The answer is, they are highly motivated. With enough desire, you can do anything, no matter how busy you are.

~

As well as rubbing shoulders with New York's financiers, I met other creative people. I attended some filmmaking courses out of interest and was offered the opportunity to work on set with some independent filmmakers making straight-to-video low-budget horror movies. The first day I arrived on set, the director was standing over an actor lying on the floor with his insides splayed over his chest. Or at least the make-up artist had cleverly made it seem that the actor's body had exploded. The director was eating a pastrami sandwich with tomato sauce oozing out of it. It was my first lesson that weak stomachs would not survive horror-movie productions.

'Hey, are you from Australia?' the soft-spoken director asked me.

I nodded.

'You're hired.'

Obviously, some sort of reputation about my home country had proceded me, and although I knew nothing about working on a film set, I was thrown in the deep end and had to learn quickly. I became the continuity coordinator. My job was to record the scenes and takes, and to make sure that the boom hadn't dipped too far into the frame and that nothing that shouldn't be in the shot was there. So, it was a bit ironic that I inadvertently ended up in a scene – holding my clipboard in the corner – of a movie about an alien invasion.

Although horror is not a favourite genre of mine, I loved the camaraderie of our group. Everybody helped everybody out, and I got to know the creepiest houses in Queens, the dankest cellars in Manhattan and the chilliest woodlands of New Jersey. I also developed a sympathy for actors, who must be able to take rejection even more than writers. The directors I worked with valued my opinion enough to ask me to sit in on auditions, but I also got the role of ringing the unsuccessful candidates (no texting to hide behind then). I found that painful, but it was a good insight into the rejection process. I saw that it was rare that anyone was rejected because of a lack of talent, but rather other arbitrary concerns such as whether the actor's appearance matched the director's vision of the character. Later, when I was a published author, I undertook some acting courses to help me with character development, and someone asked me if I was going into acting as a backup in case the writing didn't work out. I stared at them and then answered: 'You're kidding, right?'

During this period, I was credited as a writer on *Werewolf Tales*, and I also made my first short film: *Unexpected Source*. I consider it up there with the films of my favourite director, Federico Fellini, in that it makes very little sense – but only to the untrained eye, of course!

# 11

A hitch with my work visa meant I had to return to Sydney. It was only supposed to be for a couple of months, but then the attack on the World Trade Center on 11 September 2001 changed everything. The financial sector was in disarray, and conferences were the last thing on anybody's mind. The whole situation was uncertain. I decided to stay in Australia. After the long, cold winters of New York, where so much of life was lived indoors or underground on the subway, I appreciated my home city in a new way. The first time I caught a train to the city on the North Shore Line, I stood up and stared out of the window as the train travelled over the Harbour Bridge. The blue sky and the sparkling harbour seemed like magic. I also appreciated having nature around me again. Central Park was scenic, but it was usually crowded. After seeing only squirrels, rats and pigeons for so long, I was amazed by the colourful birds and unique wildlife that visited my parents' garden. I had appreciated them as a child, and now I was appreciating them as an adult. My writing career was about to take a major turn in a new direction too.

I had finished my reworking of *White Gardenia* while in New York, and my literary agent liked it so much that she decided to auction it. *Auction it!* I thought that was a crazy idea after everything else I had written had been rejected. To my amazement, not only did several publishers bid for it, but I was offered a two-book deal. Did I have an idea for a second book? No! But those publishers remembered the first novel I had submitted and which was rejected, so they had faith that, having now written two novels, I was capable of writing a third one – and more. The only person left to convince was myself. I would have to change my self-image from a struggling writer who was always going to be rejected to that of a professional author. I was going to have to get serious about my writing, too. No more flitting about the world. I needed to settle down. So I did. To prove it, I acquired the two kittens named Gardenia and Lilac.

To say that my mother was proud of me would have been an understatement. To say that her Russian friends were excited would also be downplaying things. Now all I had to do was deliver another book.

I am so grateful that, after all my struggles, my mother got to see me succeed because I had no idea that our time would be so suddenly cut short. While I was working on my second book, *Wild Lavender*, my father, who had been robustly healthy and had never even so much as caught a cold, discovered he needed major heart surgery. As it turned out, he nearly died on the operating table. During his long and difficult recovery, I stayed with my parents to help them. My father seemed to be emerging out of the woods as I was finishing *Wild Lavender*. The day the proof copy arrived, I gave it to my mother to read because I was busy with a number of publicity activities and I had to go to the monthly meeting of the wildlife group for which I was now a volunteer. She spent her entire day reading the book and, thinking that I would be back late and she wouldn't have a chance to see me, she left me a note to tell me how much she enjoyed it:

Dearest Belinda,

This is a beautiful book. I enjoyed reading it very much. I am so proud of my talented daughter and all she has accomplished.

Love,

Mum XX

As it turned out, my parents both stayed up late that evening. They were watching an old black-and-white movie, *Mrs. Miniver*, and sitting together on the sofa holding hands. I smiled when I saw them: married for forty-seven years and still holding hands. My two young cats, Gardenia and Lilac, were asleep next to them. The movie finished as I was making a cup of tea in the kitchen. I heard my mother say something about being tired and going to bed. She passed by me and told me she was going to warm up some hot water bottles for the cats. It really wasn't necessary as they slept under the covers next to me, one tucked under each arm, but she enjoyed spoiling them. She went to the laundry to get the bottles, and the kettle in the kitchen started boiling. I heard my mother call out to me and thought she must have burned her hand with the hot water from the laundry tap. Then I heard an almighty crash, as if a heavy object had fallen to the floor. I ran into the laundry to find my mother lying under the ironing board, clutching her chest.

'Mum!' I screamed, dropping to my knees beside her. Her eyes closed, and she went limp. My father came running in and held my mother and began to cry, telling her how much he loved her. His pyjama shirt opened, and I saw the massive scar that ran down his chest. I had been so worried about losing my father that I'd never even thought I could lose my mother. My neighbour came and performed CPR, and an ambulance took my mother to the emergency department, but I knew she was already gone. The doctor would later tell me that the heart attack had been so massive there was nothing that could have been done to save her.

Most of that night is a blur, but I remember how cold I was when I finally came home with my father. The hospital had given him some sedatives, and I put him to bed. I was shivering from head to toe uncontrollably, and my teeth were chattering. I put the heating on full blast, but no matter what I did I couldn't get warm. I'd gone into shock. Gardenia and Lilac stayed with me the whole night, watching me with sad and worried eyes.

I could barely fathom that my greatest supporter and truest friend was gone. It occurred to me that I had lost her in circumstances similar to the way she had lost Grandmother Alexandra.

The following morning, I found the note that she had left for me about *Wild Lavender*. I keep it in a box along with the wedding rings of my grandparents. Whenever I am about to begin a new project, I take it out and re-read it. It reminds me that my mother always had faith in me, and now I must have faith in myself too.

## 12

To be emboldened we need to have a vision and a purpose. Boldness is a forward-moving energy. It involves charging ahead bravely.

This becomes a stumbling block for a lot of us because it's difficult to get a clear picture of what we ourselves really mean by 'purpose', and often we have visions forced on us by society, parents and other influences that seem reasonable but leave us empty. It's important not to get a purpose confused with a goal. We can have a goal to make a certain amount of money, get married and own a house, but it's not a purpose. Goals can help us focus and bring us satisfaction when we achieve them, but they don't embolden us the way a true sense of purpose does. That's why so many people who have every material advantage to constitute a happy life are often miserable. They have no strong reason to be here and make the most of it. Purpose in old age is what keeps people active and interested. Without it, we fade away before our time.

We sense our purpose when our natural abilities and passions collide, producing a feeling of energy and aliveness in our spirits. When we are on the right path, we know it. In the people I've observed living with purpose, it also involves a contribution to the wider world. It's not the kind of impact that is forced or involves martyrdom. It's more that people who are energised with purpose naturally want to give to and uplift others. Their generosity doesn't deplete them.

After I went through my own upheaval, fleeing my home, I found it difficult to rediscover my sense of purpose. I'd had a vision for my life and it had been shattered. I felt like a shipwreck, and all that was left of my dreams was flotsam and jetsam bobbing in the ocean. It seemed at the time that my only purpose was to survive and become a fully functioning human being again. I took the necessary steps, but I wasn't inspired. I no longer had a vision of what my future could possibly look like. There was a twisted feeling in the pit of my stomach that a happy, purposeful life was no longer possible for me.

Then, a friend gave me a wonderful analogy. She loves to do jigsaw puzzles, and she said that when she spreads out all the pieces on her dining-room table, she always props the box up at the end of the table so she has in mind what the puzzle should end up looking like.

'It doesn't matter that your life is in pieces right now,' she assured me. 'Just start putting the pieces together bit by bit, always holding the vision of what would be a wonderful life for you, and eventually the picture will start to form.'

It was simple but sage advice. Even connecting a few pieces at a time became encouraging, and I started to trust the process and the idea that, if I kept at it, I would eventually reach my destination.

Later, while undertaking research for the novel that would become *The French Agent*, I came across the story of Virginia Hall, an American woman considered to be one of the most successful Allied agents in the French Resistance during the Second World War. Her triumph in the face of enormous difficulties illustrated to me that we can be constantly thwarted in achieving our purpose, but those setbacks – looked back on with the wisdom of hindsight – often turn out to contain all the lessons we needed to prepare us for our ultimate purpose.

Virginia's story stayed with me. It seemed some of the things that had happened to her could have made a less resilient person give up on her dreams, but Virginia pushed through and achieved something far greater and more important than her original plan had been. I thought about my own situation, and I felt for the first time that perhaps life wasn't breaking me. *Perhaps life was, in fact, building me.*

~

Early one bitterly cold morning in November 1942, a small party stood at the foot of the Pyrenees, a mountain range that borders France and Spain. Above them towered Mount Canigou. With its sharp flanks, glaciers and 2784-metre elevation, it was daunting to cross it in the summertime, let alone in winter when parts of the track would be covered in waist-deep snow. To even think of it would imply a certain desperation. But for two of the three men and the single woman in the party, there was no other choice. Their lives depended on it.

The leader of the pack was a *passeur* (guide) who had no vested interest in the wellbeing of those he was taking over the mountain pass. A smuggler of contraband, he was a gruff man of few words. Guides in the area were notorious for their lack of mercy to anyone who slowed them down on the mountains. There were rumours of people who couldn't keep up being shot or pushed over ravines. Some simply sat down to die, their frozen corpses a warning to those who followed later. Guides rarely took women, and certainly not under such brutal conditions. But the woman in the group – an American – had paid a premium price for not only herself but the other two men. She had only met them the night before, but they were fellow fighters for the Allied cause and so she wished to help them get to Spain. When the guide saw that the woman could easily pay, he agreed, knowing he could ditch her or the others if they proved too difficult.

The woman was thirty-six-year-old Virginia Hall, who for the past year had been a secret agent working for the British Special Operations Executive (SOE) in France. Virginia had coordinated everything from sabotage work to prison escapes. But her cover had been blown, and now the Gestapo was on her trail. She was listed as the most wanted woman in the whole of France by the notorious torturer Klaus Barbie. There was a bounty on her head in a country full of starving people, any of whom might have been happy to turn her in for a chance to afford black market food for their family. Originally, Virginia was due to have been taken out of France by boat, but with the German occupation now spreading into the south of France, that was impossible. To remain in the country would have meant a terrible death at the hands of the enemy.

Even so, as she raised her eyes to the path before her and began following the men, the mountain presented the very real possibility of death, too. The police were regularly patrolling the lower passes with dogs, looking for anyone trying to cross illegally from France into Spain. This meant the party would have to take the path at the highest altitude. As if the sheer drops, freezing temperatures and a bitter wind called the *tramontane* were not enough, there were bears and wolves ready to pick off stragglers. But it was not these dangers that played on Virginia's mind, it was the secret she had kept hidden from the guide, knowing he would not take her if he knew, and that he would most certainly abandon her if he found out. So vital was it that the secret not be discovered, she hadn't even confided in her two comrades. The party climbed, feeling their way up the slippery path. But Virginia could feel nothing in her left foot to help guide her. For under her baggy winter clothes she wore a wooden leg. Virginia Hall was not only a spy, she was an amputee.

~

Virginia Hall was born in 1906 into a wealthy Baltimore family. If we were to meet her in her youth, we would have found a tall and gangly woman with warm brown eyes and a ready smile. She was a tomboy who preferred riding, hiking and skiing to ballroom dancing and church picnics. Virginia was popular with her classmates, who enjoyed watching her act in plays, but she was also someone who didn't suffer fools. One of those fools was her fiancé, to whom she was briefly betrothed before realising he was a conceited jerk. Her judgement proved wise, as that ex-fiancé went on to have three unhappy and adulterous marriages. Although she was a member of the upper class and her ambition was supposed to be to marry well, Virginia felt she had a much bigger purpose than to be the helpmate of any man.

She was one of those dynamic individuals who know their own mind from an early age. Although society around her would have frowned on her forthrightness, she didn't seem to care. In her school-leavers' book in 1924, she wrote: 'I must have liberty, withal as large a charter as I please'. Her greatest supporter was her banker father, Edwin Lee Hall. Her family's trips to Europe had inspired an ambition in her. She wanted to be a diplomat, not a diplomat's wife. To this end, she convinced her parents to invest in her education rather than her dowry. She spent the next seven years attending five prestigious universities in the United States and also in Paris and Vienna. There she honed her language abilities – French, German, Spanish, Italian and Russian – not only in the classroom, but by rubbing shoulders with actors, racing-car drivers, poets and intellectuals in the cafes and salons of Europe.

She returned to the United States in 1929 deeply impressed by the artistic and social freedoms she'd experienced in Europe. Then the Great Depression hit and the Hall family fortune went into a nosedive. For Virginia, work was no longer an indulgence, but a necessity. She undertook more studies at George Washington University and applied to the State Department to become a professional diplomat. Although she possessed the right skills, she was promptly rejected, most likely because of her sex. Only six of the fifteen hundred United States foreign service officers were women.

Then heartbreak came. Her beloved father collapsed from a heart attack and died at only fifty-nine years of age. Virginia dealt with her grief by going to Warsaw in Poland, where she had obtained a clerk's job at the American Embassy, hoping to work her way up to a diplomat's position. Her role there involved processing visas, but also sending reports back to Washington about the political situation. With the support of her colleagues, who were impressed by her efficiency and self-assurance, she reapplied to do her entrance exam again for the diplomatic corps, but the exam papers never showed up and she missed the deadline.

In her disappointment, Virginia took a transfer to Smyrna – now called Izmir – in Turkey, a city surrounded by a beautiful landscape of salt marshes and lagoons. It was here that an event happened that was to change the course of her life.

~

While Virginia was in Smyrna, she arranged hunting parties to shoot snipe in the salt marshes of the nearby Gediz Delta. Snipe are long-billed waterfowl that forage for insects and earthworms in the muddy habitats. Despite my admiration of Virginia, I can't excuse her hunting animals for entertainment. Quick kills are rare, and many animals and birds suffer prolonged and painful deaths when they are wounded and not retrieved. Snipe are notoriously difficult to kill, because of their small size and erratic flying patterns. In order to kill one cleanly, you would have to be a crack shot (hence the origin of the word 'sniper').

However, Virginia reflected the views of the time. People who recognised animals as having emotions and rights were a rare breed in the 1930s. These days the Gediz Delta is protected as an important area of biodiversity by national and international legislation. It's a bird sanctuary now, and hunting is banned.

But it wasn't so that day in December 1933 when Virginia set out with her friends. The snipe came to the delta to roost and so they were plentiful. The winter weather was mild because of the Mediterranean climate, but still chilly enough for Virginia to be wearing a long coat, the hem of which was soon covered in mud as she crept through the reeds and long grass searching for the snipe, which were well camouflaged in the vegetation. She was carrying the shotgun she had been given by her late father, but she forgot to employ the safety catch. The little party came to an old wire fence. It should have been easy for everyone to climb, but as Virginia pushed down on the wire, she slipped in the mud. Her gun got caught in the folds of her coat and discharged, firing a round of pellets point blank into her left foot. White-hot searing pain ran straight up her body.

Her shocked friends hurried to staunch the profuse bleeding. They tore their clothes to make a tourniquet. As they carried Virginia back to the car and rushed her to hospital, she lost consciousness. At first it was hopeful, that despite the tissue and bone damage, Virginia's foot could be saved. It was even suggested that she might be able to return to work in a couple of months.

But one morning, when the nurses went to check on Virginia, they found her writhing in pain. Her pillow and sheets were soaked with sweat.

'My head feels like someone inside is hitting it with a hammer,' she told them. 'I'm freezing and burning at once.'

Virginia's eyes were bloodshot, and her temperature was soaring. One of the nurses undid the bandages on Virginia's foot and had to quickly turn away to disguise her horror. The smell coming from the wound was putrid.

'Doctor!' she cried, rushing into the hall. 'Come quickly. The American. Her foot has swollen and is turning black.'

The head of the American Hospital in Istanbul, Dr Lorrin Shepard, was summoned. He made the long trip by train with two experienced nurses. But by the time he reached the hospital in Smyrna, Virginia had lost consciousness and the infection was spreading. He determined that the only way to save her life would be to amputate her leg below the knee.

The hospital staff prepared Virginia for surgery on Christmas Day. 'I'd have preferred to have discussed the matter with Miss Hall first,' Dr Shepard told his surgical team. 'But if I don't do something now, there is a danger that her organs will start shutting down or I'll have to perform an amputation above the knee, which makes for a less desirable outcome for future mobility.'

~

Nothing could have prepared Virginia for the loss of her leg. The sight of the sunken void under the blanket where her limb once was left her inconsolable. At twenty-seven years of age, her life had been irrevocably changed. She lay in the hospital bed, staring at the ceiling, unable to see any future ahead of her that would be worthwhile. She had lived for the outdoor life: riding, skiing and hiking. It couldn't have helped that she was so far away from her mother and brother. Then there were the phantom pains: the ongoing physical sensations of stinging and itching of a limb that was no longer there. For years afterwards, she would play the scene of the accident over in her mind. How different things would have been if the safety catch had been in position, or if she hadn't climbed the fence. Sometimes she doubted that Dr Shepard had made the right decision. Perhaps he'd acted too hastily? Perhaps he'd done what was most expedient rather than necessary?

Among the lonely nights that followed her surgery, there were many during which Virginia was sure she would have preferred it if her friends had left her to die on the salt marshes.

~

When any of us experiences a breathtaking loss, the future looks like a gaping black hole. How we could ever put our broken lives back together again seems like a question with no answer.

What I remember most in the aftermath of my trauma was the sense of isolation and disconnection. I didn't have agoraphobia, but I did find leaving the safety of my father's home immensely threatening. But, determined to get on with my life, I accepted an invitation to a friend's book launch: my first social outing since fleeing my home. As I sat on the inner-city bus to get there, I was overcome by a strange floating feeling, as if I was watching myself from outside of my body.

It reminded me of a scene from one of my books, *Southern Ruby*, where the main character, Ruby, is conducting a ghost tour around New Orleans. She tells her tour group: 'The wraiths of New Orleans will sit with you in a restaurant and all you'll feel is a chill on your arm; they'll stand behind you while you watch the parades and whisper in your ear; they will ride with you on the streetcar and the only clue will be the breeze playing in your hair …'

I felt like I was one of those ghosts riding the New Orleans streetcar, only I was sitting on the Number 442 bus, heading for Balmain. I was a spirit with no anchor to the real world.

The life that I had known had disappeared. My mind was shattered. I had no idea what the future held and I felt terribly alone. As I watched people get on and off the bus, seemingly living normal lives – scrolling on their phones, talking to a companion, ordering takeaway – I felt as if I was looking at life from another dimension.

When people talked to me, it was as if they were speaking to somebody who had died years ago. I was no longer the person they thought I was. I experienced this sensation with everybody, including dear friends and family members. The exception was my father. He was the only person whose calm presence could turn me into a solid form again.

~

Things got worse for Virginia before they got better. Before the widespread use of penicillin, infection could be fatal if it took hold. This was the case with my father's family. While my paternal grandmother Marjorie was pregnant with my father, her young daughter Jean-Marie contracted meningitis and lingered only a few agonising days before she passed away. To add to the tragedy, Marjorie's husband John Andrew died suddenly from influenza complications a month before my father was born. She went into labour prematurely, and my father was not only a small birth weight but contracted pneumonia in hospital and was hurriedly christened because he was expected to die. The fact that he didn't, attests to his strong will and his rock-solid immune system. Sadly, his extroverted and popular older brother John wasn't so lucky. When he was twelve, he cut himself on a piece of chicken wire and contracted tetanus. The disease caused the muscles of his jaw and throat to contract, and he died in hospital struggling to breathe. Marjorie, an artist, was left traumatised by all these deaths and was often unable to get herself out of bed. My father became a 'caretaker' child.

Virginia had gone through a major operation, so when sepsis set in the sulpha drugs she was given had little effect. Sepsis is an extreme response by the immune system to an infection. It causes widespread inflammation and slows the blood flow, which means if it isn't brought under control, major organs will begin to fail. When Virginia's blood pressure began to drop, there was little the nurses could do but offer her morphine and hope that her suffering would end quickly.

One night, delirious and trembling with pain, Virginia opened her eyes to see her late father standing next to her bed.

'Come on, Dindy,' he said, using the pet name Virginia's family had given her. He pulled aside the bedclothes and lifted her as if she were as light as a feather. He sat down in a chair and rocked her in his arms. 'I know you are suffering, but you must fight this. You must keep going, because life has a great purpose for you, and you are here to fulfil it.'

Virginia wanted to speak to him. But her throat was dry and she couldn't get the words out. Her eyes filled with tears.

'It's all right,' her father told her, stroking her cheek. 'If the pain proves to be too much, I won't let you suffer. I will come back to get you.'

Virginia was a practical person and not religious in any conventional sense, but she would tell the story of her father's visitation freely, and how his love and his message galvanised every last ounce of strength she had in her to live.

Indeed, it astonished everyone when Virginia did survive the infection and was soon well enough to be moved to the better equipped hospital in Istanbul for the rest of her recovery.

~

The phenomenon of a patient who is near death receiving visits from a deceased loved one is well known to doctors and nurses. It's as if a door is opened between this world and the next when a soul is ready to pass over. I have witnessed it. The night an elderly friend of mine, Renatta, was dying, I held her hand as she slowly wound down like a clock with a flat battery. The journey started in the late evening and lasted until dawn. As her breathing slowed, she became less aware of me and began addressing her deceased sisters by name. They had quite a conversation, the kind you have at an airport with your family when returning home after many years away in a foreign country. There was a sense of excitement and reunion. As dawn broke, Renatta took her last breath. I felt the life force go from her body, and at the same time had a sense that someone else took over holding her hand for me.

People give all sorts of explanations for these experiences – some spiritual, others medical – but having witnessed that dear woman's passing, I take comfort in the idea that when it is my time to go, my mother and other loved ones will be waiting for me to show me the ropes of my new home. I am also rather excited by the possibility of being reunited with all my beloved pets – a great many of which will be cats. I will be a celestial cat lady. I only hope that one of my ethereal relatives will have had the good sense to have fed them all before my arrival, otherwise I'm going to be greeted by a heavenly chorus of a dozen hungry cats meowing and will have to open cans of cat food and clean a number of litter boxes before I even have a chance to look around.

~

Upon her release from hospital, and against the doctors' advice, Virginia drove herself hard to get back to as normal a life as possible. She resumed her duties at the consulate because she did not want people to feel sorry for her or treat her like an invalid. But she was in a country where rehabilitation and counselling after such a life-changing injury were non-existent, and she had a physical and emotional breakdown. All that could be done for a traumatised Virginia back then was to send her home to the United States.

Her mother and her brother greeted her with open arms when she arrived in New York, but it must have been a shattering experience for all of them. Virginia was altered – and not in the same way she had been the first time she had returned from Europe, enriched and inspired.

~

From my own experience and from witnessing those of others, I know it's almost impossible to go from a traumatic, tragic or life-changing experience to suddenly finding a new purpose. First, there needs to be a period of processing the shock and then moving through recovery, acceptance and adapting to the new normal.

I discovered the process is not linear. I would be doing very well and then something would trigger me into a state of paralysing fear and it seemed I was right back to where I started. When I was in the thick of trauma aftermath, I wasn't in a situation where I could lie in bed and recover or go on a world trip. I had a book tour coming up and I needed to bring in an income. I had legal proceedings to arrange, and I had to pull myself together quickly to protect my future interests. Apart from that, the events that had happened to me were so overwhelming, that if I focused only on them, I might have got stuck in my distress forever. At the same time, I had to acknowledge that I was traumatised because if I tried to go the other way, into denial, the pain would only flare up later.

What I found most useful to do was to think in terms of 'and' rather than 'or':

*I am healing from trauma AND I am creating a new life.*
*I am grieving the loss of my past life AND I am writing a new book.*

That way I could travel forward and still give myself space to heal. I do believe this helped me to recover effectively.

The other thing I did may not suit everybody, because it takes a certain type of disciplined mind – and trauma sends our thoughts into chaos – but I divided my time as if my life was a pie. A slice of that pie had to go towards legal issues. Another slice had to go towards active recovery from the trauma, such as seeking expert help. The rest of the pie was about getting on with my life: a slice for exercise; a slice for rebuilding my career; a slice for taking up new interests, and so on.

That way, I was dealing with the things that I had to deal with, but I wasn't making it my entire life project. I saw what happened to people who became obsessed about their trauma and recovery process: they identified as victims and got stuck in that identity. I would see those people years later, and they would still be trapped in the past and trying to deal with unresolved anger. I felt compassion for them because what had happened to them *was* terrible and unjust, but it was also over. The only person who could give them permission to move forward and find new purpose to life was themselves.

As I gently nudged myself forward on a daily basis, while still remaining conscious of being active about my healing, I noticed that the turn-around period from being triggered to being able to return to a state of equilibrium began to shorten. As soon as I started to feel that, it was like seeing the first signs of spring after a very long and dark winter. There were buds on the trees and baby birds singing in their nests. I still couldn't see what sort of future I could have, but I caught whiffs of new possibilities, like the scent of jasmine in the early spring air.

~

I don't know exactly how Virginia processed her own trauma, but it seems the sense of purpose the vision of her father had given her had buoyed her resilience and determination. She had to undergo more painful operations to repair her stump and make it able to be fitted with an artificial limb. The prosthetic leg she was given was not like a modern lightweight one, with microprocessor joints that can adapt to a person's unique walking style and provide good mobility. Her wooden limb was held in place by leather straps and corsetry attached to her waist. It was clunky and heavy.

Yet, despite all these disadvantages, Virginia not only got herself walking briskly but also biking, horseriding, swimming and rowing again. She practised walking with as normal a gait as possible and worked not to limp unevenly like someone with a prosthetic leg. Still, there were dozens of changes to remind her daily of the loss of her former life. She could no longer wear high-heeled shoes and pretty, floaty dresses. Modern prosthetic limbs are covered in an artificial skin that looks natural, while Virginia's leg was merely painted, and she went to great lengths to disguise it. When she later met up with old friends in Paris, she did not tell them what had happened to her in Turkey, leaving them to wonder why, even on hot summer days, she always wore thick stockings.

~

I haven't lost a limb, but when I read Virginia's story, I felt empathy for her hiding her prosthetic leg. After my trauma, I kept a major part of myself hidden too. There was a poor understanding of what I had gone through at that time – and a lot of victim-blaming – so I stuck close to people who really knew and understood me. Everyone else received a smile but was otherwise kept at arm's length.

We are told that isolating ourselves is bad for our mental health, and it probably usually is, so I don't recommend it, but I did find it beneficial in many ways. I needed that cocoon of withdrawal to process what had happened to me and to be able to stand on my own two feet about what I knew to be true. I couldn't have done that if I'd had the confusing opinions of others going around in my head while I was so vulnerable. In that sense, I needed to spend time in the metaphorical hermit's cave to figure things out for myself before I involved the whole village in my problem.

But at the same time, I didn't push away the love and support of friends. I let them know that if I wanted or needed to talk, then I would certainly turn to them. But if I didn't bring the subject up, then to keep the conversation to something else because it meant I needed a break from thinking about it.

One of the mental-health crises we face in Australia is men not talking about issues and trying to solve problems by themselves. Traditionally, it's not seen as manly to cry or to lean on others for support. As a result, men bottle things up and depression often goes unnoticed until it's too late. Therefore, it's important for men who are going through difficult times to speak either to professionals or to people they trust.

But what might be true for men isn't necessarily true for women.

I have always appreciated the social support I get as a woman from other women. I do find that we have compassion for each other and are often willing to share the load and help out in practical ways when one of us is going through a difficult time. But there can be a downside to that too. In his book *Learned Optimism,* Martin Seligman states that women are more than twice as likely to become depressed as men. He hypothesised that a contributing factor was that women tend to ruminate over problems and endlessly mull over their mistakes and imperfections. (I might add that society *also* mulls over women's mistakes and shames them for their imperfections, which doesn't exactly help either.) So it was in my consciousness that perhaps men didn't talk about their problems enough, while women talked about them *too much*. It did seem to me that the situation was magnified when women got together, and then analysed, dissected and focused on the problem to infinity and beyond.

I wanted to strike a balance between the two.

Although sometimes the time I spent by myself was lonely, painful and often overwhelming, I pushed through it. And in pushing through it, I found I got to know myself in ways I hadn't before. Very few people are prepared to confront themselves. They would rather do anything to distract themselves from really seeing who they are, as if they are afraid of what they might find. Most people go through their whole lives being strangers to themselves. We can't do that if we want to be emboldened. We have to know ourselves intimately.

I found I liked the person I am at my core once I stopped denying her and avoiding her. Out of that situation I became my best and truest friend for life. No one will stand up for me better than me. No one will bat harder for me than me. When life presents challenges and struggles, I know how to talk to myself with compassion, to push through. The only person guaranteed to be in my life forever is me.

That deeper understanding of myself has been something that has continued to grow with time. Once, I attended a belly-dance workshop with renowned Canadian teacher Florence Leclerc. She has a particularly graceful and elegant style of dancing, so I was excited about the class and wondered what routines she would be teaching. But the first hour of the workshop was spent doing exercises that were unrelated to dance and designed to create more awareness of sensations in our bodies. One of her exercises involved lying on the floor and articulating our spines one vertebra at a time, from our coccyx to the bases of our skulls and back again, several times. Then Florence would tell us to stop and observe the different sensations we felt in our bodies and to name them. Heat? Tingling? Tightness? She then went on to explain that often when we are in a class situation, we focus on imitating the movements demonstrated by our teacher. This creates an outward focus, which can be exacerbated if we are relying on studio mirrors to check our accuracy. Florence explained that we all have different body types and different personalities. We dance best when our movements emanate from inside of us. She was teaching us to rely less on mirrors (what we looked like) and to develop more awareness of our bodies in space (what we felt like).

'If you train yourself to do this, your own muscles will tell you if your arm is too low or too high for the pose. You will be able to self-correct by feeling your body rather than by seeing your body. You'll enjoy your dancing more, and you will be far more engaging to watch.'

I put her teachings into practice not only in my dancing, but in other parts of my life as well. So often we do certain things simply because we have learned to mimic other people doing them. Not many of our actions flow authentically from our deeper selves. I experimented with always checking in with myself through my body and its sensations before I did anything: writing; speaking in front of an audience; having dinner with friends. I found myself being more relaxed and present. A lot of the time we associate being authentic with being vulnerable, and I'm not a fan of being too vulnerable with people I don't know. But if anything, the more grounded I felt, the less vulnerable I felt with others. I felt so whole in myself that I didn't care how others responded to me. There can't be any fear of rejection when you aren't rejecting yourself.

I can't say whether Virginia went through a similar process in healing her trauma. But the time she spent recovering and adapting to a new life on her family's farm certainly seems have restored her sense of self-reliance. And it was this ability to be able to be alone with herself that shaped her for what was to come: a situation in which she would do more than rise to the occasion; she would become a revered heroine and discover her deeper purpose.

~

Much to the surprise of others, Virginia had no intention of spending the rest of her life on the family farm acting out the life of an invalid. She applied for a posting with the American State Department again and was given a position at the offices of the Consul General in Venice, Italy. It was a picturesque city, to be sure, with its winding waterways and Gothic-style architecture. But it was a city that presented challenges to someone with a prosthetic leg. There were no modern elevators. The narrow, cobblestoned streets were for walking – not driving – between destinations and they were often slippery. The arched bridges over the canals were difficult to negotiate if you couldn't fully bend one of your legs. But Virginia's career was more important to her than ever, and it seems in Venice she blossomed again.

The Consul General's offices were tastefully decorated in a blend of Italian and American styles, and the large staff was friendly and social. Virginia rented an elegant apartment in a palazzo that had a view over the Grand Canal, where she hosted parties again. To overcome her difficulty getting around the city, she hired a personal gondolier to take her by the canals to wherever she needed to go.

Happy again in life and work, she proved to be very good at her job and was given important consular work to perform instead of only administrative tasks. On occasion, she even stood in for the vice-consul when he was travelling. It was through her position and her voracious reading of local and foreign newspapers that Virginia learned with growing alarm how Europe was changing. Menacing dictators were springing up, and it seemed to her that there was a complacency around her in response to the danger they presented to world peace. She felt the time was right for her to make another attempt to apply for a diplomatic position. With five years' experience in consular work, her fluent language skills and the support of her colleagues, she felt certain to succeed. But to her shock, her application was immediately rejected – not because of any shortcoming on her part, but because of an American State Department regulation barring amputees from holding diplomatic positions.

Virginia was crushed by the news. We can only imagine what she felt when she was back alone in her apartment. We all know the confusion, sadness and the downward spiral it sends us into when our efforts to gain something we really wanted seem to have been in vain. Virginia was the perfect candidate for a diplomatic role, yet because of a mistake she had made one day while hunting snipe on the Gediz Delta, her dream had been snatched from her despite all her heroics in overcoming her physical disability.

But Virginia wasn't ready to admit defeat yet – and neither were her colleagues and friends. After all, the man who held the highest office of all in the United States, President Franklin D. Roosevelt, was disabled himself – semi-paralysed after contracting polio. A family friend, who knew the President of the United States well, pleaded Virginia's case with him, but this unfortunately backfired with the Secretary of State, Cordell Hull, who felt that Virginia had gone over his head. Biographer Sonia Purnell suggests that when Virginia was transferred from Venice to a less important post in Estonia not long after, it was a vengeful move on Hull's part. To add insult to injury, the man who replaced Virginia in Venice received a higher salary and a diplomat's status. In all her years of service, Virginia had never even received a pay rise.

~

Virginia tried to stick to her post in Estonia, but by the spring of 1939 she was too disheartened to continue and left the State Department to spend time with old friends in Paris. There, the lovely weather and jolly atmosphere of the city were deceptive. Despite all attempts to prevent a war with Germany, there was no choice but for Britain and France to declare war on the country when Hitler's armies brutally invaded Poland on the first day of autumn in 1939. It was clear that both countries were now in Hitler's sights.

Never one to stand by idly, Virginia put herself on the front line. She took a role driving ambulances in France. The country had been badly prepared for the German assault, and the *service de santé des armées* was so desperate for volunteers that the organisation didn't seem to care that Virginia was a foreigner or a woman, much less an amputee.

Although having to use her artificial limb to work the clutch of her ambulance caused Virginia a great deal of discomfort, she continued to drive the injured to hospitals even as France fell rapidly to the Germans, and streams of refugees and soldiers fled in the opposite direction.

Virginia had not witnessed a war first-hand, and the scenes were confronting. She was required to perform basic first aid on horrifically injured men, some of whom had lost limbs, before rushing them to field hospitals or to better-equipped hospitals in towns. Her ambulance was little more than an adapted delivery van, and the suspension was poor. She had to focus all her attention on driving through rough terrain and shut out of her mind the agonised screams of her passengers and the smells of blood and gore. But it wasn't just the soldiers who were suffering. As the Germans approached Paris, there was a mass exodus from the city. The road south was crowded with terrified people driving any sort of vehicle they could get their hands on – taxis, horse-wagons, bicycles or even coffee-vendor carts. Others fled on foot, pushing wheelbarrows or prams in which might be sitting an elderly parent, frightened children or perhaps a beloved pet. If this wasn't bad enough, the German fighter pilots mercilessly strafed the fleeing refugees.

Based on the many eyewitness accounts I researched, I included such an incident in my book *Wild Lavender*. Simone Fleurier, a music-hall star, is fleeing Paris with some friends when she witnesses an atrocity:

For the next hour, we drove through open fields. Minot amused us with tales from behind the scenes at the Adriana, including gossip about the Paris stars, and I tried to lighten the atmosphere by singing a couple of numbers from my last show. I was crooning the theme song from 'Les Femmes' when a blood-chilling wail cut through the sky.

'Merde!' said Minot, peering up through the windscreen. 'What is that?'

The traffic stopped ahead of us. People leapt from their cars or dropped their bicycles and fled across the field towards a grove of trees. Those with carts dived under them.

The schoolteacher and her assistant jumped from the truck, pulling the children down after them. The driver rushed out of the cabin to help. I stepped from our car. A Dutch man in the field turned and screamed out 'Stukas! Stukas!' for the benefit of the French people who didn't understand what was going on and were looking at each other. Then I saw them: two German planes heading towards us.

But they were military planes, looking for military targets. They wouldn't fire on unarmed refugees. The planes lowered altitude. My heart cramped in my chest. Minot and Madame Ibert dropped to the floor of the car. 'Duck!' screamed Minot. But my eyes were fixed on the children trying to make their way to the trees, pushed and urged on by the teacher and her assistant. The driver was running with two toddlers under each arm.

'No!' I screamed.

There was a rattling sound like stones hitting the road. Dirt jumped up in puffs. The little bodies shook and dropped to the ground. The teacher froze, jerking to the left and the right, trying to shield a girl from bullets before she and the child toppled down. The assistant fell a moment later. The driver was still running ahead, weighted down by the children he carried. A man ran out from under the trees towards them and grabbed one of the children. They had almost made it under cover when one of the planes turned back. It cut all four of them down in a hail of bullets before regaining height and disappearing into the sky on the tail of its mate.

My legs would only carry me as far as the edge of the road. Nobody else moved, terrified that the planes might come back. I stared at the huddle of bleeding bodies in the grass. At that low altitude the pilots would have known their targets were children. They had hunted them for sport.

Galvanised by witnessing such atrocities, Simone Fleurier returns to Paris to fight in the Resistance. It seems that what Virginia experienced driving ambulances did the same for her. So, when Marshal Philippe Pétain seemingly gave in so easily and signed an armistice with Germany, Virginia was outraged. All those French soldiers had died for nothing! The armistice divided France into two sections: the north, including Paris, to be occupied by the Germans; while in the south a collaborationist French government would rule from the spa town of Vichy. The new French government was a little brother of the Nazi regime – it was authoritarian, antisemitic and right wing. Women lost many of their rights and were denied access to birth control. Abortions were punishable by guillotine.

In Virginia's eyes, the Nazis were the epitome of evil. She would do anything to bring them down. But as it seemed that the French people had given up the will to keep fighting, she had no choice but to leave the country along with other foreigners and refugees while the borders were still open.

It was at this point that all Virginia's experiences, including her deepest lows and most frustrating failures, were to come together to show her the great purpose that her deceased father had promised her in the vision she had experienced. She was about to meet a man who would change her destiny.

# 13

Failure and rejection feel awful when they happen: that sinking feeling in our stomach, the prickles around our hairline, the way our heart starts to beat erratically and our throat goes dry. Then that rush of nasty self-talk that tells us how unfair the world is, that our life is ruined, that we can never hold our head up again. We want to run away from the world and be alone.

MRI studies have shown that when we experience failure and rejection, the same areas of the brain that alert us to physical pain are activated. Interestingly, some studies have suggested that because of this, over-the-counter painkillers may relieve some of the discomfort we feel. If only I had known that a couple of aspirins might have taken the edge off the crushing disappointment I'd felt when my manuscripts were rejected or my heart was broken!

But there is no doubt that most of our emotional suffering around failure and rejection is self-inflicted. It is the story that we tell ourselves about the meaning of the failure that will influence whether we decide to persist or give up. Psychologists tell us that the best way to respond to failure is to see it as an opportunity to grow and increase our mastery of life. That view is far less painful in the long run than seeing the world as unfair or ourselves as inherently and irrevocably flawed in some way.

Blaming things we can't change – or personalising failure – is the fastest way to demotivate ourselves. Focusing on learning and improving – something that we do have control over – not only feels better but will often give us that final oomph we need to push ourselves over the finish line and reach our goal.

One of the good things I have found about getting older and maturing is that I have more failure under my belt. Seriously! Because when I look back over my life and remember some of my most significant successes, I recall all the failures and rejections that led up to them. I had ten years of constant rejection of my writing before I was published. It made me a better writer and probably a better person because, when I did finally succeed, I appreciated it – and still do. For others, it turns out to be the toxic marriage that led them to later creating a happier, more fulfilling partnership with someone else. Three unsuccessful business ventures might provide the persistent entrepreneur with what they need to know about making the fourth one take off.

Many of us wish we could put our arms around the shoulders of our younger, discouraged selves and say, 'Hey, don't take this so badly. Keep going. This is all going to work out.'

Jeff Bezos, founder of Amazon, redefined failure when he set up Amazon Fresh, the company's new grocery delivery service. Instead of hiring executives who had been successful in grocery delivery services in the past, he picked ones who had been responsible for a spectacularly failed one, Webvan, which after initial success filed for bankruptcy in 2001. Bezos' logic seems to be that these executives had thought long and hard about what went wrong, what they would have done differently, and now would do anything to redeem themselves and rebuild their reputations. In his mind, executives who had failed but learned from their mistakes made better prospects than those who had never fallen down.

Sometimes, things we pursue with all our hearts fail because life has something bigger and bolder planned than what we were aiming for. This certainly seems true in the case of Virginia Hall. If she had reached her dream of becoming a diplomat, she would have gained a front-row seat to world events. She may have had some influence representing her government in delicate negotiations. But it would have been unlikely she would have been a real player in changing the course of the Second World War.

When destiny called, Virginia was in the perfect position to use all the experience she had gained in detailed consular administration work, as well as the resilience she had built up from the pain and isolation she had endured after her amputation.

~

After the retreat at Dunkirk, the British lost contact with France and were desperate for information about what was going on inside the country. Were the French living under duress or had they formed an allegiance to Germany as their government had appeared to have done? A British intelligence agent named George Bellows was posted on the border of Spain and France. His assignment was to hang around the train station, striking up friendly conversations with the refugees and foreigners pouring out of France, and casually question them about conditions in the country.

'*Bonjour, Madame*, you look lost. What frightful chaos this all is. Can I help you with your baggage? Have you had a long journey? Are the trains all running as usual?'

Bellows had to be careful. Although Spain was ostensibly neutral, it was ruled by another Fascist dictator, General Franco, who had Nazi sympathies. Virginia, attractive and forthright, couldn't have failed to catch his attention. He heard her American accent when she went to the ticket office to buy a train ticket to Portugal.

'Can I offer you any assistance?' he asked, sidling up to her in line. 'Wartime travel is a nightmare. I'm a salesman, and I've learned the ins and outs of getting around.'

Intelligence agents are skilled at getting people to offer more than they might usually do to a complete stranger, and Virginia, tired and frustrated, would have to learn the importance of not getting tricked in the future. Happy to hear a British accent, she told Bellows about her ambulance-driving under fire and her anger at the armistice.

It was obvious to Bellows where Virginia's sympathies lay and that she was passionate enough to have volunteered in a dangerous and unpleasant role in the aid of the Allied cause, although her own country was keeping out of the conflict. As Virginia described how France had been divided, about the food rationing and the atrocities she had witnessed, it was also obvious that she was a person who paid attention to detail. Bellows realised that he had done more than glean some useful information for British Intelligence from Virginia: he had found a perfect candidate for a more direct role in the war effort.

'I wish you well,' he told her, when it was time to part. 'By the way, when you get to London, please do look up a friend of mine. Here is his card. I'm sure that if you decide to stay in England, he will be able to find you some interesting work.'

Virginia thanked him and put the card away in her purse. She saw it as nothing more than British courtesy. She didn't realise at the time that the 'friend' Bellows was referring to was Nicolas Bodington, a senior officer in a new section of the British Secret Service.

~

'F Section' was the French arm of SOE. It was the brainchild of Winston Churchill, who saw the need for a form of 'irregular' warfare that would specialise in sabotage and subversive activities, with the aim of weakening the enemy's ability to launch a defence against an Allied attack on the continent. Despite Churchill's instruction for SOE to 'set Europe ablaze', the section had yet to successfully infiltrate any agents into France after six months of trying.

Virginia called Bodington in London and he invited her to his elegant home in Mayfair for dinner with his American wife. Virginia thought she was merely accepting a pleasant invitation as a diversion from the bombing of London and the pervasive fear that Britain was in real danger of being invaded. But as Bodington listened to Virginia, especially to her plan of getting back into France to help the Quakers' refugee relief effort and to let Americans know what was really happening in the country by reporting for newspapers, he realised that she would have several unique advantages as an agent. She not only spoke French and German, and had an intimate knowledge of France, but she was intelligent and courageous – the kind of person, motivated by morals rather than money. As a citizen of a neutral nation, she would have more freedom to move around France, especially if she was given the cover of a news reporter. There wouldn't be any need to clandestinely parachute her into enemy territory. She could simply arrive by rail with her appropriate papers.

Bodington could not wait to tell his SOE colleagues about Virginia. The section's glamorous and chain-smoking intelligence officer Vera Atkins had met Virginia at a social occassion and agreed with Bodington's assessment of the American. She invited Virginia to a meeting and put forward the following proposal to her: that she be sent to France with the task of clandestinely coordinating the work of SOE agents along with the activities of the local Resistance. She would be the first female F Section agent, and the first liaison officer of either sex. Her cover would be as a correspondent with the *New York Post*, and in her published articles she would be able to communicate to SOE the state of affairs inside France.

'It is terribly risky,' Vera told her. 'I'm not going to water down the fact. Sabotage work is particularly dangerous. You won't be protected by the Geneva Convention, as are ordinary members of the military. This means that, should you be caught, the Germans can do what they like with you and we won't be able to help you.'

Vera's words were true. Eventually, Hitler would become so enraged by the activities of Allied agents that he would issue a directive known as *Nacht und Nebel* – Night and Fog – by which agents who were caught would be made to 'disappear' in such a way that nobody, especially their families, would ever be able to find out what had happened to them. Of the estimated 470 agents SOE would eventually send into France, 118 would not return. They met terrible fates – brutally tortured, deported to concentration camps and executed.

But how could Virginia not be tempted? It was clear that SOE was putting a tremendous amount of faith in her capabilities. It was more credit than she had ever been given by the State Department in all her years of diligent work. As an SOE agent, she would be making a vital and tangible difference to the war effort. A role that, in fact, should she succeed, might even be key in helping Britain to win the conflict.

As it turned out, once Virginia accepted the offer, SOE cared so little that she was an amputee that it wasn't even made note of in her records. After all, she had driven an ambulance in wartime conditions. She could also swim, ride a bicycle and even ski – what other proof of her physical ability could they possibly need?

~

Despite her sex and her prosthetic leg, Virginia was not spared the demanding training required of SOE agents before they could be sent into enemy territory. Her life and the lives of those she would be in charge of depended on her being fully prepared. At a country house in the New Forest, recruits were trained in fitness, weaponry, use of explosives for sabotage, unarmed combat and the art of silent killing. They were also taught spycraft: map-reading, Morse code, how to make invisible ink and how to use disguises. Particularly intriguing, I think, was the art of searching a desk without leaving a trace, even to the point of replacing any dust that might have been disturbed.

Virginia was the only woman training alongside ten men, but soon others would follow: legends such as Odette Sansom Hallowes, Violette Szabo and New Zealand born Australian Nancy Wake. While there had been initial resistance to the idea of sending women into Europe for such dangerous work, the women of SOE showed aptitude and dedication in carrying out their assignments. Also, they had the advantage of the element of surprise. Because they were underestimated in their abilities and stealth, they were less likely to be as scrutinised by the enemy as were their male counterparts. But that didn't mean if caught they would be spared brutality, so no one could be complacent.

It was one of the reasons Virginia's cover as a journalist would be so vital to SOE's efforts. The organisation needed to know every detail of French life – that women were not allowed cigarettes as part of rations, that alcohol was only served on certain days, which goods were in short supply – otherwise, highly trained agents could be lost on their first day in France if they made the slightest slip. For this reason, while on the course all trainees were to keep up their cover names and cover stories and practise them to perfection. But while it was one thing for an agent to maintain their cover during dinner, it was quite another to maintain it under duress, and that led to the part of training that recruits hated the most.

~

A light shone into Virginia's sleeping face. She opened her eyes and squinted painfully into its blinding glare. She had been in deep sleep, dreaming of her mother back in Baltimore – the mother who knew she was involved in war work but not the exact nature of it. Virginia had no idea what the time was or how long she had been asleep. It felt like the early hours of the morning. Suddenly, a deluge of cold water splashed over her with such force it stung her skin like needles and sent her into shock.

'*Aufstehen!*' A German voice barked at her. 'Get up!'

But Virginia was too stunned to move, and two soldiers in Nazi SS uniforms yanked her violently from the bed. She struggled against them, but it was hopeless. She couldn't stand without her prosthetic leg. She was dragged down some stairs and along a corridor with a glass door at the end of it. Figures moved menacingly on the other side of it, and Virginia stiffened with fear, realising that she was in the hands of the Gestapo now and nobody could save her. Her hour of testing had come. The door opened, and more stern figures in uniform waited for her. She was roughly pushed into a chair.

One of the officers held a pistol in his palm and toyed with it.

'What is your name?' he demanded.

'Brigitte Lecontre,' she replied, giving her cover name.

'You are lying. You are a spy.'

Virginia shook her head. 'I'm not lying. And you have no right to hold me here.'

'I'll give you one more chance!' the officer said. 'Who are you working for? Give me names.'

Virginia remained stubbornly silent. The officer nodded to a thug that she only now noticed was waiting in the corner.

'*Fais-le!*' the German said to him in French. Do it!

From somewhere in the back of her mind she remembered being told that the one who would torture her would be French. That way, the Germans could claim to have never tortured a French citizen themselves. She heard water dripping and saw that there was a large barrel filled to the brim next to the desk.

'One more time!' the officer said to Virginia.

But she refused to talk.

Suddenly, the thug pulled her off the chair. She tried to grip the slippery floor with her right foot, but it was impossible. He grabbed her hair so tightly she thought he would pull her scalp off. With her face one inch away from the freezing cold water, she could make out her reflection and saw the terror on her face.

'Names!' the officer shouted.

Virginia shook her head, closing her eyes and steeling herself for what was to come. She knew it would be painful and that she would be gasping for breath as her lungs filled with water. Drowning was supposed to be agonising.

'All right, that's enough,' said the interrogating officer, reverting to a warm and friendly British accent. The relief in the room was palpable. The 'thug' lifted Virginia's face away from the water and released his grip on her hair. A blanket was thrown around her shoulders and she was helped chivalrously back into the chair.

'You did well,' said the training officer who had played the part of the German interrogator. 'But you know it will be worse than this if they catch you.'

'I don't intend to be caught,' Virginia told him firmly.

'All right then,' he said, with a polite but curt nod. 'Goodnight. Get a good rest. We start physical training again at five in the morning.'

~

Virginia was sent back into France through Lisbon at the end of August 1941. She was thirty-five years old. She was to be SOE's first representative in France to set up a type of warfare that had never been fought on the scale envisioned. As her biographer Sonia Purnell points out, the training SOE had given was largely guesswork, and Virginia would have to learn in the field. We can only imagine the intense isolation she felt on her secret mission. She was no longer the vivacious Virginia Hall, but her more circumspect cover, 'Brigitte Lecontre'. France was not the delightful country she had known. The signs of the brutal occupation were everywhere and she saw the fear in the faces of the people. By the second year of the war, many French people were borderline starving. The Germans were extracting large amounts of produce from the country. Farmers lost the motivation to continue cultivating. Why should they, if their labours were going to Germany? This, combined with the loss of imports, led to severe rationing and resulted in the average French adult receiving fewer than 1180 calories a day. Infant mortality rapidly increased, along with incidences of malnutrition, tuberculosis and diphtheria, and stunted growth for children and adolescents.

It was the desperation of the citizens that made Virginia's undercover work especially dangerous. The German military were brutal, but it was easy to recognise a soldier in uniform. Even the secret police, the Gestapo, usually looked like the thugs they were. But it was those Virginia would be approaching to join the Resistance network she was trying to set up who presented the most danger. The only way to survive was to buy on the black market, but this was expensive. The Gestapo took advantage of this desperation by offering large cash rewards for informing on resisters and foreign agents. The Germans were the masters of motivation. This meant Virginia had to look at everyone as a potential informer: the nice old lady in the apartment downstairs; the clerk at the post office; the woman who cut her hair. It must have been a very difficult way to live, especially for Virginia who genuinely liked people.

The town of Vichy was the centre of collaborationist France. Informers and spies were everywhere. Virginia would most certainly have been noticed when she went to the gendarmerie and registered herself as an American correspondent.

Meanwhile, back at SOE Headquarters in London, the intelligence officers waited for some news from her. They were at war and there were sacrifices to be made, but F Section officers held their agents in regard. They hated the thought that anything might happen to them, especially Virginia who was well liked and was prepared to fight in a war that wasn't hers. The radio silence was unnerving.

Then suddenly an excited clerk burst into the room unannounced. 'We have contact!' he cried. 'She's filed a story via the Western Union cable.'

The intelligence officers gathered around to see Virginia's first report, titled 'Bathroom Offices in Vichy'.

The article was outwardly about how Pétain's government had requisitioned every hotel in the town for its offices, even using the hotel bathrooms for space. But peppered within the article were important facts that the other agents coming into France would need to know: a ration book allowed only a small amount of meat and bread a week and absolutely no rice, pasta or chocolate; all correspondence was read and censored; telephone calls were tapped.

The intelligence officers let out a cheer. Vera Atkins decided it was a cause for celebration, and whiskey was shared around. After nearly two years of knowing next to nothing about the situation in France, SOE must have felt as excited as Mission Control did when Neil Armstrong stepped onto the moon in 1969.

~

Before other SOE agents could arrive in France, Virginia needed to set up a network of safe houses to receive them, where local people sympathetic to the cause would be able to support the agents' cover stories. It was fortunate for SOE that Virginia had a natural trait that no amount of spy training could have bestowed on her. She was genuinely likeable, with an ability to inspire confidence in others. People of integrity recognised her integrity and wanted to join forces with her, despite the danger to their own lives. She wasn't asking anyone to do what she wasn't prepared to do herself. It should be no surprise, then, that the network Virginia put together, aptly named 'Heckler', became one of the most successful in France.

Her cover as a foreign correspondent gave her access to officials in the Vichy government itself. Through her interviews, she was able to ascertain how an official might truly feel about the German and French collaboration, aside from the official line. When she suspected Allied sympathies, she would slowly work towards winning them over to her side. Other vital contacts included officials working at the American consulate and members of the Vichy police, who could warn Virginia of potential arrests.

Despite these successes, it soon became clear that the town of Vichy had too many collaborators to be a safe base for Virginia's network. Instead, she moved to Lyon, a hotbed of French patriotism. Small cells of rebellion had already organically sprung up there after the armistice, in the bars and bistros, in factories and private homes. Here she found that anti-Nazi tracts were being distributed, and the people were resentful of having their country pulled back into the Dark Ages by Pétain's conservatism. In Lyon, Virginia would find rich pickings in the form of contacts from every stratum of society willing to help her – from industrialists to shopkeepers, from doctors to hairdressers. But in true Virginia style, she started with the most unlikely resisters.

Accommodation in Lyon was scarce due to the influx of refugees from the north. The only accommodation Virginia could find on her arrival was with a group of cloistered nuns at the Sainte-Elisabeth convent. The nuns became her first recruits in Lyon when they agreed to hide SOE agents in the convent grounds. After Virginia moved her headquarters to a hotel in the centre of town, she started recruiting from the other end of the social spectrum.

~

Virginia climbed the sweeping spiral staircase slowly. The surroundings were luxurious: marble flooring, Venetian chandeliers, and neoclassical paintings. A scent lingered in the air that seemed to be a blend of sandalwood, cigars, champagne and something else. Musk? When she reached the top floor and knocked on the door, there was a long period of silence before a maid answered it.

'I will tell Madame Guérin that you are here,' she told Virginia, ushering her into the drawing room.

Virginia sat on the edge of the velvet sofa and looked around her. The apartment was like an elegant Romany caravan, with tapestries, beaded cushions and wooden treasure chests with gold coins and beads spilling out of them. A tingle ran down her spine. Although she was the only one in the room, she had the uncanny feeling she was being watched. Then she saw it: a large black cat sitting directly in front of her on the coffee table and slowly blinking its golden eyes.

'Where did you come from?' she asked it.

Something batted her right foot. She looked down and from under the fringe of the sofa cover came a small furry paw. It swiped at the shiny buckle of her shoe. Promptly a black kitten slipped out from under the sofa, followed by another two. They scampered across the carpet and disappeared into the corridor. There was a black cat on the windowsill cleaning its ears and another asleep under a potted palm. Virginia was sure that if she kept looking, she would see black cats *everywhere*. She turned towards the door, but instead of another cat she saw a darkhaired woman with smoky eyes regarding her. She was perhaps a couple of years older than Virginia, and was wearing an evening dress although it was only four o'clock. Diamonds offset by rubies, emeralds and other precious stones sparkled like stars from her ears, her arms and fingers. Wholesome, clean-cut Virginia in her tailored suit dress had never seen anyone quite like her. She was looking at Germaine Guérin, a successful businesswoman and a part-owner of one Lyon's most luxurious brothels.

Virginia took a moment to collect herself. 'A certain RAF officer says that you have been most helpful to him,' she ventured.

Germaine watched Virginia carefully with her cat-like eyes. Why should she trust this upstart American? Germaine had been running a successful Resistance network of her own. Her clients were the who's who of Lyon: not only Vichy officials and wealthy businessmen, but even high-ranking German officers. They supplied her with blackmarket goods that were hard to come by, such as food, petrol and coal, with no idea what Germaine was doing with them. No idea that she was helping downed Allied pilots get back to England and Jewish families to escape from France. Her sabotage activities may not have involved bombs and explosives, but they were effective. In conjunction with a local gynaecologist and dermatologist, Dr Jean Rousset, she had given prostitutes with syphilis the papers to confirm they were 'disease-free' so that they might infect German officers. Others of her working girls were getting the upright Aryans addicted to cocaine. But even more important than those activities, the women who worked for Germaine were dealing in a very valuable commodity: 'pillow talk' which meant they were often privy to top-secret information.

But slowly, over cups of real coffee served in exquisite cobalt-blue and gold Limoges cups, Germaine's attitude towards Virginia began to soften. She saw how useful she and her girls could be to this 'Heckler' network and liked the idea that the British were planning to supply weapons to an army of French resisters. Germaine owned apartments all over the city, and the nature of her business meant that men coming and going from them would not necessarily raise suspicions. She could supply not only accommodation to SOE agents, along with food and the correct papers, but she could also pass on the information about military operations directly to Britain via SOE's radio operators.

A slow smile came to Germaine's face. 'All right,' she said. 'I am a good judge of character and I've decided that I like you, Mademoiselle Lecontre. Firstly, I must introduce you to Dr Rousset, whose loyalties to the Resistance you can completely trust.'

~

Although Germaine would one day pay dearly for helping Virginia, her assistance was invaluable to the Heckler network. She was what we would now call a connector. She was able to put Virginia in touch with people who had transport permits to travel around France, which meant that fields suitable for Allied supply drops could be found. She was also able to squeeze favours out of officials and wealthy businessmen who relied on her discretion.

It seems that the many things that had happened to Virginia in her life had prepared her for her role as SOE liaison officer in Vichy France. When SOE agents arrived, mostly by parachute drops but sometimes by boat, they would make their way to Virginia, who would set them up with accommodation, the correct papers and money. All that visa processing and red tape she had found boring in her consulate jobs now made her an exceptional coordinator, able to keep track of everyone and everything while working under extreme pressure.

~

Unlike Germaine Guérin, Dr Rousset trusted Virginia the moment she came to see him at his surgery. He was a jovial, moon-faced man with an optimistic and energetic demeanour. He had helped Jewish families and he had hundreds of anti-German pamphlets stashed away in his rooms. He admired Virginia's courage and appreciated the fact that an organised Resistance network would be more effective than informal allbeit passionate, cells of activity. He was popular with his patients, and that was an asset to Virginia. With Rousset's introduction, people were more likely to trust her than if she had approached them on her own. He saw no problem in taking orders from her, and willingly became her loyal 'second-in-command'. If only all men could be so humble, Virginia's work in France would have been much easier.

Virginia was well respected by many men in SOE for her abilities, including celebrated agents like Peter Churchill and Ben Cowburn. However, she did come up against that old bugbear that female CEOs and heads of departments in male-dominated fields still find themselves facing today: staring down the dreaded male ego.

Although they were on the same team, an important SOE agent named Georges Duboudin did not like being outshone by a woman. This seems ridiculous considering that Virginia's role was to keep him safe and help him to succeed. But Duboudin constantly criticised her to SOE in London, believing that he should oversee the operations in the region. To this end, he made exaggerated claims that he already had the loyalty of ten thousand men who were ready to take up arms. SOE, desperate for good news of any kind, believed him.

It was Virginia who was slapped on the wrist by SOE Headquarters for steadfastly refusing to hand over the contact details of the network she had so painstakingly built up. She felt too much responsibility to the people whom Germaine Guérin and Dr Rousset had introduced to her to put them in the hands of so cavalier a man.

The group of resistants Duboudin led was careless and undisciplined. Far from waiting patiently for the right moment to launch an attack, his recruits were doing foolish things like blowing up newspaper kiosks. Such activities only served to draw the attention of the authorities and had no effect on disabling German military capability.

Whatever other qualities Duboudin possessed – and he was considered a star agent by headquarters – his need to be admired was a dangerous liability. He put the entire network at risk by frequently bragging to anyone who would listen. At a supply drop one night, Duboudin and his men drew attention to themselves with their loud talking and were arrested. However, the policeman who detained Duboudin was sympathetic to the Resistance and let the agent go. Instead of appreciating the gesture (if found guilty, he could have been sent to a concentration camp) and remaining quiet about the favour, Duboudin boasted about his powers of persuasion, which resulted in the policeman who had been lenient on him being arrested and tortured.

To add to the troubles he caused Virginia, Duboudin was also a serial womaniser. In a breach of security on the night Duboudin and his group were arrested, he had taken along his mistress, Germaine Jouve. Now she was sitting in a jail cell, and would remain there for the next six weeks, while he was free. Virginia had no idea where the woman's sympathies lay, and it seemed she knew about the other agents in Lyon and where the weapons supplied by the British were being hidden. To make matters worse, Germaine was sharing her cell with the wife of a collaborator. Instead of placating his mistress, Duboudin wasted no time finding himself a younger woman, whose brother-in-law ran a Resistance group. Virginia anticipated how furious Germaine would be when she was released. Indeed, when the members of the brother-in-law's network started being arrested, Virginia was put in the awkward position of having to ask SOE permission to possibly eliminate Germaine Jouve. But by the time the deadly cyanide tablets arrived from London, the disgruntled mistress had done her deadly damage and slipped away.

Male agents fraternising with women of dubious sympathies, or getting drunk in bars and publicly boasting of their Resistance exploits, were a constant nightmare for Virginia. Even one of her favourites, gay wireless operator and former music-hall entertainer Denis Rake, whose favourite motivational line was 'Pull yourself together, duckie', gave SOE grief when he temporarily took up residence in Paris with a lover he'd met in a bar – an aristocratic German officer, who had no idea Rake was working for the British.

Surprisingly, Virginia doesn't seem to have resented any of these men, even Duboudin. Rather, she attributed their rash behaviour to the enormous stress of being in the field. Agents who had appeared mentally tough while in Britain found the daily uncertainty a strain, and sometimes behaved suicidally.

## Purpose

~

Recruiters of intelligence agents cite one of the important qualities of someone able to work effectively undercover is the ability to live without the need for accolades or praise. Virginia was perfect for the role because she could work on her own without the need to brag about what she was doing. In fact, after her service, when she was awarded the Distinguished Service Cross for extraordinary heroism against the enemy by the Americans (whom she worked for at the end of the war), she chose to receive the medal quietly in the office of the director of the intelligence service rather than from the president, with all the pomp, ceremony and publicity that would have entailed.

I believe Virginia's ability to thrive in the loneliest of roles, far away from her home in enemy territory was partly due to how she had responded to the trauma of losing her leg. Only she could understand the full extent of the devastation she felt; only she could decide that life was worth living again.

I know from my own experience that, as much as our friends and family may love us, they cannot fight our battles for us. They cannot push us through our dark nights of the soul. Also, sadly, there may be times when our friends desert us, or may not be available, and we have to find a way to carry on by ourselves. When we learn to self-soothe our strong emotions, to be our own best friends, we often find that we come out the other side stronger and more confident. While having a community of supporters is wonderful, there is a certain satisfaction knowing that if no co-pilots are available, we can fly our planes on our own.

Life as an SOE agent in France was a lonely one. Surrounded by a brutal enemy and living under a cover name, Virginia could never allow herself to become too close to anyone. Agents needed to work in independent cells and use couriers for communications between each other. This protected the arrest of one agent leading to the collapse of the entire network.

Agents used dead letterbox drops – places they could leave messages for each other to avoid meeting directly. In her time in France, Virginia used several cover names and often changed her appearance. It was almost impossible, in fact undesirable, to make close friends while working for SOE.

As it turned out, it was the sense of isolation and loneliness that almost brought the whole operation down in the first few months.

A group of highly skilled agents – half of them French, the other half British – responded to an invitation purportedly sent by one of them to meet at a villa in Marseilles. Although it was strictly against protocol for agents to gather together in one place, there had been little contact with London so far, and the agents were growing restless. Virginia understood the need for patience. There was no point to Resistance activity until the Allies were prepared for the invasion. She listened to her intuition on this matter and didn't go to the meeting. She was right, as it turned out. It was a trap set by the Vichy counter-terrorism force, who promptly arrested the agents. For SOE this was a major setback, as they lost nearly all their highly-skilled agents and wireless operators in one sweep. On top of this, the men would most likely be subjected to torture, and then executed.

But all was not lost. Virginia, quiet and methodical, ended up coordinating one of the most daring escapes of the French Resistance. She and one of the French agent's wives, Gaby Bloch, hatched a plan to rescue the men who were being held in Beleyme Prison in Périgueux, which was notorious for its atrocious conditions.

At first, it seemed there was a chance to spring them when Virginia found out that they were going to be transferred from the prison to an internment camp, but then she discovered that, after months of harsh treatment and malnutrition, the men were too weak to escape. However, the conditions in the camp were better, and the men focused on rebuilding their strength. Afternoon games of boules allowed them to calculate the time they would need to reach the camp's barbed-wire fence from their barracks, and in what positions they would be out of view of the watchtowers. Meanwhile Gaby, with coaching from Virginia, recruited guards willing to assist with the men's escape. Inside the food parcels and hollowed-out books Gaby took to the prisoners, she and Virginia had hidden files, screwdrivers and hammers. Virginia used her extensive contacts to create a network of safe houses to get the escapees out of France via the Pyrenees mountain range. Her loyal network worked at full speed. The network included a priest in a wheelchair who had lost both legs in the First World War. He managed to sneak a wireless set into the camp by hiding it under his cassock. Members of SOE in London were more than astonished to find themselves receiving messages from inside a French internment camp. The radio allowed Virginia to send word to the men via London about the final plans for the escape. It was ingenious, and although roaming German detector vans picked up signals coming from the camp, they could not believe anybody could have smuggled a wireless set into it and searched nearby houses instead.

After extensively training and drilling for every contingency, and a few tense moments when one guard backed out of the plan and another prisoner threatened to denounce the group, the twelve men managed to run to the wire and escape with split-second timing. They were spirited away in a lorry by one of Virginia's recruits to an abandoned house in the woods, where she had supplied clothes, razors and soap so they could pass as civilians rather than escapees.

The escape went down in SOE legend. Virginia had once again proven her outstanding ability to coordinate a major mission. However, while this event had been pleasing to the British, it certainly wasn't to the Germans. They now knew there was a highly effective agent operating in the unoccupied zone of France. They didn't yet know who *he* was, but they were determined to find out.

# 14

Thanks to Virginia's exceptional organisational skills, as well as her ability to win people over to the Resistance cause, her secret army began to grow. Perfumers, hairdressers, shopkeepers, hoteliers, lawyers, gendarmes and entertainers joined her network, couriering messages, hiding weapons that had been sent into France by night-time parachute drops, offering transport and supplies, and assisting agents with clothing and disguises if necessary.

However, her position was to become much more difficult after the Japanese attack on Pearl Harbor brought the United States into the war in December 1941. Besides that, Virginia's efficiency in the French free zone, especially after the prison break, was turning a spotlight onto her.

Hugo Bleicher, the suave and persuasive 'spy-catcher' with the *Abwehr* (the intelligence unit of the German army), eventually ascertained that the person they were after was a woman with a slight limp, who was possibly Canadian or English. Bleicher had refined tastes in music, food and women. He'd once had the ambition of becoming a concert pianist. He detested brutality and preferred to catch spies with clever games of cat-and-mouse. Once they had been caught, he used his charm and persuasion to convince them to change sides and work for him instead. His favourite game was to catch a network's radio and send false messages to Britain. Whoever this clever woman was, he rather admired her and was determined to find her. But he intended to be patient in order to capture those who worked with her as well.

In competition with Bleicher was Klaus Barbie of the Gestapo, the German secret police. He was a psychopath who had been dubbed the 'Butcher of Lyon' for his brutal treatment of resisters. He was known to burn and disfigure them, sexually assault them and worse. He'd issued wanted posters with a lifelike drawing of Virginia across France, along with the words: 'THE ENEMY'S MOST DANGEROUS SPY: WE MUST FIND AND DESTROY HER!'

Recognising the deadly circle that was now closing in on Virginia, SOE recalled her to London. She had already spent longer in the field than most agents, and it was time to come home. But Virginia refused. She wasn't foolhardy about her safety – or the safety of others. Every time she left her apartment, she always made sure that she wasn't followed. She used backstreets and left messages in secret locations. Unlike other agents, she was meticulous about the use of passwords and security checks. She never told anyone – even those she trusted – more than they needed to know. She felt there was much more that she could do, and the tide of the war was at a crucial point and things were starting to turn in favour of the Allies.

Britain was no longer fighting alone. With the greater resources the Americans brought to the table, the way was now clear for the Allied forces to launch an attack on Europe and take back the countries Germany had invaded. The parachute drops of arms, explosives and agents into France rapidly increased, which meant more reception committees had to be organised and more safe houses found. The sabotage targets were to become more daring: entire railway networks, fuel depots, industrial sites and even military targets.

But then one man brought Virginia undone. He was a narcissist: a wolf in sheep's clothing.

~

It's been said that even after two hundred years of modern psychology, we still don't have a grip on abnormal and evil behaviour. It is only in the last few years that narcissistic personality disorder and the devastation inflicted on the victims of people with this disorder has come to public light. A few years ago, terms like gaslighting, coercive control and stonewalling were not widely recognised. Now they are understood everywhere from corporate offices to reality TV shows.

The hallmarks of pathological narcissism are a lack of empathy, a grandiose self-image of being special and not bound by normal rules of behaviour, and a sense of entitlement. It is not a mental illness. Narcissists do have a degree of choice and control over their actions. It is simply that they have learned somewhere along the line that manipulation and deception get them what they want, and what they want is power and control. They are experts at manipulation – both overtly and covertly. Experienced and skilled narcissists painstakingly take their time to set their victims up before they reveal their true intentions. For the victim, they often won't realise what is being done to them until it is too late.

I have encountered two narcissists who had significant negative impacts on my life. The first was the classic kind – charismatic, very concerned with appearance and status, able to convince a team of flying monkeys to do their bidding, a pathological liar. If I'd been more aware of what the red flags of narcissism were, I might have seen that one coming. The second one was entirely different. They were what is sometimes referred to as a 'communal narcissist': to all appearances warm, kind and mentally stable. They're the sort of person we turn to in a crisis, and who has a large network of friends ready to vouch for their honour and trustworthiness. It's often this kind of narcissist who has the most devastating impact because their manipulation and lies are so well hidden behind social proof.

That second narcissist was able to intentionally steer me off my purpose one degree at a time, like slowly turning a ship from its course. By the time I realised what was happening, my ship was heading towards the rapids and a waterfall. It was too late to turn around, and I plunged straight off.

A memorable life lesson!

One of my favourite novels by one of my favourite authors is *Rebecca* by Daphne du Maurier. The story was published in 1938 and has never gone out of print. It remains a bestseller to this day. I first read it as a teenager, and then later watched the classic 1940 film, directed by Alfred Hitchcock and starring Joan Fontaine and Laurence Olivier. The story is gripping because it employs, to dramatic effect, a fiction technique known as a 'mid-point reversal'. This is when everything the writer has led us to believe about the story so far is suddenly turned on its head by the revelation of new information. From that point on, the narrative will move quickly in a completely new direction as it plunges towards a shocking climax. We will hang onto our hats chasing it while we realise that the author skilfully gave us misdirection after misdirection in the first half of the story, but now everything makes perfect sense. We start seeing all the 'red flags' we missed but could not have interpreted accurately without the information given to us at that mid-point. The mid-point reversal in *Rebecca* isn't situated at the halfway point of the novel, it's closer to two-thirds of the way through, but its effect is electrifying.

Du Maurier's Gothic psychological thriller poignantly describes a relationship between a narcissist and her victim. When the story opens, Maxim de Winter, a dashing forty-two-year-old widower, is holidaying on the French Riviera. The novel is told through the eyes of a young unnamed narrator, currently employed as the companion to a rich American woman, and who will eventually become Maxim's second wife. At first, Maxim seems to be the classic romantic hero – strong, silent, brooding. In the eyes of others, Maxim is a man in deep mourning for his beautiful, accomplished first wife Rebecca, whom we are told drowned tragically in a boating accident the previous year. The truth, as we will later learn, is that Maxim de Winter is a man whose life has been shattered by his marriage to a narcissist, and he is a shell of his former self.

Later in the novel, when the narrator learns the true cause of Rebecca's death, du Maurier has Maxim deliver an artfully rendered account of a victim's reaction to a narcissist revealing their true intentions. Maxim believes that he has married a beautiful socialite of good breeding and similar values – someone who will be a perfect partner to him, and help him in his responsibilities as a member of the English gentry to his parish and to his splendid ancestral home, Manderley. Everyone around him has the same impression of Rebecca, telling Maxim he is the luckiest man alive to have married 'breeding, brains and beauty'.

But once Maxim and Rebecca are married, her sexual depravity and her true intentions come to light. Rebecca can reveal them now, because she has Maxim exactly where she wants him – trapped. He cannot divorce her without bringing shame and destruction to everything he holds dear – his family name and his heritage. Besides that, he suspects no one would believe him. They would shun him for smearing Rebecca, whom everyone adores and venerates. All he can do is watch helplessly on while Rebecca revels in what he now realises is their farcical marriage:

'She was clever of course,' he said. 'Damnably clever. No one would guess meeting her that she was not the kindest, most generous, most gifted person in the world. She knew exactly what to say to different people, how to match her mood to theirs. Had she met you, she would have walked off into the garden with you, arm-in-arm, calling to Jasper, chatting about flowers, music, painting, whatever she knew to be your particular hobby; and you would have been taken in, like the rest. You would have sat at her feet and worshipped her.

Du Maurier runs the description of Rebecca's confessions and Maxim's reactions for several pages, and our stomachs turn along with Maxim's at each revelation. One of the reasons we as readers so intensely feel Maxim's shock and distress is that we too, for the first part of the novel, have been taken in by Rebecca. This sensation is heightened by the fact that du Maurier doesn't give the narrator a name. We live the story through her eyes. She could be any one of us.

~

Abbé Robert Alesch was a young and striking-looking priest. The pictures I've been able to source of him remind me of Hurd Hatfield, the actor who played the lead character in the 1945 film adaptation of *The Picture of Dorian Gray*, with his handsome face and piercing eyes. At the time Virginia encountered him, she was assisting an MI6 intelligence network, WOL. It wasn't in her line of duty, and SOE wasn't particularly thrilled about her helping a competing intelligence organisation, even if they were on the same side, but the information the network was gathering in the form of maps and photographs was vital to the Allied invasion. Virginia was also familiar with some of the network's members, including Jeanine Picabia (daughter of the

Surrealist artist, Francis Picabia), with whom she had driven ambulances at the start of the war. When some of WOL's members were arrested, including their wireless operator, Virginia took on the role of making sure their microfilms and messages reached London. She also conveyed funds from London to WOL.

Alesch arrived one day at Dr Rousset's surgery, telling him he was acting as a courier for WOL. Rousset exercised all the caution Virginia had instilled in him, quizzing Alesch for passwords and codenames. But it was most likely Alesch's priestly robes that lead to Rousset, a devout Catholic, trusting him. Those robes combined with a winning manner and an ability to quote the Word of God, had led to an entire congregation in Paris putting their faith in the man whom they saw as a brave resister. It didn't hurt that each Sunday, from his pulpit, Alesch openly and seemingly courageously preached against the evils of the Nazi regime.

'Put on the full armour of God,' he beseeched his devoted flock, 'that you may be able to stand against the schemes of the devil.'

Inspired, the young men and women of the congregation would come and tell him that they had joined the Resistance, and Alesch would bless them and assure them that he would be praying for them. 'Be strong in the Lord, my children. Trust in his might.'

Then he would go to the *Abwehr*, for whom he was working, and give the names of the resisters and the details of their contacts and networks that they had confided in him. For this treachery he received a generous salary plus bonuses. And when the young men and women were dragged from their homes, shot, hung, guillotined or sent to concentration camps, Alesch would preach again from his pulpit the following Sunday about the evils of the Nazi regime and comfort their grieving parents.

Alesch had no allegiance to the German cause. He had no allegiance to anyone. He offered his services to the *Abwehr*, Gestapo and Resistance networks alike, taking money from all of them as well as fleecing his own congregation. He used these funds to live the high life. Leaving his congregation and their faith in him behind, he would walk to the 16th arrondissement of Paris, with its wide avenues and expensive restaurants, and on to his eight-room apartment in a grand 19-century building, where he kept two mistresses, as well as a collection of fine wines and artworks that had been stolen from Jewish families.

It seems that in Alesch's mind, the life of a young man or woman from his congregation was a fair price to pay to acquire for himself a painting by Degas or Matisse, or perhaps to enjoy a bottle of France's most exclusive wine, *Romanée-Conti*.

When Rousset introduced Virginia to Alesch, she recoiled at the sound of his thick German accent, which he quickly explained was due to being from Alsace, on the border with Germany. But as he spoke to her amiably and warmly, her stomach kept pinching and rolling. Something wasn't right.

'I don't trust him,' she confided in Rousset later. 'He gives me the chills. Those eyes—'

'You have been in the field too long,' Rousset assured her. 'You don't trust anybody anymore. His whole congregation speaks highly of him. He risks his life every Sunday to speak out against the Nazis. Would he do that if he was one of them?'

Virginia desperately needed to re-establish steady contact with WOL. Could Rousset be right? Had she become so used to distrusting people that her gut instincts were not as sharp as they used to be? It was certainly true that Alesch vehemently denounced Nazism. The Germans would not have tolerated that in one of their agents.

As it turned out, the *Abwehr had* remonstrated with Alesch for discrediting the Nazi cause in his sermons, but after a while they conceded it was an effective tactic in getting resisters and their families to trust him. So, they let him continue to do it.

Alesch must have sensed that Virginia wasn't as trusting of him as Rousset and the others, and he set about convincing her.

'The "Hun" shot my father in the Great War,' he told her one time, with a tremble in his voice and tears in his eyes. 'I will not let his death be for nothing. France must be free again.'

In truth, Alesch's father was alive and well.

Virginia didn't take anything anybody said at face value. She herself was operating under a false name with a false backstory. But despite her suspicions, she made the fatal mistake that many of us have made regarding narcissists: trusting them by proxy. Virginia trusted Rousset – he had proved time and time again to be exceptionally loyal to the cause – and because he trusted Alesch, she was willing to put aside her own doubts. She welcomed Alesch into the network, showing her trust by giving him a significant sum of money to take to WOL. He was designated the codename 'Bishop'.

The *Abwehr* could not have been more pleased with Alesch. He had infiltrated the network of the spy whom everybody was after. But while Klaus Barbie of the Gestapo ranted and raved about what he would do to that 'Canadian bitch' when he caught her, the *Abwehr* did not arrest Virginia straight away. They understood the value of patience. It would be far more effective to use her first to mislead the British. Then they would make sure they knew who all her contacts were and bring down the entire Heckler network that way.

~

When more members of the WOL network, including their leader, were arrested, Virginia became suspicious of Alesch again. The next time he visited her, seeking more money, she casually questioned him.

'Did you pass on the money I gave you to WOL yet?'

'I have,' he assured her.

'I haven't met their second-in-command. What does she look like?'

'Tall and blonde,' Alesch told her.

Virginia's stomach tightened. Jeanine Picabia could never be described as tall and blonde. She was a tiny, middle-aged woman with dark hair.

Virginia took her suspicions to SOE. They did a background check on Alesch but came up with nothing. The only advice they could give her was to proceed cautiously.

Alesch realised he had made a mistake and had to win back Virginia's trust. With the *Abwehr*'s assistance, he provided intelligence photographs of the German defences on the Atlantic Wall. They would enable the Allies to make an effective attack.

Unbeknown to Virginia, the *Abwehr* had doctored the photographs. But having them go through Virginia's hands gave British intelligence the impression that the information was from a highly reliable source. With this belief, they organised a surprise commando raid on the coastal port of Dieppe, in the Normandy region of northern France. It was a total disaster because when the commandos arrived, the Germans were waiting for them. Four thousand men were needlessly lost – killed outright or taken prisoner.

~

When I first became aware of narcissists and suffered the devastation they brought into my life, I became, I must admit, a bit of a vigilante. I learned absolutely everything I could about the disorder. I think the fear of the false friend – or, at least, false ally – has been a theme in nearly all my books. It wasn't until I wrote *The Invitation* and *The Mystery Woman* that I knew exactly what a narcissist was, but I can see they are there in some form or another in *Wild Lavender*, *Tuscan Rose*, *Golden Earrings* and *Sapphire Skies* in all their evil glory. When those narcissists wrought their horror on me, it was as if my worst nightmare had come true. The moment when a narcissist takes off their mask, and reveals what is underneath, is bone-chilling.

They destroy good things, good causes and good people. That is why I cannot emphasise enough that in becoming emboldened, we must educate ourselves about their methods and actively keep them out of our lives, charities and businesses.

The role of narcissism in what we now call coercive control in abusive relationships was brought home to me when one of the finest human beings I know was nearly murdered by one.

Paola is a vivacious, warm-hearted ball of energy. She's a smart entrepreneur who takes excellent care of her clients. I met her when I used her business, and then we stayed in touch. She's the kind of woman I admire. She has a strong sense of ethics and serving the community, using her business to employ people with disabilities and support charities (including starting her own).

I hadn't seen her for a few years when we got together one day at a cafe, because we'd both been busy, but I had occasionally seen her Facebook pictures come up in my feed and smiled when I saw the posts of Paola with her partner and young daughter. They looked the picture of a happy, young family.

The day we met I was limping after having overdone it at a dance class. Paola and I got to talking about health and yoga, and she told me that she had recently been given the all-clear after being diagnosed with stage 3 breast cancer, for which she'd received the full dose of aggressive medical treatment. I commiserated with her, especially as she had recently attended the funeral of a friend who had died from the disease. Then I asked her how her partner was doing. She answered that he was on eighteen months community correction service for violent behaviour towards her.

Of all the things I was expecting to hear that day, that was not one of them.

She then shared with me a harrowing story. When she was sick from chemotherapy and scared for her life, her partner was screaming at her and punching the wall near her head. The night she was in hospital prior to major surgery, he was supposed to be at home looking after their young daughter, but instead he picked up a woman at the local supermarket and brought her home – with his young daughter there – to have sex with. Paola would find out about it when her daughter innocently pointed out the woman when she saw her in the supermarket.

Paola looked at me, and I can imagine my expression was one of shock. 'Belinda, it happens a lot more than you might think. My story isn't uncommon. Do you know there are women who aren't being taken to their medical appointments by their abusive partners? They are being denied treatment.'

Someone else listening to that story might think Paola's husband had some extreme reaction to the stress of having a wife with a life-threatening illness. And a cancer diagnosis is stressful in every way – the shock, the fear, the huge financial burdens, as well as the extreme nature of the treatment. Or they might think he was just a low-down poor excuse for a man. But I formed my own opinion about what had happened based on the research I had done into narcissistic personality disorder. Paola was supposed to be her narcissistic husband's 'supply'; she wasn't supposed to get sick. *He* wasn't supposed to be looking after *her*. His rage was fuelled by the fact that she wasn't giving him the things that he'd set her up for. Even worse, in his eyes, she was spending money (that she had earned through her business, but he saw as his) on expensive medical treatment when it should have been spent on him.

After Paola had fought for her life and beat the disease, she had to ask herself if she really wanted to stay married to someone who had deserted her in her darkest hour. Of course, she didn't! But when she left her partner, he became so incensed that his victim should object to his treatment of her, he sent her a video suggesting his intent to commit suicide, and the next thing she knew her house was on fire with her in it.

Paola and I talked some more, and I told her about my own experience with narcissists and their devastating effects. She looked at me and said, 'You are a writer, you have to tell people about this.'

After Paola and I said goodbye to each other, I sat in my car with my head resting on the steering wheel. *You are a writer, you have to tell people about this.* My mind was reeling. Paola is the kind of woman society needs more of, and yet she was nearly finished off by a narcissist. Every week Australians are shocked by another woman being bludgeoned, strangled, shot or set on fire by an intimate partner after enduring months and even years of coercive control. But for each woman killed there are thousands more women – and men – who nobody sees. The ones who commit suicide because they believe there is no other way to escape their tormentor. Their deaths are not listed as being caused by domestic abuse, but as something else: depression or an inability to cope with 'life's stresses'? Then there are those whose minds and spirits are so broken they can't hold down jobs or have become homeless, while others who have worked hard all their lives now face poverty in their twilight years. There are the victims Paola mentioned who are very sick, in pain and terrified, but are being denied access to medical treatment by their abusive partners. I haven't been in that situation. I don't even know anyone personally who has, and yet, out of all the horrors I have mentioned above, for some reason that one disturbs me the most. How could people be getting away with that? Isn't that a kind of murder?

I don't think the connection between narcissistic abuse and coercive control is made often enough. So yes, I am something of a vigilante when it comes to narcissistic personality disorder. But I think I have good reasons and Paola is definitely one of them.

And perhaps the fact that Virginia Hall, whom I admire so much, had the good work she did in France brought undone by one irks me too. The cost to the Allied war effort and the number of lives lost by this fatal mistake was significant.

~

Virginia had trusted a narcissist and now she was being played by the *Abwehr*. Even worse, seeing that Virginia had placed her trust in Alesch, the other members of her network felt safe to do so as well. Not only did Virginia pass on Alesch's military reports, she also made the fatal error of giving him a precious SOE radio. This, of course, went straight to the *Abwehr*, who began to play their favourite game of *Funkspiel*, plying London with false information while pretending to be one of Virginia's contacts.

As important agents around her began to be arrested, SOE warned Virginia that her cover had been blown. She had to concede that staying in France would only endanger members of the Heckler network, including Rousset and Germaine Guérin. Virginia originally planned to leave the same way she'd entered France, keeping up her cover as a correspondent for the *New York Post*. She'd felt this would draw less suspicion to her network than for her to suddenly disappear.

But the desire to protect others put her at greater risk. It was difficult to obtain the necessary visas and papers, let alone a flight out to Lisbon. Anybody who has dealt with bureaucracy knows how frustrating this can be even in peacetime. But now, with Klaus Barbie bearing down on her, Virginia was quibbling with pernickety visa clerks about her passport as Resistance networks were crumbling like dominoes around her and their members were being carted off for interrogation and torture.

Although SOE agents were warned against forming close relationships with fellow resisters, it's almost impossible for human beings not to bond when they have faced dangers together in pursuit of a common cause. It was anathema to Virginia that she was being recalled to the safety of London while other valuable agents were in prison. She felt responsibility particularly to a dapper young wireless operator whom she had sheltered: Brian Stonehouse, codename Célestin. In his civilian life, Brian was a fashion illustrator for *Vogue.* After being parachuted into France, he had hidden his wireless set under a bundle of fashion illustrations. But he was poorly protected by the leader of the Resistance circuit to which he had been assigned, and Virginia had helped him. When he was arrested, he gallantly refused to reveal anything about her, even under torture. Now she would return that favour by rescuing him from prison. Her plan was a particularly audacious one, involving agents dressing up as gendarmes and Gestapo officers, and arriving in a vehicle that could pass for a German staff car driven by another resister dressed in SS uniform, claiming they had orders to move Stonehouse and the other British prisoners to another jail.

Such a strategy involved meticulous planning and rehearsal. It turned out that the gendarme uniforms were particularly hard to source, so two genuine gendarmes, supporters of the cause, were recruited instead. But this added a further complication in that they and their families would have to be shipped out of France by SOE afterwards, as the reprisals for the jail bust would most certainly mean death.

While drilling the agents for the escape, Virginia was still tangled in red tape, trying to obtain her visa and ticket out of the country. Then one of her contacts at the American consulate gave her a tip-off that turned her plans on their head. 'Operation Torch', the Allied invasion of occupied North Africa, was imminent. If the Allies were successful in gaining a stronghold, they would be able to launch themselves from there into southern France. The Germans would soon be swarming into the unoccupied zone to crush any Resistance activities that might help the Allies. With them would come Klaus Barbie, who now had more detailed information on the 'terrorist' who went by the name 'Marie', another of Virginia's cover names. She had no choice but to trust the other agents to get the British prisoners out of jail and go. But leaving by conventional means in the circumstances had become impossible.

There was only one way out of France for her now – and it was a terrifying one.

# 15

And so we come back to where we began, with Virginia about to make that formidable climb over the Pyrenees with a reluctant guide and two other resisters whom she did not know.

There was little time to waste. The Germans had already stormed over the demarcation line, and within hours they would be in Perpignan, the town at the foot of the Pyrenees. Between the treacherous mountain range and the clutches of Klaus Barbie, Virginia had to choose the lesser of two evils. The party would depart before daybreak.

At first the climb was gradual. The group walked in silence, careful not to alert the inhabitants of nearby villages to their presence. By early morning, the snow was swirling around them and the frigid wind bit through Virginia's clothing and into her skin, like millions of tiny cuts. The straps of her heavy rucksack cut into her shoulder. Unlike her companions, she couldn't change the side she carried her bag on because she could only bear extra weight on her right leg.

The guide turned back to check the progress of his charges. His dark eyes scrutinised them for any lagging, any signs of weakness. His gaze settled on Virginia, but she nodded and waved, hiding the discomfort she was already in so early in the journey and not daring to think about what lay ahead.

Indeed, the climb grew ever steeper. Soon Virginia and her companions were struggling for breath as they reached the 7900-foot mark. The snow was now knee-deep and Virginia could not walk normally. Her limp became more pronounced. She had to use her good leg like a ski pole to dig into the snow and drag her prosthetic one behind her. When they came to a steep and slippery ravine, her courage almost failed her. There was only a narrow ledge and the climbers had to practically hug the mountain as they crossed it, a sheer drop to one side of them. The amount of will and courage needed for Virginia to continue can't be glossed over. The nerve communication between our feet and our brains is vital for balance. When our feet sense stability and send that message to the brain, we have the confidence to move forward. Virginia only had her right foot to stabilise her. Now, more than ever, when the tiniest slip or misstep could result in a fatal fall, she had to draw on her mental strength.

~

When faced with something overwhelming, the outcome of which is uncertain, it is common for us to freeze, to feel that the challenge is beyond our capacities, and perhaps even in some cases – as the frozen corpses that littered the Pyrenees attested – give up and wait for fate to solve the problem for us.

Virginia faced all those feelings and still pressed onwards. What kept her going?

Friedrich Nietzsche wrote: 'He who has a why to live for can bear almost any how.'

When Virginia was climbing that mountain, she was doing so with a tremendous sense of purpose. It wasn't merely her personal survival she was aiming for, but to reach Spain and then find a way to continue her war work and help others to survive.

But the 'how' is also important in this story. A few years ago, I read about Navy SEALs undergoing what is arguably the toughest training regime in the military. To qualify, candidates go through a number of arduous physical tests, including having to complete a 2.4-kilometre run in under ten minutes wearing boots and pants. Trainers found that it was not necessarily those who held the big goal in their minds of becoming a Navy SEAL who succeeded, but rather those who broke the tasks down into smaller chunks. *I only have to run to that next post ... to that next tree. I only have to bear the pain another minute ...*

It seems it was that thinking that allowed Second World War Soviet fighter pilot Aleksey Maresyev to survive after being shot down over enemy territory. He broke both his ankles on impact and suffered other serious injuries. Frostbitten, starving and in agony, he made the eighteen-day journey back to Soviet territory by thinking that he only had to crawl to the next rock, and then the next stream and so on. He ended up having both his legs amputated due to gangrene, but he was able to return to flying a fighter plane, completing eighty sorties and shooting down seven German aircraft before the war ended. After his retirement from the military, he obtained a PhD in history and lived to the good age of eighty-five years.

During the writing of this book, my beloved ninety-one-year-old father became seriously ill. After his heart-valve operation eighteen years before, he had been in robust good health. My mother had been the love of his life, and after her death he could have given up on life. Instead, he made a deliberate decision to reinvent himself. For the past eighteen years he had continued to work in various consulting capacities, went to the gym a couple of times a week, enjoyed a variety of social activities and was involved in environmental protection projects. When I started this book, he still had his full driver's licence and was so busy that I almost had to make an appointment if I wanted to see him.

But all this changed in one day, when I found him sitting outside in the freezing cold, breathless and delirious. He was rushed to hospital, where the doctors told me that his heart valve was starting to deteriorate, causing severe anaemia. There was a possibility of replacing it, but then his kidneys proved problematic. On top of that, there was a problem with his bone marrow and a haematologist warned me it was very likely age-related leukaemia. Everything was going wrong at once. I had been looking forward to an exciting year with some great opportunities coming to fruition, including my first real holiday in years. But all that went out the window as my life became caring for my father who could do very little for himself. He had been my rock throughout my healing from trauma. I'd enjoyed our conversations and his sage advice. Now I could barely have a conversation with him that made any sense. The days became dominated by hospital visits, then home care, endless lists of medications and appointments with specialists. I wasn't sleeping more than a couple of hours a night, and I was stifling my big emotions – my grief and fear about losing the one person I completely trusted – in case they became so overwhelming I wouldn't be able to cope.

To manage it all, I had to let a lot of opportunities go and I was letting people down, something that I hated. I tried to maintain a positive attitude, but everything felt dark and bleak. Then I remembered that time many years before, when I had fled my house and was feeling traumatised and overwhelmed. I'd read a book by Victoria Moran, *Creating a Charmed Life*, in which she suggested in times of stress to focus only on doing the 'next indicated thing'. I stopped overwhelming myself and focused on the most important thing I had to do, and then the next, and the next and so on.

Gradually, I found myself getting into a rhythm, as if I were pacing myself in a marathon. I accepted things I couldn't control and kept my focus on what I could, and I did what I could one step at a time. Over time a sense of order and peace found its way back into my life.

This approach works well for us not only in times of extreme stress, but also when life is good. When we are fully present, life becomes not only more manageable but more pleasurable too. Time seems to slow down, or at least we seem to be getting more juice out of it instead of feeling we are always striving and never arriving.

When I was learning a ballroom dance routine once, my teacher told me to focus on each step instead of the whole routine at once. 'When dancers think about the next step rather than the one they are currently performing, they don't finish off their steps properly, and everything begins to look sloppy, and they get on top of the beat and slightly out of time.'

Break it down and do each step well, seems to be the way.

This is an important principle for becoming emboldened. We may not change our lives in one gigantic leap. Rather, we might have to take small but continuous steps towards our goal. Or if we do end up taking that gigantic leap, we will go further if we have had a good run-up of smaller steps first.

If this approach works for Navy SEALs and worked for Virginia Hall in extreme circumstances, then it is very likely to be helpful in our daily lives too.

~

It was with tremendous relief to Virginia that she survived the first day of the climb. The guide led her and her companions to a small cabin where they could rest. While the men took off their boots and warmed their aching feet by the fire, Virginia couldn't take off her prosthetic leg and the corsetry that held it. She had to hide under the cover of her blanket and look at the welts of painful blisters that had formed where her prosthetic leg met the stump. But she was simply glad to still be alive.

The next day, as the party climbed again, this time to 7650 feet, Virginia tried to calm her fear by taking in the rugged beauty of her surroundings, to think of nature not as her enemy but as her friend. One of the men complained that his left foot was so cold he couldn't feel it. Virginia could only nod at the irony. As the climb continued, she faced more difficulties. Her prosthetic leg was only designed for normal living, not an arduous mountain climb. The rivets began to come loose and she couldn't stop to tighten them without holding everyone up, or worse, revealing her leg.

Their next stop was at a safe house in a village. Virginia was astonished and delighted when her hosts produced a wireless set, and she was able to communicate to London that she was on her way back and was bringing two other resisters with her. When SOE Headquarters asked her whether there were any other important matters that they should know about, Virginia famously informed them that 'Cuthbert' (her pet name for her prosthetic leg) was causing her some difficulty but that she could handle it. Not sure who 'Cuthbert' was, but perhaps assuming he was a troublesome agent or informer, headquarters transmitted back that if Cuthbert continued to be difficult, she had permission to eliminate him.

We can only imagine Virginia's jubilation when, the following day, the party reached the Spanish side of the mountain range and looked out at the view of neutral Spain. It was here that their guide left them to go his own way. Virginia breathed with the elation of one who has survived a great ordeal. There was another day's walking ahead, but while the men grumbled about their stiff legs and fatigue, Virginia urged them to continue on until they reached the town of San Juan.

~

On Virginia's return to London, SOE felt it could no longer safely send her back into France as an active agent and offered her other intelligence roles within the organisation. But determined as ever, Virginia trained as a wireless operator and offered her services to the Office of Strategic Services, the nascent American intelligence service which was a forerunner of the Central Intelligence Agency (CIA). They sent her back into France in the disguise of an elderly woman, and she was active in organising military drop zones ahead of the successful Allied invasion. After the liberation of France, Virginia travelled to Lyon to find out what had happened to the Heckler network after she left. Sadly, Alesch's information had led to most of them being arrested and sent to concentration camps, where many died. But Germaine Guérin and Dr Jean Rousset were among those who had survived. Alesch was caught and put on trial. In 1949 he was executed as a war criminal.

Due to her outstanding war service, Virginia became one of the first women employed by the CIA. Although her activities with the organisation remain confidential to this day, many female CIA operatives credit Virginia as their inspiration to participate in intelligence work.

What Virginia did, all of us can do. That is, face an obstacle that we think we can't overcome, and then overcome it, step by step, stumble by stumble, until we reach the other side. What I believe Virginia did was draw on something deep inside of her, something that is quite supernatural and yet accessible to us all, and that's what I'm going to talk about next. In flamenco it's called *duende*, the little demon or the little angel: a passionate connection to something greater than ourselves.

# PASSION

# 16

It's impossible to become emboldened without being passionate about life at the same time, or at least some aspect of it. Passion fuels our inner fire. It motivates us to push through difficulties when they arise. It makes us feel alive.

But where does that fire come from? And if our life currently feels like a passionless wasteland, how do we ignite ourselves?

In my novel *Golden Earrings*, Paloma Batton is the granddaughter of Spanish refugees who fled Barcelona after the Civil War. A disciplined student with the School of the Paris Opera Ballet, Paloma lets little get in the way of her career, until she receives a visit from an other-worldly being who leaves her with a pair of golden earrings. Sensing that she has been given a quest, Paloma begins exploring her own Spanish heritage and makes the connection between the visitor and 'la Rusa', a woman who rose from poverty to become one of the great flamenco dancers of modern times.

I based la Rusa on the flamenco dancer Carmen Amaya. She was born in 1913 and grew up in a slum in a district of Barcelona. The *barrio del Somorrostro* was where the city's Romany population, numbering in the thousands, lived. It was a dirty beach, littered with industrial waste, and the sand was stained black by coal dust. There was no sewer.

The only fresh water supply was a couple of meagre fountains. Each year, death mercilessly swept over the area. If it wasn't floods, it was dysentery, cholera or typhoid fever. Infant mortality was high in the slum. Only the toughest children survived. Carmen's mother, Micaela, had already lost several babies at birth before her squalling daughter was brought into the world on the night of a fierce storm. There is some contradiction among the Amaya family over whether Carmen was born in a flooded tent in the *barrio del Somorrostro*, as is often claimed, or in her father-in-law's home in another poor area of Barcelona, or under a wagon in the countryside. But all accounts agree on the wild weather that accompanied her arrival. To the highly superstitious Romany people, the arrival of a new soul during a storm foreshadowed a powerful destiny. Indeed, from a very young age it was clear there was something special about Carmen.

From the time the little girl could stand on her two thin, dark-skinned legs, her father, the flamenco guitarist José Amaya, only had to start strumming his instrument for his young daughter to naturally move to the rhythm. No child in the *barrio del Somorrostro* was exempt from work, and one of Carmen's tasks was to fetch water from the fountains and collect sticks for firewood. Many who witnessed her going about these duties said that she always danced rather than walked. In many ways this is understandable as Carmen was surrounded by dancers and musicians. But it was something about Carmen's way of moving, a vigour that emanated from within her, that suggested an otherworldly presence. It was a force that would only become more apparent as she grew older.

~

Flamenco is the music and dance of Andalusia, the southernmost region of Spain. The first time I saw a true flamenco performance, I was in the city of Seville with my parents. Although I had travelled to many interesting locations with my work for the conference company, it was the first time I had managed to persuade my parents to leave the familiar comfort of their home and travel with me. Somehow, touring Spain in summer, when the midday temperatures reached forty-three degrees Celsius and everything stopped for a long afternoon siesta, seemed like a good idea when we planned it. I think the only reason my mother agreed to it was because she was beginning to fear that I might never return to Australia.

Up until that time, my vision of flamenco was probably something along the lines of Sono Osato's rather corny dance of seduction for Frank Sinatra in *The Kissing Bandit*, or Rita Hayworth swanning around in *Blood and Sand*. My mother was an avid fan of films from the Golden Age of Hollywood, and it was from watching classic movies with her from the time I was a child that I received my first introduction to dance. My mother often told me that she had been attracted to my father because of his resemblance to Gene Kelly.

Sure that the only way to see the 'real Spain' was to avoid hotels and stay in family-run pensions, I'd convinced my parents to join me in a historic house in the centre of the city where the staff spoke only Spanish. It had no air-conditioning, but the rooms featured high wooden-beamed ceilings and opened onto a tiled central patio complete with a fountain (the sound of which, my father later told me, inspired him to make several trips to the bathroom during the first night). One evening, I told our hosts that I would like to take my parents to a 'flamenco show' and after some animated discussion among themselves, the father of the family wrote down an address and called us a taxi.

The previous day, my father had secretly bought me a flamenco doll (or 'flamingo doll' as he called it) and that evening presented her to me over dinner. She was a dark-haired señorita with a yellow flared dress and black lace mantilla. My father and I have always been at odds with each other over the souvenirs we collect from the places we visit. I like to buy art or jewellery, and he likes salt-and-pepper shakers or snow-globes with 'Greetings from —' printed on them.

I stared at the doll, speechless, and wondered what I was supposed to do with it. My father nudged my mother. 'Look at that,' he said, chuffed. 'She can't take her eyes off it!'

Indeed! As gauche as the señorita appeared to me at the time, she gradually grew on me, and I have never given her away in any of my frenzies of decluttering. She travelled with me from Spain back to New York, then for long journeys in France and Russia, before returning back to Australia carefully wrapped up in my luggage. She sat on my desk when I wrote *Golden Earrings*, her frozen Barbie-like smile beaming at me. Even when my life was falling apart, and I was trying to save far more valuable heirlooms from destruction, I could not forsake her. Hidden in a biscuit tin, I handed her to my neighbour. For in her, I saw all the joy my father had in choosing her and presenting her to me. I was the grown woman whom he would always see as his precious little girl.

That night in the taxi, as we sped away to our evening out, I expected that I was taking my parents to see a dance and music spectacular with snappy castanets and exotic women draped in fringed shawls. However, we seemed to be driving out of the *barrio de Santa Cruz*, the heart of the city, with its Gothic cathedral, winding streets and museums, to somewhere further afield where the houses were run-down and the restaurants less glitzy. The taxi stopped outside a dingy looking tapas bar. A smell of stale garlic and fried fish hung in the air. The people waiting in line were mostly Spanish. There were some foreigners among them speaking English or German, but they were not the usual tourists sporting polo shirts or capri pants that you might find wandering around the Alcázar Palace or the Plaza de España. There was no buzz in the air, no pre-concert excitement. It seemed to me that everyone was whispering – highly unusual in Spain – or quietly contemplating something. A young woman showed us to our seats at a small round table. My father took his camera out, but she frowned at him and shook her finger. I assumed her refusal was due to copyright laws or because camera flashes could distract a performer.

'It's all right, Dad,' I told him. 'I'll buy you the show program.' But when I looked around, there wasn't a program-seller in sight.

The stage was small and narrow. Two chairs and two stools were set up on it in a semicircle. I was glad we were in the front row, because otherwise it might have been difficult for my mother to see if she was stuck behind some lofty German. The show was to start at 7.30pm, but it was 9pm before anything happened. By then my parents, both lifelong teetotallers, were a little 'happy' on the glasses of sangria that had been placed before us, without any of us having ordered them.

From the moment the performers arrived on stage, it was clear this wasn't going to be the cabaret-style performance I had anticipated. Two scruffy-looking men dressed in black and four women in bright but worn polka-dot dresses took their places on the seats, arranged in what I later learned was *cuadro flamenco*, where the dancers, singers and guitarist are seated in a semicircle and accompany each other with *palmas* (handclapping) as each takes a turn dancing or singing. All the performers were middle-aged and slightly-haggard looking. The women were not the glamourous long-limbed beauties of the Folies Bergère in Paris. The men, with their scuffed shoes with worn-down heels, looked more like stagehands than performers.

One of the men stood up, and a hush fell over the audience. The guitarist started strumming something that sounded familiarly Spanish. The women began clapping a vibrant rhythm. I smiled at my parents, who looked excited that the show was about to begin. Then the music and the clapping came to a complete stop. The singer opened his mouth and emitted a sound that resembled a cross between an animal moaning in its death throes and somebody gargling. From the corner of my vision, I saw my father's eyebrows shoot up. The singer continued with long mournful laments, bending notes I never knew existed and contorting his face as if each word he uttered was causing him pain. I glanced at the other audience members, but they sat there leaning forward, enthralled. The singer's voice was rough and unpleasant, and the effect he was producing was gut-wrenching and primordial. It many ways it was 'awful' and yet strangely alluring at the same time. The more I listened, the more I thought I understood. While the performance wasn't what I had anticipated, and I wasn't sure if either of my parents was going to thank me for subjecting them to it, I decided to do what I always did when travelling and found myself confronted by something I didn't understand: I went with it.

~

Flamenco, is the music of the outcast. Flamenco dancing is often confused with Spanish classical dancing, which, like ballet, had its origins among the noble classes. Indeed, most flamenco dance teachers of Western students will offer something of a hybrid of the two styles, because pure flamenco, as I was to learn, is an acquired taste and needs some historical and cultural context to be appreciated. Spanish classical dancing is graceful and more pleasing to the Western eye (and ear), because the patterns and music are familiar to what we know. This is the style that introduces embellishments like fans, hats and castanets.

Traditionally, flamenco is not concerned with sounding or looking pretty. At its core it is about expressing a strong feeling and having that emotion understood. That is why older performers are venerated and appreciated: they can convey the deep emotions that come with life experience. In fact, the rougher a singer's voice, the more they are seen to have lived life. Nobody is going to respect a squeaky teenage *cantaor* or *cantaora*. The ravages of age on a dancer's face only make her more beautiful in the eyes of those who watch her, because each of those lines represents wisdom.

According to flamencologist Robin Totton, while flamenco is closely associated with Romany culture, which has certainly developed it and ensured its survival, the music originated in the melting pot of Andalusia. It was heavily influenced by the Moors, who ruled there for almost eight hundred years (the word *Olé!* is derived from the Muslim interjection, 'By Allah!'), and also by Jewish religious songs and Byzantine Gregorian chants.

The Spanish Inquisition saw the Moors and the Jews persecuted, forced to hide in the hills and caves alongside the Romany people, who had always been the outcasts of society. It was then that the many influences that we now find in flamenco fused together to become the form we see today. It was secretly performed as an underground movement, hidden away in private homes, the countryside or in the caves of the Romany. Later, it would emerge again and be performed out in the open, in taverns and at fiestas.

We could say then that flamenco is the perfect artistic expression of the resilient. It is the song of the survivors.

~

That night in Seville, the more I deliberately peeled off my expectations and layers of judgement and surrendered myself to the moment, the more I felt I was participating in something ancient and otherworldly. The dancers, when they took their turns, were spectacular, but not in the way of cabaret performers and showgirls. They would move fiercely and then softly and quietly, then fiercely again and come to a moment of such stillness it was as if time had stopped.

So much of any kind of 'performance' is about pleasing the audience. The flamenco dancers with their strong, proud stances but downcast eyes were not interested in whether they were delighting anybody. Indeed, their fierce facial contortions were sometimes ugly and would not have been acceptable in other environments. They seemed to be moving in a trance and yet, far from being zombie-like, were acutely aware of everything. A pure flamenco performance is always improvised. The dancer will dance to the emotions she is feeling at the time. Unlike other dance forms, the guitarist will follow her. Because nothing is choreographed, the dancers will usually not dance together. You won't see them performing synchronised steps or orchestrated stagecraft. The best way to approach such a performance is without any expectations.

Even though I had stumbled upon this gathering of flamenco aficionados with the clumsiness of a foreign explorer falling into a ditch, what I saw that evening stayed with me. A curiosity was born inside me, a desire to better understand what I had experienced. But it would be many years before I would return to it. As for my parents, they too had been seduced by the performance. It was understandable in my mother, who was used to moving fluidly between cultures. But my father was also moved by the performance. Now, even in his nineties, he describes it as one of the most memorable nights of his life.

~

Carmen Amaya's father recognised his daughter's talent and was quick to exploit it. Child or not, the family needed money to survive. Even the smallest children from the *barrio del Somorrostro* were sent to the markets to steal fish. Dancing was a preferable – and more profitable – employment for Carmen, and from the time she was a very small child, José took her to the bars and cafes of Barcelona to dance for the patrons. This was a risky undertaking, as Barcelona's child-labour laws were progressive for their time, and making children work late at night was punishable with heavy fines. While Carmen danced, José had to keep one eye on his daughter and one eye on the door in case the *Guardia Civil* appeared. One memorable night, they did, and José had to make a quick exit out the back door while tiny Carmen hid herself in the folds of another performer's coat. She had been given the flamenco name 'La Capitana' because of her seriousness about her dance and her determined, confident nature.

Barcelona is the capital of Catalonia, a region that merged with the rest of Spain in the 1400s but remains culturally separate in terms of language and traditions. It was also the industrial and business heart of Spain in Carmen's time, and many Romanies from the south migrated there to find work. *Las Ramblas* is a long boulevard that runs down the centre of the city. Far from sedate, it is vibrant with flower markets, bars and restaurants. Street performers abound and the atmosphere is always bustling. It was a short walk from here that José brought Carmen to an upper-class restaurant near the docks, Las Siete Puertas. The owner sometimes let Romanies perform there for entertainment. With the reflection of its hundreds of gas lights sparkling in its gilded mirrors, it was the place that the city's millionaires and magnates came to eat with their wives and mistresses. The atmosphere was tinged with the salty-saffron smell of Catalan cooking, along with the scents of French champagne and fine Havana cigars.

The sight of all those important people decked out in expensive silks and velvet might have been intimidating to a small child who lived in a shanty town and wore threadbare clothes. But Carmen wasn't intimidated. She danced on the chequered tiled floor, often barefoot if her shoes were hurting her feet. Waiters bustled past with plates of steaming paella, and her dance was sometimes obscured by the Ionic columns and ferns. Carmen didn't let any of that bother her because she knew that after a few steps her dancing would bring the conversations to a stop and all eyes would turn in her direction. People were mesmerised not because of her child-like cuteness, but because of her extreme focus and animal-like fierceness. 'That child,' they would whisper to each other, 'she has something.' They would not only reward her exceptional performance with applause, but would also toss her dollars, francs and pound-sterling notes. If anyone should throw her coins, Carmen would not pick them up. Even at a young age, and desperately poor, she knew her worth.

~

When Carmen was older, José took to her to Madrid and the Villa Rosa, a tapas and wine bar where the very best of the flamenco dancers performed. The patrons – wealthy businessmen, celebrity bullfighters, politicians and intellectuals – understood flamenco intimately and appreciated its artistry. However, Carmen encountered some cultural snobbery. What could a girl born so far from the flamenco heart of Spain have to offer? A child who had only her family and the rhythms of the ocean's waves as her teachers?

Still, Carmen was undaunted.

> La Capitana remained impassive as a statue, arrogant and noble, with racial nobility beyond description, focussed inward and oblivious to everything happening around her. Suddenly she leaped to her feet. And the *gitana* was dancing. Indescribable. Soul. Pure soul. Feeling

in the flesh. The stage was vibrating with unheard-of savageness and incredible precision.

    Paco Sevilla, *Queen of the Gypsies: The Life and Legend of Carmen Amaya*

~

As part of my book tour for *Golden Earrings*, I was giving a talk at a library. In the audience that night was a group of women who, from their style of dress and hair, were clearly flamenco dancers. They had come with their teacher, Carmen Maravillas, who had read my book and loved it. It is always a great compliment when an expert in the field confirms the accuracy and authenticity of my writing. Set during the Spanish Civil War, *Golden Earrings* was well received by Spanish readers. Carmen delighted in telling me that many of her Spanish friends had read it and were convinced that I had Spanish heritage or had lived there for many years.

    Carmen Maravillas is a former ballerina who studied Spanish dance in Madrid and fell in love with both the classical style of dance as well as flamenco. She had spent the last fifty years, together with her guitarist husband Juan, as a flamenco performer in Australia and Europe. She was in her seventies when we met at the library, but was, in fact, ageless. Graceful and beautiful in both appearance and character, she was extremely knowledgeable. We spoke about Carmen Amaya and connected immediately. There is a lot of conjecture and argument in the flamenco world: what is pure flamenco? Do the Romany people have a right to claim it as their own? Should foreigners be allowed to learn it or does that constitute cultural appropriation? But I've never met anyone who disagrees that Carmen Amaya was the greatest flamenco dancer. Even sixty years after her death, she brings arguments to an end and unites people.

But it wasn't always so. In her lifetime, Carmen Amaya was highly controversial. Traditionally, women were 'upper body' dancers. They used their torsos, arms and hands to express the dance. The rhythmic foot-stamping (*zapateado*) was the domain of men. Carmen used her feet with a technical precision that used to send her audiences into a frenzy. She eschewed the voluminous frilled skirt (*bata de cola*) for pants so that the bullet-like precision of her feet could be better appreciated and she could spin unhampered. In Romany culture, a woman wearing pants was sacrilegious, as the sexes were kept distinctly separate. Carmen's dancing was anything but traditionally feminine.

My experience in Spain and my research for *Golden Earrings* had stirred a desire in me to learn to dance flamenco. I told Carmen Maravillas that and she gave me her card.

'When you are ready, please come and see me. I would love to be the one to teach you.'

'And you are the one I want to learn it from,' I told her.

For five years I kept Carmen's card in my wallet. To study flamenco dancing was a yearning that didn't dim, but I had several writing and family responsibilities, and I couldn't make the time.

Then, when my life began to turn into a nightmare, I had to create for myself a mental escape before I could make a physical one. I believe it was an important factor in saving me: for one hour a week, every Monday night, I went to Spain.

~

I would arrive an hour before my flamenco lesson and park my car around the corner from Carmen and Juan's house. It was a pretty street lined with liquidambar trees, which in late autumn were losing their leaves. No one could see me sitting in my car there, and I'd watch the fallen leaves swirl in the wind and try to take stock of my ever-downward-spiralling life.

Leaping into the unknown is difficult enough if you've planned it. Even those who have prepared well to leave a job to build their own business or to write a book feel a certain level of fear before they take the final leap. I had to plunge headfirst into a future that I could not picture. I was positive enough to believe that great leaps of faith often produce spectacular results. But I was also realistic enough to know that leaps into the darkness can also result in broken spines and fatalities.

As the time for my flamenco lesson drew near, I would dry my tears, reapply my make-up and step out of my car. I had to find the strength somehow. After all, my personal heroine, Carmen Amaya, had to make a leap of faith of her own too.

~

After her performances at the Villa Rosa, word about Carmen began to spread throughout Spain and she made a name for herself performing with various touring dance companies. She came to the attention of Luis Buñuel, who would come to be considered one of the best and most influential filmmakers of all time. He cast her in the tragic *La Hija de Juan Simón*, about a young girl who falls in love with an actor who has come to her village to make a movie. As her star rose, Carmen never forgot her family. Now able to afford an apartment in Madrid, she moved all of them in with her – about twenty-five in number.

In 1936, things took a shocking turn in Spain. There was a nationalist military uprising against the elected Republican government. When the coup failed to take complete control of the country, a bloody civil war erupted. The Republicans were supported by those with liberal sympathies – the educated middle class, the intelligentsia, and many artists and entertainers, as well as urban workers and agricultural labourers. Those in favour of the Nationalists were the Roman Catholic Church, monarchists and those with conservative and fascist leanings. Many historians regard the war as the 'dress rehearsal' for the Second World War: the Allies failed to adequately support the Republican government, while Germany's Nazi government supported the Nationalists. The war became a testing ground for many of the weapons the German army would later use in its invasion of Europe.

Carmen was on tour with some of her family in Valladolid when the military seized her car. Left without transport to her next destination – a theatre in Lisbon, Portugal – she had to go there by bus. She arrived late, only to discover that the impresario who had employed her had cancelled the contract when she had failed to arrive on time. Finding herself in Portugal without enough money, Carmen had no choice but to resort to the tricks she and her father had used to find themselves work in the cafes and restaurants of Barcelona when she was younger. At the upmarket Café Arcadia, the usual entertainment was a sedate quintet. Carmen, along with her father and brother, managed to persuade the waiters to let them perform. Carmen donned her finest dress and sang and danced, enthralling the audience and charming the owner into giving her company a contract.

Word about Carmen was spreading internationally, and she soon received a proposal from a theatre in Argentina, offering her one million pesetas for three months of performing. It was more money than Carmen could have ever imagined when she was a young barefoot girl dancing on a dirty beach. There was only one problem: she and her family would have to travel over the ocean to get to Buenos Aires. It seems Carmen's clan were very superstitious about ocean travel, and she had already refused a lucrative offer to perform in New York, complaining to one reporter that she would have gone if the Americans had built an underwater tunnel between Spain and the United States.

Carmen claimed that her seasickness began the day she bought the tickets for herself and her family. White-knuckled and muttering prayers, the Amaya family, including Carmen's grandfather and her diabetic mother, boarded the gangplank to the ship that would carry them to South America. The ocean voyage was not uneventful: one of the other passengers did go overboard and the ship stopped for eight hours to search for him. To Carmen's horror, he was never found. Later, when the ship ran aground, Carmen's family did not attribute the accident to a navigation error, but rather saw it as proof that the sharks were trying to stop them reaching their destination.

The day the company arrived in Buenos Aires, the impresario who had invited them searched for the great Carmen Amaya among the disembarking passengers. When he found himself standing opposite a tiny woman of swarthy appearance, he was so sure that the show was going to be a disaster that he refused to attend the opening night. Instead, Carmen's performance stirred the audience into such a frenzy that the next night, as people fought to gain entry to the theatre after hearing about the dancer, the police and fire brigade had to be called to hose down the crowd. From Argentina, Carmen went on to make tours all around South America.

When asked how she liked Buenos Aires, Carmen replied that she liked it so much she wanted to stay, just so she never had to cross the ocean again. But if she and her family hadn't overcome their fears and made that trip to South America, Carmen wouldn't have been seen by the impresario Sol Hurok, who would take her and her company to the United States. Carmen became a worldwide star and a very rich woman, changing not only her own destiny but that of her family. All that began with her leap of faith.

But in case you think that fame and riches might have changed Carmen, you will be heartened to know that she never forgot her humble roots. While staying in the exclusive Waldorf-Astoria hotel in New York, the Amaya family alarmed both the other guests and staff by building a fire in their suite and frying fish, just as they had on the beach of the *barrio del Somorrostro.*

~

Arriving at the home of Carmen and Juan Maravillas was like stepping into a piece of Spain. The villa-style house had little in common with the other suburban houses around it. After walking through a wrought-iron gate, I passed a brightly tiled courtyard complete with a tiered fountain and overlooked by Juliet balconies with fiery red geraniums spilling over the railings. Carmen and Juan used to own a Spanish antique shop and their house was full of Gothic-style walnut furniture and tapestries. In the corner of the living room stood a full suit of armour from Toledo, affectionately named 'Jorge'. Their dance studio in their converted garage was decorated with mementos and autographed photographs taken from their time as performers, as well as a collection of Juan's racing bikes, which at eighty-three years of age he was still riding every morning. Carmen's art, which she was doing more of now she had retired from dancing, hung on the walls. It was a magical house, and Carmen and Juan were a magical couple who seemed to exist in a different realm. Carmen resembled a medieval queen. Always immaculately turned out, I couldn't imagine her popping down to the supermarket in a tracksuit.

They had agreed to come out of retirement to teach me, and only me. I was very aware of the privilege I'd been granted and knew of other students who were envious of it. I intended to work hard, not only for my own satisfaction but out of respect. After years as a professional dancer, in which she had spared nothing of herself, Carmen now suffered from rheumatoid arthritis and had some bone deformities in her hands and feet. We had originally agreed that she would demonstrate the steps once, then she would sit down as I danced and she would correct me. But that agreement didn't last very long. I don't think it even went past the first lesson.

Flamenco is not a dance you can do by halves. Your whole body is involved. The dancer is a percussive instrument. Her feet keep the rhythm while her upper body and arms move more slowly to express her emotions. Those emotions run the full gamut: *Sol y Sombra*: sun and shade. As soon as Juan started playing his guitar, Carmen would get up and throw herself into the dance, putting everything she had into her feet and body. Faced with the energy of a dynamo in her seventy-ninth year, I could hardly prance around at half-speed. I had to give the dance my all too.

Flamenco is the dance of the proud. The unbroken. All dancers have excellent, upright posture but the *flamenca*'s stance is unique. Her shoulders are placed slightly backwards, which thrusts her chest forward, opening her ribs and thereby exposing her heart and her solar plexus, which to the Romany is the centre of the universe. Her chin is slightly lifted, showing her throat. It's not a stance we make when we are hurt and fearful. In those moments, we hunch our shoulders forward to protect our vital organs. The *flamenca* is almost daring you, throwing down the gauntlet. She knows she can expose her vulnerabilities because no matter what you do to her, you can't hurt her. Life has thrown her heartache, tragedy, difficulty after difficulty, and she has risen above them all. You can crush her body, but you cannot crush her spirit.

Flamenco dancers are not crowd-pleasers, although the effect they have on audiences can be electric. The dance itself is in many ways introverted. The eyes may be proud, but the gaze is downward. The dancer looks within rather than without. For all her explosive performances, Carmen Amaya was reputed to have been quiet and self-contained offstage.

While Carmen Maravillas corrected my posture and the tilt of my chin, it occurred to me that you cannot dance flamenco in the mindset of a helpless, discombobulated victim.

~

Sometimes people confuse passion with obsession or an addiction that destroys one's equilibrium. Indeed, the word *passio* in Latin does mean suffering, hence 'the Passion of Christ' is the suffering of Christ. Or we associate it with doomed love affairs, great lusts that are sure to burn out, like Heathcliff and Cathy in *Wuthering Heights* or Anna and Vronsky in *Anna Karenina*. However, lately it has come to mean something positive. So positive, in fact, that, like the word 'trauma', it can be overused in situations, even job interviews. *I am passionate about meeting the service expectations of our most demanding clients, and improving crisis and issues management.* Really? You'd throw your heart and soul into that?

Passion is a path – a journey with a view to mastery. It is ongoing. It is never about a goal. It's not about overworking or overachieving either – that is perfectionism and not passion. Passion embraces failure as part of the process. Without failing and trying again, there can be no mastery.

Being passionate is an act of self-love. It's never about crowd-pleasing or showing off. We become so absorbed in something that even the ups and downs of it bring us a sense of fascination and joy. When I am fully engaged in a passion – my writing or dancing, for example – I'm far more balanced in my life than when my days feel monotonous and pointless. I sleep better. I take good care of my health. I'm happier and more present around other people. That sort of passion is something I pursue out of love. Not because I'm trying to meet deadlines or produce a bestselling book. It emerges when I find myself fully absorbed in what I'm doing and it isn't motivated by external desires or, even worse, *fear*! It's always about the process and not the end goal.

There is a paradox to that, too. The more completely immersed we are in something, and the less concerned we are with admiration and outward success, the more likely we are to be successful. The things that we produce out of pure love are always superior to those produced out of fear or ambition. It's as if our projects become infused with the energetic quality with which we created them.

Passion is closely linked to purpose because when we are feeling passionate about something, we know we are in the right place at the right time and doing exactly what we are supposed to be doing. It's spiritual, in that passion satisfies our deepest soul desires.

It's also linked to resilience. We understand nobody becomes a master of their pursuit after their first attempt. It takes time and dedication – and much failure. Mastery comes from failing and learning from those failures.

Confusing an obsession with a passion is a bit like confusing limerence with unconditional love. I might add that we can never be passionate about another person. To really love someone, we have to afford them the freedom to be utterly themselves. We cannot 'master' them.

Also, we don't have to know what our passions are from birth, and they can evolve and change over our lifetimes. The less we worry about 'finding our passion', the more likely it is to sneak up on us as a delightful surprise. Simply allowing ourselves to follow pursuits that bring us pleasure, and learning all we can about them with a sense of exploration, is a fruitful way to coax a passion into life. The more knowledge we gain, the more passionate we often become about our pursuits.

~

Carmen Amaya was not merely an accomplished dancer. She was a legend. While she displayed unsurpassed technique and brazenly preferred pants over dresses for her performances, what has flamenco aficionados unable to forget her was that there was something supernatural about her dancing. An important part of flamenco is to communicate a feeling, but how the audience receives that feeling is equally important. Carmen was famous for sending her audiences into riots of ecstasy. She seemed to be channelling an other-worldly energy, and not spontaneously but with intention. It appears she had discovered a way to regularly produce in almost all her performances a state that in flamenco is called *duende*.

*Duende* in folklore refers to mischievous but benign spirits that are humanlike in appearance. They often inhabit houses but are also found in fountains, caves and rivers. Despite their impishness, they are usually kind and helpful to humans, guiding the lost through forests or helping fishermen row their boats in stormy seas. But *duende* when used in a flamenco context has a different meaning. It refers to a point where the dancer becomes so focused and such a master of her art that she conjures up from inside herself a supernatural force that makes her one with all that is. It is in that moment of supreme emotion that the dancer and audience transcend life and its suffering. They can draw on enough strength to face anything.

Perhaps it could be compared to the flow state known as 'the zone', when a person is so fully immersed in performing a certain activity that they feel energised and fully involved. But it is still more than that. It is being in a state of flow and a state of awe. When we are feeling awe, we usually feel so overwhelmed by the wonder of something that we seem to connect to something bigger than ourselves. It is also a spirit of evocation. In flamenco, the audience must feel it too and it must produce a deep emotional reaction in them.

~

Flamenco employs the full body and mind. The rhythms of the different musical forms are not the familiar 3/4 and 4/4 timing of Western music. On top of making me think about my feet, body, arms, hands and gaze, Carmen Maravillas was adding props – I had to use my skirt a certain way in the dance and not only hold a fan but open and close it on exactly the right beat. After only a few lessons she was already talking about adding castanets. Flamenco means nothing without expression. You have to draw up your feelings, and those emotions must be present in and able to be felt in every part of your body. They can't be faked, stagey expressions. They must come from your innermost being.

Neuroscience tells us that when we rehearse and perform an action over a period of time, there are structural and chemical changes in our brains. Power posing – the idea that standing in a superhero pose before a job interview makes you feel more confident and therefore more likely to succeed – is controversial among researchers. But conditioning the mind and body is well studied. It's the basis of hypnosis, cognitive therapy and sports training. When changes in beliefs are combined with confident poses and practised along with powerful rhythmic music, and when this is regularly rehearsed and reinforced, it can produce effects in how someone feels and thinks and therefore reacts to certain situations.

There was no choice but to be utterly present during my lessons. When I was dancing, nothing else existed. There was no past or present. My problems disappeared from my mind. Of course, they still existed in real time, but not while I danced. As the nails in the soles of my flamenco shoes slammed down on the floor, I was stamping out the sense of powerlessness that had taken over my life the way you might stamp out the last embers of a fire.

~

I've always believed in the sacred power of three. As Juan played, Carmen clapped and I danced, we were conjuring up some powerful magic. I don't want to give the impression that I am a great dancer. I'm not a natural, and I don't have long, sinewy limbs. But I have always loved dancing, and often desire and passion are more important than natural talent. I would practise everything that Carmen taught at every opportunity, so it would be perfect by the following week.

Then one day something quite supernatural happened while Carmen and I were dancing together. I don't claim it was as lofty as *duende* because I wasn't a master of flamenco by any means. But at that moment my heart was so immersed in what I was doing that nothing else existed. I would have thought that if ever I was going to have a mystical moment while dancing flamenco, it would have been in one of the soulful, deeply expressive *soleares*, or even a magestic, defiant *siguiriyas*. But my magical moment of oneness came in dancing a lively, vibrant *alegrías* – the dance of happiness.

The *alegrías* is elegant and refined, with varied footwork. It is a vivacious dance that expresses joy, but it also has some solemn, reflective moments.

In the studio, Carmen and I were working on the *escobilla* – the section of the dance that involves climactic, virtuoso footwork. I loved watching Carmen dance it, and then I followed, doing my best to imitate and incorporate her precision and tap into my own spirit of happiness. We went over and over the section. Juan was playing and Carmen was urging me on when, suddenly, I was a little girl again, dancing on the back patio of the family home. The sky was clear blue and the sunshine was sparkling around me. I was so happy and so full of joy. A dandelion floated on the breeze towards me. My mother had told me that dandelions were fairies and that when I saw one coming towards me on the wind, I should gently catch it, make a wish and then let it go again. And that is what I did.

The whole vision was only a matter of seconds and yet the effect was electric.

'Are you all right?' Carmen asked me. 'Do you need to sit down?'

I had stopped dancing and must have looked shaky on my feet. 'That was the weirdest thing,' I told her. 'I just time-travelled. For a moment I was a little girl again.'

~

Later, over tea, Carmen told me about an experience she'd had of being transported to another realm when she was dancing an *alegrías*. She and Juan were on their way to perform at a re-enactment of a famous Andalusian festival in the Clare Valley, South Australia. Their guitarist friend Angel was with them. The festival was a pilgrimage, where the Virgin of the Dews was to be taken into the countryside in processions and fiestas that would last several days. It was a celebration to give thanks for being alive. It was a particularly poignant time for Carmen and Juan because they had been in a car accident a short while before and were still suffering chest injuries. On their trip along the dusty road to the festival, they stopped for a while. Juan and Angel started playing an *alegrías*. Suddenly, Carmen was swept up in the splendour of the natural beauty around her.

'I danced without any concessions to an audience or performance restraints,' she told me. 'I felt my spirit soar above the dry soil and the majestic eucalypts of the Australian bush.'

As I drove home, I thought about what had happened to me during the lesson. The life I was living had become so dark, so full of fear and dread. I was suffering, and had little hope that things would get better. That flash of a vision had woken me up.

For I knew very clearly what that little girl had wished for when she caught the dandelion and let it go. She had wished to be free.

~

Carmen Amaya once said that if she could no longer dance, her life would not be worth living. The longevity of her career is proof of her vivacity and genius. People never grew tired of seeing her perform. In 1963, while dancing in Mexico, Carmen collapsed on the stage. She had been suffering from sclerosis of the kidneys, and her only functioning kidney was enlarged. Carmen had believed that her kidney failure was due to an inability to eliminate toxins, and that by dancing furiously she would be able to rid her body of them through her sweat. Her belief doesn't stand up medically: you can't sweat out toxins, and strenuous exercise can worsen kidney disease. But I don't think that even if Carmen Amaya had known the facts, it would have made any difference to how she lived her life.

Dancing was her joy and her passion. She lived her life exactly as she wanted to live it. How many of us do that, even when faced with the knowledge that every single one of us – no matter how safely or dangerously we live – will eventually die?

A quote often attributed to Hunter S Thompson is:

> Life should not be a journey to the grave with the intention of arriving safely in a pretty and well preserved body, but rather to skid in broadside in a cloud of smoke, thoroughly used up, totally worn out, and loudly proclaiming 'Wow! What a Ride!'

Passion is surrender. It's giving up everything that gets in the way of it. Passion is in all of us, but we don't find it until we are willing to let go.

The best passion to develop, I believe, isn't necessarily for certain activities or interests. It's to have a passion for life. To love it fully, including all the pain and the joy. I think if we develop that, we become truly emboldened.

# CONNECTION

# 17

'Gardening is about the future. One plants a seed dreaming of what it will become. It requires patience. It requires faith.' So writes one of my characters, Diana White, in *The French Agent*. Diana is a forward-thinking landscape designer, active in postwar Sydney. She and innovative architect Harry Scott have a dream of making Sydney the city with the most beautiful suburbs in the world. She has also been given a quest by her recently deceased Aunt Shirley to restore her mother's picturesque garden in Killara. The garden had been lost in an act of violence, and Aunt Shirley believed that by restoring it, Diana would be able to heal her past trauma.

My inspiration for Diana was a pioneering garden designer named Edna Walling, active in Australia from the 1920s to her death in 1973. She was born in York in northern England in 1895, but spent her formative years in Plymouth in the county of Devon. Her father's work brought the family to Melbourne, Australia, in 1915 where Edna enrolled in the Burnley School of Horticulture. She was an artist in every sense, creating a combination of plants and stonework, light and dark, that evoked different moods in the gardens she designed. Her signature features were inviting flagstone paths and flights of stairs, reflective ponds, stone walls draped with clematis, and pergolas with honeysuckle and wisteria climbing their posts. She liked to frame a house with trees to lend an enchanting air of mystery, rather than leave it naked and on display for all to see from the street. She would often leave part of a garden in its wild state to reflect the surrounding countryside. She later became one of the first designers to incorporate native Australian plants into her plans. Edna was so sought after that people boasted of having an 'Edna Walling garden' the same way they might boast about owning a painting by Tom Roberts or a sculpture by Norman Lindsay. Indeed, her patrons not only received a beautiful garden from Edna but also their garden plan, painted in delicate watercolours, which was work a of art in itself. She was the gardening writer for *Australian Home Beautiful* magazine, a photographer and a passionate environmentalist, who was still writing letters to local newspapers about roadside plantings until her last day.

Edna was able to be who she was thanks to the influence of her parents, William and Margaret Walling, who were liberal in her upbringing and education. When she was a young child she contracted pneumonia. As part of her rehabilitation, her father took her for long walks on the moors and woodlands of the surrounding countryside. Edna's red hair would blow in the soft breeze as her lungs grew stronger and her legs sturdier with time. Father and daughter would sit down on a log and eat the lunch packed for them by Margaret and Edna's older sister, Doris. All the while, Edna's nut-brown eyes surveyed the quaint villages, the stone bridges, the mosses and lichens that grew on rocks, and the profusion of bluebells that carpeted the forest floors in spring. Like all children who experience an enchantment, she would try to recreate the magic of those days in her adult life.

Edna's parents were supportive of her in other important ways. While Doris was a natural homemaker, Edna was uninterested in sewing and dolls but fascinated by the tools in her grandfather's ironmongery workshop. William encouraged Edna's natural predilection by giving her materials with which to design and build things. When she grew older and showed no interest in boys or getting married, Edna didn't have beaus forced upon her by her mother. Instead, Margaret encouraged her to draw and gave her books by renowned garden designer, Gertrude Jekyll.

Oh, how our parents influence us by what they give us to read!

~

The books my mother gave me when I was a child shaped me in ways that still influence me and the stories I tell today. Jo March's burning desire to be a writer and an independent woman in *Little Women* ignited those desires in me too. As the March sisters grew from young girls into women, they faced many desolate and exultant moments. Even though I was far too young when I first read the book to understand the complexities of romance, let alone marriage, I thought that Jo's rejection of Laurie's proposal showed courage. Although I wouldn't have been able to put it into words then, I understood that Jo had decided against what might be easy in the short term in favour of what was true. The poignancy of *Black Beauty*, an equine coming-of-age story that follows a horse from the time he is a foal to his retirement, and the cruelty and kindness he experiences on his journey, taught me that life is not all roses and rainbows. It has violent storms and dark nights, but it also has achingly glorious beauty, just like a splendid garden. My mother's selection of books were often stories that illustrated the importance of resilience and also of becoming an emboldened human being.

An author whose work was a great influence in both my life and my writing was May Gibbs and her superbly illustrated stories about two gumnut brothers, Snugglepot and Cuddlepie, who go on adventures that bring them into contact with bush flora and fauna. One of the tales set me up not only for a passion but for a purpose. Cuddlepie is out in the bush one day when he hears a pitiful cry. He comes across a brushtail possum that has been caught in a steel-jaw trap. The possum is weeping in agony:

> 'Oh! poor dear Possum! Who did this to you?' asked Cuddlepie.
> 'Humans,' said the Possum. 'They set these traps at our very doors and we run into them before we see them.'

The possum is dying, and Cuddlepie is too tiny to open the trap. He tries to revive the injured animal but fails, so he goes running to Snugglepot for help:

> 'See! Oh, see what the Humans have done.'
> Snugglepot was filled with grief and the tears ran down his cheeks, while all the Bush creatures cried in their own way. Nothing could be done. No one was strong enough to open the great trap. The poor, gentle Possum must stay there till he died.

They hear a 'monster Human' approaching and all the bush creatures run away in terror. The monster Human sees the possum, and the bush creatures gasp in horror, sure that the human will kill the possum. But this happens instead:

> The monster Human opened the trap with his strong hands and gently lifted out the little Possum. Then he bound up the poor broken leg, and they heard him say, 'These rotten traps, I hate them.' And he pulled up the stake and flung the trap into the stream.

I'm not embarrassed – or maybe I am just a bit – to say that even as an adult woman that story still moves me to tears. Of all the writers I have read and enjoyed, it is with May Gibbs that I feel the deepest connection. When I visit her house of forty-four years, Nutcote, which sits in a lush garden on Sydney Harbour's foreshore, I feel that I am going to see an old friend.

My mother would also have liked her. I grew up surrounded by majestic bushland with magnificent trees – looming, giant ones with wide canopies. I'd climb them with my brothers or settle underneath the shade of one to read a book. My mother taught me to have respect for trees as living things. You never 'vandalised' them, which was her term for carving your initials on them or peeling off their bark. 'How would you like it if someone tore off your skin?' she asked me. Both writer and mother instilled in me a deep and abiding love of natural beauty and Australian wildlife. I never wanted to be a 'monster Human' to the animals or the bushland. I would be a 'friendly Human' who would help them if they needed it, but who would otherwise appreciate their magic and beauty without encroaching on it.

Anyone who reads my books will always find in them a deep affection and respect for nature and all living creatures.

~

At one time in my life, I found myself living in a suburb in North-West Sydney. It was for convenience purposes as I was working towards another goal, and I had only intended to be there for a short time. The people were nice, it had good facilities and it was safe to walk around at night. The house I lived in was modern, roomy and had a pleasing flow to it. North-West Sydney is considered to be a green area compared to the rest of the city, but my suburb was devoid of natural beauty, or at least the spectacular beauty I had grown up with. There was no tree canopy to speak of and consequently not a lot of wildlife. It was not a suburb of gardeners. The gardens were mainly lawns and shrubs with very few trees. It wasn't long before it started to depress me. I found myself *physically aching* for natural beauty. Living without trees and wildlife was like living without friends.

I was also soon to discover that the suburb baked in summer. If you went outside from mid-morning onwards, it was like being cooked alive. I lived in a cul-de-sac where the tarmac would become so hot you couldn't go anywhere near it, and it would radiate heat all night. There was no southerly buster to freshen the air in the evenings, just a hot wind blowing from inland. Unless people went away on holiday, summer was spent inside with the air-conditioning running. I was saddened that a whole suburb of people thought spending an entire summer like that was normal, or even worse, they were teaching their children it was.

Despite the modern ducted air-conditioning, I was horrified to find that things kept on the top floor of the house sometimes melted. I'm not talking about items like make-up and hand cream. The plastic components of my hairdryer, which were supposed to be resistant to heat, collapsed into goo. My storage containers wouldn't close because the lids had twisted out of alignment.

My father suggested I get whirlybird fans installed on the roof and was dismayed when he learned there was no ceiling insulation. To my father, ceiling insulation was house-cooling 101. He'd been advocating for double-layered insulation in Australian homes since the 1970s. He had been a senior engineer with the Department of Public Works. While my mother enthralled us with stories of exotic China at the dinner table, my father would talk about his engineering projects, including one that involved harnessing the methane gas produced from sewerage plants to run the boiler plants in hospitals and prisons. He'd always been concerned about the environment and the careful use of resources. His stories didn't seem half as exciting to me as my mother's, but I must have absorbed more than I realised, because there was one thing he said that stayed with me: 'People don't realise that heat will kill more people in this country than bushfires or floods.' He wasn't talking about somewhere out in the desert. He was talking about Sydney.

There wasn't much that could be done about the structure of the house other than to get the roof covered in heat-reflective paint. It was modern and typical for its time, with large paved surfaces and small eaves. It desperately needed the cooling effect of a garden.

Edna Walling thought that trees were one of the most important elements in a garden, particularly an Australian one. She used them to shade driveways and to cast pleasing shadows to soften the harsh afternoon sun. She believed that a house with a backdrop of trees was far more appealing than one with an 'unrelieved' roofline. In her later life, when Edna was constructing her holiday home on a hill above Victoria's scenic Great Ocean Road, she built around the existing trees rather than cutting them down. She believed such a process not only kept the natural landscape as intact as possible, but also produced more interesting housing designs than the standard box-like cottages of the time.

Where I grew up, people loved lush gardens and trees. It was only later that I would learn about the 'garden manicurists', or that some people regarded nature as some sort of anathema.

~

After Edna graduated from the Burnley School of Horticulture, she found work as a 'lady gardener' at the same time as Australian suburbs were expanding. This was fortuitous as it created a demand for people who could design and construct suburban gardens, and Edna gained experience quickly. Although she had a great love of trees and shrubs, she preferred to leave the planting to others while she concentrated on the structural aspects of a garden. It was always stone walls, pergolas and sculptures that she started with whenever she was designing. She was, at heart, a builder. Despite that early bout with pneumonia, Edna grew up to be physically robust. She enjoyed the hard labour of building. She wasn't a woman adverse to pushing heavy wheelbarrows of soil or lifting bags of cement. In the 1920s, she was striking to look at too. Some would even say shocking. Tall with pale English skin and pinches of ruddiness on her cheeks, her daily uniform was a pair of jodhpurs, a tailored shirt and a pair of sturdy men's shoes. But Edna was comfortable with her own unconventionality and never apologised or made excuses for it. Eventually, people were won over by her charm and good manners and simply gave her the affectionate nickname of 'Trousers'.

'Edna, dear, don't you tire from all that digging?' asked Mrs Jones, a new client who had requested a lily pond for her garden. She handed Edna a glass of homemade ginger beer.

'If everyone gardened there would be no wars,' Edna replied, wiping the sweat from her brow and eagerly accepting the refreshment. 'Nobody would have the time or mental capacity to make such evil plans.'

Edna was well read and thought deeply about things. She kept a journal in which she wrote down quotes from philosophers and literary luminaries. While she wasn't religious, she did have a quiet faith in God and believed in angels. It was this ability to see deeply and to care so much for the natural landscape that saw her contributing articles about gardening to newspapers and magazines, and eventually writing books on the subject. New home owners who had never had a garden before, and were without the means to hire professionals, lapped them up. Her engaging, conversational writing style and confidence in her own opinions won her a following. She was soon viewed not only as an expert but as Australia's premier garden designer. This was something that was to prove both a blessing and a curse. Edna grew such a strong fan base, that people would appear on her doorstep wanting gardening advice. She was friendly but she was also an introvert who valued her privacy. The attention proved so exhausting that Edna would eventually build herself a small secondary cabin on her property to use as a bolt-hole to escape to whenever uninvited guests appeared, leaving her gardening assistants to invent excuses for their boss's sudden disappearance.

~

As Edna's reputation grew, she gained a following of wealthy clients down the eastern coast of Australia from Queensland to Tasmania, including the internationally acclaimed opera singer Dame Nellie Melba, and newspaper proprietor Sir Keith Murdoch and his wife Dame Elisabeth Murdoch. But she also enjoyed the challenge of a small garden. It was to Edna's techniques on making a garden seem larger that I turned to when I was about to tackle my own humble suburban plot. My main challenge was the front garden, which faced west and bore the brunt of the relentless afternoon sun. It needed shade desperately, but it was also small and narrow. If not for that, I would have loved to have planted a landmark tree: the kind of tree that defines a house and gives it personality; the tree a family sits under to have afternoon tea or on whose branch they hang a swing. But even if I'd had the space, a large tree would have been out of place in the cul-de-sac where I lived, as there were no trees at all in the front gardens. Everything was highly manicured, and there was no shade – a look favoured in much of the suburb. I didn't expect to live in the house more than five or six years (but through circumstances ended up being there longer), and I hated the idea that the next person who lived there might cut a beautiful mature tree down. So instead, I planted a number of smaller trees like Little Gem magnolia, prunus, photinia, and small lilly pillys, which were elegant, but had more contained root balls that were less likely to lift pavers and footpaths.

I wanted to keep the front garden formal yet inviting, but the stone borders that Edna liked would have only added to the radiant heat effect, so I used hedges instead. For the flowerbeds, I followed her advice on avoiding too many colours. For a visual cooling effect, I used gardenias, lavender, white grevillea and plumbago, which all grew well in the local soil. I placed a birdbath under the magnolia tree and planted agapanthus around it.

I had to keep up the watering until everything established, but once the garden got going it looked lovely. It softened the house, which without a garden had appeared monolithic, and lent it a pleasant elegance. Each time I came home I'd stop to admire it a moment before driving into the garage. Sometimes when my father came to visit, he would bring an elderly Italian friend who would pluck some of the flowers and hand them to me when I opened the door. 'Your garden is lovely,' the Italian gentleman would tell me. And that was quite a compliment, because his late wife had been a superior gardener who had regularly won competitions.

The back garden was much bigger, and I had more freedom with it. Because it was bordered by five houses, the painted steel fences typical of the suburb were mismatched and that did not make for an attractive view from the house. Following Edna's style of planting thickly around the border of a garden to create a sense of depth, I went to town on the native trees and plants, and then brought a greater sense of formality closer to the house with more hedges and deciduous trees to shade the patio: prunus, Japanese maple and crepe myrtle, which all grew quickly.

I placed a wrought-iron bench in the corner beside a romantic-looking birdbath, although I didn't expect to see any native birds and animals apart from the ones I had in care as a wildlife volunteer. I had two dome-shaped vintage green aviaries to house possums in until they were ready to be released back into the wild. I planted deciduous trees around them, so the possums would have shade in summer and sun in winter. Although Edna loved a sense of naturalness to some aspects of a garden, the kind of place a person would have to 'fight through' as she once described it, I was careful not to overplant and make the garden too high-maintenance or *too natural-looking*, aware that I was not creating a forever garden solely for myself but also for whoever might live in the house after me. It all looked so elegant and tranquil, I hoped that they would appreciate it, because the house now had a pleasing outlook from every window. Although I didn't expect to have that garden forever, I did put my full heart and soul into it.

All the while I worked on the garden, I kept Edna's books on my bedside table. They were something beautiful to read before bed. It seemed a great pity to me that they were out of print and could only be bought – expensively – second-hand. Edna's designs still have much to offer Australians, especially after she started incorporating native plants into her plans. If more people had Edna Walling gardens – even scaled-down versions – our suburbs would be so much more beautiful and environmentally appropriate. I also agree with Edna's larger view that if we all understood the value of nature and its beauty, there might be fewer wars and other strife.

~

A garden is like an artwork that constantly changes. I felt not just pride in the garden I had created, but a tremendous love for it as a living, breathing entity. The sight of it, and the way it was progressing, was a true source of joy. I'd grown up with a bushland garden and any gardens after that were the courtyard and balcony variety. I didn't have naturally green thumbs, and I had to learn from my mistakes and ask much more experienced gardeners many questions. I spent a lot of time looking at gardening books and visiting the local nurseries. But it gave me such delight. Eventually, it took on the quiet informal elegance I was aiming for. 'Gosh,' my friend Lisa said to me one summer, when we sat in the garden looking at the fish pond and actually feeling refreshed rather than boiled alive. 'This has totally changed. It used to be a yard and now it's a garden. I feel like I'm in some charming guesthouse in the Blue Mountains.'

Which was exactly the feeling I had wanted to evoke.

~

People were not the only visitors to my garden. The local wildlife that had seemed non-existent at first glance arrived as if my garden was Noah's Ark. During one heatwave, when the temperatures were in the high thirties for several days, different species of birds that would normally avoid each other – magpies, rainbow lorikeets, galahs and crested pigeons – sat in my birdbaths all together, trying to cool off. With that many birds together, it was important to keep the water clean to avoid disease, so I became their personal valet, coming out every few hours to refresh the water and always cleaning the baths thoroughly at the end of the day. Blue-tongue lizards regularly made their way across the patio. A kookaburra came in the mornings to swoop on bugs, and in the evenings his shift was taken over by a tawny frogmouth. One night I went out with a torch to inspect the ringtail possums I had in the aviaries. At first I thought they had escaped, because I could see three sitting in the

Summer Beauty eucalyptus I had planted. But when I shone my torch inside my aviaries, my possums were still inside. The following year, I looked outside my window and saw a big, fat brushtail possum sitting on the garden bench.

With more shade and water sources, frogs appeared: green tree frogs; dwarf tree frogs; marsh frogs. All types. It was a thrill, as Sydney's frog populations were in rapid decline due to loss of habitat and the use of pesticides. Not in my back garden. I made a froggy pond for them outside the room where I had my piano. I'd play classical music and they would croak. What music we made together.

I've never had much patience with people who say they can't sleep because of a frog croaking in the garden, and yet can fall fast asleep with the television blasting out disasters and horrors. How removed from nature is that? I was at another wildlife carer's home one evening when something rather funny happened. She had a verdant garden full of amphibian life. While I was there, her neighbour came over to ask her if she could kindly quieten her frogs because it was now after nine o'clock. Instead of answering that the woman's request was impossible to fulfil, the carer told her: 'I have to listen to your kids jumping on their trampoline for hours, and I don't ask you to turn them down. Frogs keep populations of flies, mosquitoes, cockroaches and spiders in check. Tell me, can your kids do that?'

~

One year, the council green team came around and planted street trees in the suburb. They had gone through a process of thorough planning first, choosing species of appropriate trees and marking beforehand where they were to be planted to avoid any root problems with driveways and drains. The trees they put in were already quite large, so there was some expense involved. They sent a water truck around for the first few weeks and then left notes in everyone's letterboxes, asking us to keep watering the trees until they were established. I was so excited that they had been planted and I imagined how beautiful the avenues of trees would look when they matured. They would soften the sterile look of the suburb and they would bring welcome shade to the footpaths and road surfaces. They would also provide nesting places for birds and create safe lines of travel for small arboreal mammals like possums.

As I walked around looking at the new trees, I could only think how much Edna Walling would have approved, although the method she used to plant trees was to take a bucket of potatoes and toss them into the air and then plant the trees where the potatoes fell. This was how nature randomly dropped her seeds and would give a more natural look to the planting. However, even Edna conceded this approach wasn't always practical, especially when planting along driveways. Once she fell in love with native trees, her favourite planting was an avenue of lemon-scented gums. These quintessentially Australian trees would not only offer shade and were suited to the environment – lending sensual beauty with their white trunks and flowers, and the glorious scent of their leaves – but they also gave a sense of place. If you were to be suddenly dropped into Tuscany or Provence, you'd know where you were by the dirt roads lined with cypress trees that have been planted for hundreds of years to protect vineyards and fields from strong winds. If you were to stroll through Paris with your lover – or poodle – in the summer, you would be delightfully shaded by the plane trees that line the city's elegant boulevards. In New York it would be linden trees, while in New Orleans the majestic oak trees stretch their branches across streets and pavements to soften the city's intense southern heat. So, when I saw that my local council had planted avenues of street trees, I felt the suburb was about to transmogrify from its prepubescent awkwardness into a place of beauty.

I called the green-space manager at the local council to thank him for the trees.

'What a beautiful suburb you are creating for us,' I told him 'It's going to look magnificent!'

He sounded stunned to have heard from anyone.

My excitement was not to last. As soon as the council water truck stopped coming around, residents began pulling out the trees in numbers. Many of those that were left were not watered by the residents, so a lot withered and died. But the strangest thing I saw was the people who chopped the trees to knee height and then topiarised them into lollipops! Those poor tortured trees reminded me of the inhabitants of CS Lewis's Narnia who had been turned to stone by the White Witch. I only hoped the evil spell they were under could one day be lifted, and they would be able to become proper trees again.

A real-estate agent came knocking on the door, asking to see if I wanted to sell the house anytime in the near future. I told him about what had happened with the street trees, because I could not make head nor tail of it. I have always thought tree-lined streets were beautiful aesthetically, a sign of excellent taste, but I'd also heard that a leafy street immediately added 10 per cent to house values, which in Sydney is no small amount.

'Oh,' he said. 'You're not from around here, are you? Don't you know what they call people in this suburb? *The tree-haters*. They see a tree, they cut it down.'

~

I rang the green-space manager and told him what had happened. 'When so many trees in New Orleans died as a result of being in salty flood water after Hurricane Katrina, the residents cried,' I told him. 'With all their other losses, they *cried* for the trees. What's wrong with the people in my suburb?'

He commiserated with me. 'I've come to the conclusion that there are two categories of people,' he said. 'There are those who appreciate nature and understand that we are part of it. They are willing to put up with inconveniences like having to clean out leaves from their gutters or sweep their pathways. For them, living around trees is more important. Then there are the others who cannot tolerate any intrusion by nature into their lives. A leaf on their driveway makes them angry. To them, birds singing in the morning is annoying. Nature is something they need to impose their control over. If they see a bee, they will reach for the insect spray with no appreciation that without bees the human population will starve. They'll go to a National Park, but nature is always *something out there*, and they have no deep connection to it. It's got nothing to do with formal education, how much money they have or what country they are from. It's got everything to do with how they grew up and what they learned from their parents.'

~

There were people in the suburb who liked trees and valued them. You could tell from the little patches of trees that remained and were well-cared for. But tree-hating and tree-fearing were both certainly prevalent in a way I had never seen before, and instead of the beautiful avenues of trees I had imagined, the suburb looked like a strange chequerboard of tree-lovers vs tree-haters.

*Tree-hating*. I had not even conceived of it. Who could hate a tree? I remembered being six years old in my leafy school playground and my teacher making us gather around a tree that stood at the centre of it.

'The tree breathes in the carbon dioxide we exhale,' she told us, 'and then it breathes out the oxygen we need. Trees are the lungs of the Earth, and we are alive because of them.'

As we stood there, sucking our little cheeks in and out, we imagined the tree breathing in unison with us. Then the lesson continued as my teacher explained that the animals and birds that lived in the trees kept us alive too. They ate the berries and deposited the seeds in their droppings, or carried pollen on their fur and feathers, and helped more trees to grow.

I thought it was all wonder and magic, and yet another reason to love nature.

Where had the tree-haters been when that lesson was taught? What did they think sustained human life on Earth? Shopping malls and chain stores?

~

Not long after my conversation with the green-space manager, a terrible incident happened a few streets away from me. Someone deliberately laid out poisoned meat for the local magpies. As a wildlife carer, I knew this kind of horror happened all over Sydney from the North Shore to the Eastern Suburbs, but coming so quickly on the back of the street trees saga it broke my heart. Each orphaned baby bird rescued by a wildlife carer represents hours, days and weeks of dedicated care. A 'monster Human' had wiped out thirty of them in a single day.

It seems bizarre to me that as a society we spend so much time and money on our personal appearances and pursuing dreams of happiness by internet shopping and scanning social media, while completely ignoring our connection to the very thing that sustains us. Even worse, we participate in its wanton destruction. Australia is among the worst land-clearage nations in the world, and the worst for animal extinction. In the year the magpies were killed and the street trees massacred, twenty-three football-sized fields of koala habitat were being bulldozed in the state of New South Wales *every day*. Animals and birds were dying in their millions, and the residents of my suburb couldn't even share some trees and space with those that still remained?

When our mental, emotional and physical health deteriorates, we turn to psychologists and a medical system to help us, when many of the answers we need are right outside our door.

Yet sometimes we remember: when we look at the stars with wonder, or go for a walk with an azure-blue sky stretching above us and warm sunshine on our backs, or we dip into the saltiness of the ocean and feel it breathe in time with us.

To be emboldened we need to be connected to a larger force than ourselves. That might sound woo-woo to some people, but that is simply how it is. Otherwise, we are like appliances with no electrical supply. Much of our pain comes from being disconnected from this larger Divine entity that makes its presence known in nature. When we reconnect with it, our peace and joy come back to us. From that state, everything we do, we do as emboldened people.

~

One day I saw a rainbow lorikeet in my garden that appeared at first sight to have something wrong with its wing. It flew over my back fence, and I walked around the block to find the house of the garden I thought it had gone into. I rang the doorbell and was greeted by a vivacious lady, Rita, who looked to be in her sixties. At her feet was a sweet elderly terrier. I told Rita that I was concerned about a bird that had flown into her garden, and she invited me to have a look around. I followed her out into her back garden and discovered a beautiful paradise there, with all manner of birds flitting about and a blue-tongue lizard sunning itself on a rock. There was a special ramp in the pool so that if an animal should fall in, it would be able to climb out. I'd had no idea that this beautiful garden was there because it was screened by a tall hedge of cypress pines. We found the bird and discovered it was quite all right. Then Rita and I struck up a conversation about gardening and wildlife. She showed me back inside and introduced me to her pet bearded lizard who was basking on a log in a large tank in her living room. Her house was stylish and immaculate with a coastal feel about it. I was surprised to discover she had several reptiles in it, including a snake curled up in a terrarium. 'Oh, that's my son's,' she said. 'I'm just babysitting it.'

Rita had a beautiful energy, and it looked like everything she cared for thrived. We had been brought together by a bird that had flown over the fence.

Nature not only connects us to something bigger, it connects us to each other.

~

Edna Walling was a woman who deeply understood the need for a like-minded community. In 1921, while out walking in the countryside with a friend from her horticultural schooldays, she discovered a piece of land that was on offer for subdivision. It was being advertised as suitable for small farms and weekend homes. It had long been Edna's dream to build her own cottage and to have land enough for a plant nursery. She wasn't the only woman to have a dream of a cottage and garden. In the 1920s, there was a movement of professional and artistic women buying their own plots of land and living in cottages. What was behind this movement? We have to remember, in that era women often had to make a choice between a family and a career. Marriage for many was a burden rather than a pleasure. Without reliable contraception, the number of children a woman might have could add up to an entire soccer team – or more! Without the convenience of household appliances – or even running water and electricity in many homes – domestic chores occupied most of a woman's time. Even if she was wealthy enough to have servants, a woman in high society was often even more burdened by expectations to stick to the domestic sphere and be her husband's 'helper'. For women who wanted something else in life, it seemed the best choice was to get away and have their own space as a way of declaring independence. Those with some means or an inheritance often bought the ready-made cottages offered by timber mills and had them assembled for them, something like the 'tiny houses' of today. Others acquired the huge wooden crates that aeroplanes were delivered in and used them as the base for their cottage, adding rooms when they could afford it. If this all sounds a bit desperate, it's important to understand that perhaps only a century before, the only way a woman could escape marriage and children was to become a nun.

Edna was only starting in her career and, having spent all of her savings on a deposit for the piece of land she had acquired, she hadn't considered all the difficulties posed by the site she had chosen. Firstly, the land was almost 5 kilometres away from the nearest train station – Mooroolbark – and was situated on a hill with no road leading up to it. The cost of bringing any materials to the site – ready-made or not – was formidable. So, Edna had to put her dream on hold until she could earn some more money.

It was her mother Margaret who offered a solution to the problem. She travelled out to the site and saw that it had an abundant supply of natural stone and many slender saplings that could be used to build a cottage. With the words 'build it yourself' in her mind, Edna's excitement for her project was reignited. She acquired a horse and sledge to carry supplies she needed from the station, but otherwise she built her cottage from what was available to her on the site. While her mother sat on a rock observing the process, Edna built her home stone by stone. She was a recycler, too. The roof was made from packing cases that her father donated to the project from those left over from his warehouse. When she was done, Edna found herself the occupant of a delightful, rustic cottage. She named it after one of the villages that she had passed through with her father on their excursions together: Sonning.

The cottage had one main room with double glass doors that opened out onto a piazza, a kitchen and a bathroom, and a bedroom that was up one step because the cottage was situated on a slope. Edna's style was to make her houses to fit the land, rather than having the naturalness of the land destroyed to fit the house. Like many Australian homes of the time, her lavatory was outside and there wasn't piped water or electricity. But Edna did give herself the luxury of a porcelain bath along with a wood-fired heater, so she could soak her tired muscles after a long day of gardening or building. But she was happy there with her books, her gramophone and her pets – a dog named Brian Boru and two black cats.

The progress of the garden that she planted around Sonning was shared with her many delighted readers of *Australian Home Beautiful*. But as time went on, and Edna became more successful in her career, she was faced with another problem. The various subdivisions around her were in danger of being sold off to pig farmers – or, perhaps even worse in Edna's mind, to property developers who would clear all the land and build 'cookie-cutter' suburbs. She needed to secure at least 12 acres to preserve the beautiful views that her property offered of the undulating hills and peaks of the Dandenong Ranges. But Edna couldn't afford to buy all that land on her own.

That's when she hit upon the idea to become a property developer, but not the usual sort who is concerned with maximising profits and who disappears when the cracks in the houses they have built start to appear. Instead, Edna dreamed of a village of 'like-minded people' where the cottages would be built in sympathy with the landscape and as much of the natural setting as possible would be preserved.

Her first customer was the friend who had been assisting Edna to get her accounts in order, a pharmacist named Blanche Scharp. As Edna set to work on Blanche's dwelling, she took into account some of the mistakes she had made with her first building project. For example, Sonning's bedroom window offered a perfect view when Edna was lying in bed, but not when she was standing up. Later, the mother of Edna's gardening assistant, Gwynnyth Crouch, would have a charming cottage named 'Winty' built for her and two of her other daughters. Lorna Fielden, a teacher at the Methodist Ladies' College in Kew and a poet, was attracted to the community. Lorna would become the ideal collaborator for Edna's gardening books, as well as a lifelong friend.

From this start, Bickleigh Vale came into being. Unlike the soulless, treeless suburbs springing up elsewhere, the village, which still exists today, evoked the atmosphere of *The Wind in the Willows*. At first the residents were nearly all female professionals, single or widowed. Later, men would also join them. This was not a commune by any means, the residents maintained their independent lives, but it was a community. Edna included in the development an outdoor theatre with terraced steps for cultural events, where various fundraisers were held during the Second World War to raise money for the Red Cross. The entertainment on those occasions included famous ballerinas and theatre actors. Edna's name had become a drawcard.

~

While my own suburb was hardly a 'like-minded' community to me, I realised that holding a negative attitude wasn't going to make things any better. I did my best to focus on all that was good, and the nice people I was meeting, and even tried to be more understanding of the tree-haters. And I really do believe they deserve compassion. I imagine their lack of connection to something that supports their very existence must feel a bit like going through life after a lobotomy. I was at a loss to explain how someone could look directly at the wondrous beauty of nature and feel absolutely *nothing*.

Wildlife carers are also educators, and we usually encourage people to green up their gardens to create supplementary wildlife habitats and corridors. That's a good strategy if most of the residents in the area are wildlife-friendly. But it's preferable to steer wildlife away from people who don't feel a connection to nature, otherwise the animals could end up being poisoned or harmed in other ways. It is better to provide them with safe habitat elsewhere.

I received a sign of sorts, you could say. I was standing in the local shopping centre car park when a ringtail possum fell out of the only tree there and landed directly in my arms. It was a boiling hot day, and the poor thing was gasping from heat stroke. I took it home until it recovered. The whole suburb needed more tree canopy, but if people weren't willing to green up their gardens and share them with wildlife, the next alternative was to do something about the parks.

The area actually had a lot of parks, but they were barren patches of grass and not at all inviting. In the middle of the suburb was a huge park that was all eroded soil, weeds and a few straggly, sick-looking gum trees. It spanned several blocks, but you never saw anybody walking in it. With such sparse vegetation it was useless to wildlife. It looked like a neglected paddock and it was something of an eyesore.

Edna Walling was a letter-writer. Until the very last days of her life, even after several strokes, she was still writing letters about the importance of roadside plantings to avoid soil erosion. So I took a leaf from her book, so to speak.

I wrote to my local councillor and said it would be great to turn that park into a bird sanctuary, as it was otherwise wasted space. I suggested that maybe even a local business would sponsor the planting because it could be a lovely centrepiece for the suburb, and I listed all the benefits to animals and people.

I can't remember his reply exactly, but I think it was the usual: 'Thank you for your letter, but no thank you, we have other priorities … and yes I have passed your letter on so it can be lost in a file somewhere forever.'

But a couple of days later, a woman from the council rang me and asked me about my idea and I explained it to her. She was sympathetic, but she said that it was such a big park with so much erosion that, 'You could throw a lot of money into trying to plant in that park and it wouldn't make any impact.'

I was disappointed but I told her I understood, thanked her for her time and thought that was most likely the end of that idea.

A few weeks later, I drove past the park and saw some earthmovers digging up the soil. A huge mountain of bark had been delivered and a truck pulled up stacked with plants and trees. After they all left, I went and had a peek at what had been done. A large area had been planted in one corner of the park where there were already some existing gum trees. Over the years, the council kept adding to the area planted, and before long, trees that would become canopy trees began to reach for the sky, while the mid-storey and understorey trees began to thicken and spread. It became a wonderful paradise for all sorts of local birds, and soon that once barren place was filled with birdsong. Over time the council also added pathways with shade trees, a fenced dog park and a children's playground. It became a beautiful space for people and wildlife alike. The plantings were thick enough for the wildlife to feel hidden, and the paths and other facilities kept human activity at the other end of the park.

After that positive experience, I joined in the annual Planet Ark National Tree Day plantings that took place in the suburb. There were never more than ten volunteers, but it was good to see other barren parks in the suburb start to green up and become attractive. The local council was also active in restoring creek beds and created some inviting tree-shaded bicycle paths. One of my neighbours came up with a word for whenever an area of the suburb was planted, whether I had any participation in it or not, 'Oh look, that park has been *Belinda-rised*.'

It made me especially happy to see the children playing in those parks. Perhaps they wouldn't grow up to be scared of trees and birds. Perhaps they wouldn't think that living an entire summer indoors was normal.

I joined in a special Mother's Day planting, where people came together to plant trees in memory of their mothers. Years later, I went to visit it again. I stood there among the trees and felt their soothing energy. The air was cool and fresh, and the sunshine was dappled. Little birds flitted everywhere. It had once been a dry, dusty place, but now it was beautiful and full of life. My mother would have loved it.

As for my own garden, the trees had grown and it had turned into something verdant and leafy. When I woke up in the morning, I went out into it to breathe the oxygen it offered and to look at the birds and plants. Before I went to bed, I'd go out, even on cold winter nights, to look for frogs and possums. In the end, I was very sorry to have lost it.

# 18

'You know the land Harry and I were trying to save out west? It's all been cleared now. I saw the photographs in the newspaper. The woodcutters moved in and everything we tried to preserve is gone now. When I read about it, my heart broke and I wondered if darkness and greed will always win.' She paused a moment to gather herself before continuing. 'All my life I have tried to protect beauty because it is the best antidote I know to evil, and when evil wins and vanquishes beauty, we must get up and revive her again.'

Belinda Alexandra, *The French Agent*

I related to Edna Walling not only as a gardener and conservationist, but as a woman who had to rebuild again after something precious to her was destroyed.

I can imagine that Edna felt about Sonning very much as I did about my garden. So one winter morning in 1935 when disaster struck she would have experienced pain similar to mine as she picked herself up and started again.

The air was crisp outside, but Edna was snug inside. She was working on a design for a new garden plan, sitting at a table with a cosy fire burning in the grate. Her animals were with her: her beloved Irish terrier

Brian Boru, her elderly black cat and a recently adopted black kitten. Brian and 'Old Black Cat', as Edna affectionately referred to her, were asleep by the fire. The kitten was on top of a cupboard, having staked her claim on a place where she could benefit from the rising warm air and also get a bird's eye view of the room. Like me, Edna loved to listen to classical music when she was working, particularly Beethoven. So, although she didn't mention any music in the events that unfolded that day, I'll take some poetic licence and add the *Moonlight Sonata* playing on a gramophone in the background.

Gwynnyth, her assistant, was at work outside, tending to some seedlings. It was a day like any other, and Edna was already dressed in her gardening clothes with the intention of joining Gwynnyth as soon as she had finished with the plan. She had made several attempts, but the ideas weren't flowing. Leaning back in her chair, she closed her eyes and thought about her October article for *Australian Home Beautiful*. Then, she remembered she needed to speak to Gwynnyth about the Italian lavender cuttings.

Edna strode out the front door with Brian following her. She found Gwynnyth in the nursery, but before she could say anything, her assistant pointed in horror towards the house. Smoke was pouring from the windows and the curtains were ablaze. It seems likely that when Edna opened the door, she didn't notice that the breeze sweep her papers from the desk and into the fireplace. Airborne embers had then set the furnishings alight. Edna ran to get the hose while Gwynnyth heroically dashed inside the house to save the cats. She broke a window with her bare hands to help them escape, badly cutting herself in the process.

With a lack of foresight unusual for Edna, there was only one tap near the cottage. The hose, as it turned out, barely reached one of the windows and the water pressure was too low to have any significant effect. The heat forced the women back, and the roar of the flames and the sound of breaking glass was terrifying. Black smoke poured from the home where Edna had been peacefully working only a few minutes before. It was all over in less than half an hour. Sonning was nothing but a burnt-out shell. The women and the animals were safe, but Edna had lost everything. Her library of books and her artworks, as well as her daily household items.

~

Edna would tell her readers later that, unable to sleep that night, she got to working on a plan for 'Sonning 2'. While it is true that Edna did build a better constructed house than her first, it didn't have the wonky charm of the original. Edna put on a brave face about her loss and tried to be philosophical about it, but I understand her pain. It's not just the material things that you have lost, but something of your essence. It was those moments with her mother that could never be repeated; the sweat and satisfaction Edna felt when she finally got the roof on straight; the laughter of friends who had come to lend a hand; the quietness of the place when Edna finally climbed into bed. She had put herself into that cottage, as I had put myself into my garden.

It was not the first – nor would it be the last – time that Edna lost a home to fire. The first time was when she had been a child in Plymouth, and her grandfather's ironmongery workshop caught fire and was razed to the ground. The family's finances went close to bankruptcy and Edna had to be taken out of her exclusive school before the family eventually had to move to New Zealand and then Australia to follow her father's career selling scales. The last time was when her beloved holiday home at East Point near the township of Lorne on Victoria's Great Ocean Road was burned down in a bushfire. It was a place she had enjoyed building so much that she was planning to publish a memoir about it entitled: *The Happiest Days of My Life*.

There would be a Sonning 2 for Edna, rising from the ashes. And in her later years, Edna would move to Queensland with plans to recreate another village-like community there. Edna felt pain over her losses for sure, but she was a woman who saw struggles as part of the journey and always had her eyes firmly set on the future.

# 19

The notion wasn't lost on me that when I was catapulted from my former life, I landed in the place of my childhood, with its majestic natural beauty and abundant wildlife. Cockatoos and king parrots became my companions when I read on the balcony. When I went for walks, I'd look up at the pure blue sky through a canopy of towering trees.

There were signs of 'friendly Humans' too. A few of the houses had fences that had been specially built so that mature trees would not have to be removed. In one place in particular, round holes had been cut in a fence so the branches of a jacaranda tree could poke out from it. Little street libraries abounded, suggesting the voracious reading habits of my neighbours, and, every so often, coming from an open window was the sound of someone playing a piano or violin. One day on one of my walks I heard someone playing the harp, and I stopped a while to listen to the heavenly music.

But it was a long time before I could connect to other humans. I avoided new ones and stuck to only those I knew very well. The ones I felt I could trust not to turn into someone else entirely. But most importantly, having had my autonomy and my sense of self so deliberately destroyed, I had to reconnect with myself before I could connect with anyone else in any healthy way.

~

Complex Post Traumatic Stress Disorder (CPTSD) is the result of prolonged and repeated trauma. If there was one good thing that came out of my experience, it was a fascination with the brain and how it works. I knew the cause of my trauma was over and I was safe, and that now my suffering was being caused by how my brain was functioning. It was mostly neurological. If I could heal my traumatised brain, I'd be able to get on with my life.

CPTSD leaves you hypervigilant and constantly anxious, and I understood that it was a result of my brain trying to keep me safe. It was forever scanning the environment for danger, and it didn't have an off switch. I only saw a psychologist briefly. She confirmed that I was doing all the right things to heal, and that my mindset and my attitude to life were good, so there wasn't much more that psychological therapy could offer me.

My path out of CPTSD turned out to be meditation, and a particular kind of meditation. I had experimented with guided visualisation, hypnotherapy and breathing meditations in the past and I wasn't very good at them. I was one of those people who claimed that they couldn't meditate. I would start off okay, but after a few minutes I would be thinking about my writing, or what I had to do next, or composing shopping lists. My mind was too busy, and meditating seemed like such an effort when I could go for a walk or to a dance class and get the same amount of stress relief with a lot less mental effort.

So, it would seem contradictory that I would find myself gravitating towards meditations designed by Dr Joe Dispenza, a lecturer and researcher on neuroscience and quantum physics. His guided meditations run about an hour, sometimes longer, and involve quite a vigorous type of breathwork and deep concentration. His approach combines neuroscience with spirituality, which is a good combination for me with my Russian-Australian background. The Russian part of me is open to the idea of the mystical and inexplicable, but the Australian part of me demands something that I can logically understand and has some sort of practical application. In terms of neuroscience, Dr Dispenza says his research shows that when we are in a constant state of stress, our brain functions erratically, switching between our different senses as it scans the environment for threats to our survival. The aim of his meditations is to get the brain functioning more holistically.

I discovered my claim that I couldn't meditate was a bit like someone saying 'I can't speak French' or 'I can't crochet'. Of course we can't if we have never learned those skills. They take time and practice. One hour out of a busy day was also quite a commitment on my part, but I discovered what one meditation devotee said about the practice to be very true: 'Everyone should be meditating at least ten minutes a day, except for very busy people who should be meditating for at least an hour.'

Although an hour was a significant slice of time for me, and I had to get up early in the morning to fit it in, meditating made me more productive, creative and focused, so an hour spent meditating probably ended up giving me an extended three or four hours of productivity each day.

But the benefits went well beyond that. Having experienced the hypervigilance and triggers caused by trauma, as well as having a mild but persistent anxiety most of my life, meant that to have a peaceful, calm and observant mind for the first time was a revelation. The sense of connection with myself, and life, and also something greater was so profound that I would not have swapped it for a Ferrari or a mansion on the French Riviera if someone had offered those to me in exchange.

~

Edna Walling liked people. She liked community. But she was also a person who needed her own space. Like a lot of people with a definite sense of aesthetics, myself included, she was very sensitive about her surroundings. Edna could get out of sync with people who didn't share her tastes, so the community she created wasn't without squabbles, mainly caused by Edna and her dogmatism about design. When Lorna Fielden gave specifications for the cottage she wanted built, Edna didn't have any qualms about altering them as she went along without discussing the changes with Lorna first.

Still, their relationship not only survived but blossomed. Lorna was not a handywoman, so when something needed repairing in her cottage, Edna would fix it. Likewise, Edna was a terrible cook and homemaker, so Lorna would often prepare dinner for her, so she had something to eat after a hard day's gardening. Lorna also edited and collated some of Edna's books. When, in her old age, Edna moved to the warmer climate of Buderim in Queensland, Lorna eventually followed. The two of them are buried next to each other under two silky oak trees at the local cemetery.

Edna could get moody when she was in between creative projects, and she did take it out on other people. Her assistants, often bore the brunt of these outbursts and Blanche Scharp once summed up a particularly difficult morning with the diary entry: 'Edna Ghastly!'

Reading about Edna's faults only makes me like her more, as they did the many people who knew her over her lifetime.

There was a study published by the *British Journal of Psychology* that offended a lot of extroverts by suggesting that many loners – rather than simply being socially awkward – were more intelligent than the general population. The study suggested the reason for this was that loners tended to be self-reliant and able to solve problems on their own, while less intelligent people needed a group effort to solve theirs! While that study was controversial, it did make some sense to me. Intelligent people need to be alone sometimes to incubate their genius and their masterpieces. They get exhausted by small talk. Somebody who is creating great art or working on a cure for cancer probably doesn't want their mind cluttered with inane details about the Kardashians, gossip or conspiracy theories. Unfortunately, that sort of resistance to 'participating' and 'chit-chat' often sees them labelled as 'loners', 'aloof' or just plain 'snobs'.

Studying Edna's life brings this into clearer perspective. She once wrote to a friend that 'socialising' was a crashing bore and she hated it. Yet, she had no shortage of sincere and lifelong friends. Edna meets the very definition of an emboldened person: she did exactly what she was most passionate about and had a great sense of purpose to her life. But while she was certainly her own person, with a unique point of view, she didn't achieve all she did without support. The most important thing she emphasised in her life was not community as such, but the importance of a *like-minded* one. Edna was very selective about who she kept company with. If she didn't like someone – or thought they were a fool or their ideas were dull – she moved on.

We are constantly told that we are made for community, and social connections are very important. I do believe that's true. But Edna's approach highlights something else that needs to be considered: a community is only as healthy as the individuals within it. There are plenty of sick communities that insist everybody conforms to a certain way of thinking. They are not safe places for anybody original or different. So, when it comes to being connected to others, there is something of a paradox here: to be able to make deep and true connections with the right people for us, we must know ourselves first, which often means we have to get very comfortable with being *alone*.

~

Isolation and solitude are not the same thing. When we isolate ourselves from others, we are cutting off contact with them for some reason, perhaps because we feel hurt or unable to relate to them. When we are in solitude, we are communing with a deeper part of ourselves and life. Even when Edna was by herself, she wasn't suffering loneliness. She had a deep connection to nature and to her sense of God. It was in this state that ideas would flow to her. By her own admission she did sometimes imagine that perhaps it would be nice to have an intimate partner with whom to share the ups and downs of life, but then she'd consider how horribly wrong that might actually turn out, and continued on her own merrily independent way.

Young people, in particular, were attracted to Edna because of her self-assurance, her fresh ideas and because she was so ahead of her time. In the 1960s, Edna supported the feminist movement and the movement for rights for Indigenous Australians. She spoke up against the Vietnam War. She remained an ardent conservationist, concerned about Australia's wanton destruction of bushland and disregard for its unique wildlife. The young assistants who worked with her would often hear more enlightened views from her than the ones they were getting at home from their parents.

When Edna was staying at her holiday home at East Point, she had a slightly antagonistic relationship with one of her neighbours, a retired army lieutenant colonel now working as a banking inspector. Edna had acquired 16 acres of land for the property, but decided against turning it into a garden or a village when one day she spotted a wallaby in the bushland. She squinted, at first thinking that it was a young man in a grey flannel suit walking between the trees, but when she recognised it was a wallaby she was moved. Wallabies live in social groups and Edna realised that the land around her was the animal's home, and she lost all desire to change the landscape. Later, when she relocated from Victoria to Queensland, she bequeathed the property as a wildlife sanctuary.

Edna was pleased that she had left the landscape in its natural state. Her greatest joy at East Point was to observe the wildlife around her, and to photograph it. It was a particularly good place to birdwatch and Edna spent delightful hours observing the tiny wrens and thrushes that flitted about. A ringtail possum had taken up residence in the space between the wall and the cross beam that was left exposed in the kitchen doorway, and Edna enjoyed its antics so much she saw no reason to evict it. But her neighbour, Mr Smith, was a man of 'progress' and had other ideas.

'Mr Smith is coming up the hill again,' said Joan Niewand, Edna's young apprentice gardener and building assistant.

Edna put down her camera. 'Is he?'

If there was one disadvantage to her new property it was that Edna hadn't yet had a chance to build herself another bolt-hole so she could 'vanish' when unwanted guests arrived.

'Shall I put the kettle on the stove for tea?' Joan asked.

Edna nodded. She didn't dislike Mr Smith. His wife and children were polite and welcoming, and she and Joan had often been invited for afternoon tea in the Smiths' home. But his *ideas*. The man could be so irritating!

Mr Smith arrived on the doorstep, puffed and dabbing at his flushed face with his handkerchief. 'Good morning, Miss Walling. Good morning, Miss Niewand. I've brought you some of my wife's apricot jam.'

'Oh, how kind,' said Edna, taking the jar from him and ushering him into her home, a two-level structure which from its position on the hillside offered a spectacular view over leafy green eucalypts and gullies of ferns towards the vast blue stretch of ocean known as Bass Strait. It was to this view that Mr Smith was instantly drawn.

'You know, Miss Walling...'

Edna braced herself for what was coming. She'd heard it from him the last time he'd visited. And the time before that.

'Call me Edna, why don't you?' she said, hoping the offer of familiarity might get Mr Smith to change tack.

But Mr Smith lurched on regardless.

'You really ought to cut down all these trees,' he said. 'Then you'd have a view straight to the sea.'

There, he'd said it. Exactly the thing that usually hit Edna's nerves like an electric shock. Joan braced herself. When irritated, her boss could be acerbic. But Edna was in her fifties now. She'd learned to calm her tongue somewhat and win people over to her ideas slowly. 'You attract more bees with honey than vinegar,' her friend Lorna was always telling her.

'But Mr Smith,' Edna said, 'The view of the ocean framed by the trees is *exactly* the view I want. Isn't it just grand? Green-on-green then out onto that spectacular teal-blue water.'

But any subtlety was missed by Mr Smith. In his mind, Edna simply wasn't hearing him correctly.

'Who wants to see trees when the ocean is right out there?' he said. 'I'm installing a picture window in my living room so I can look at it every day.'

Edna sucked in a breath and slowly let it out. 'If I want the full expansive view of the ocean, I only have to walk a few yards down the track to get it. And, quite frankly, I think building a "picture window" is a very bad idea. Once you've captured the view like that you *stop seeing it*. You take it for granted. To appreciate something, you have to do a little work to get it.'

~

'You know she's a nice lady, that Miss Walling up the hill,' Mr Smith later told his wife, as he sat at his kitchen table drawing up his plans for the picture window. 'But she has some funny ideas.'

As he related to his wife what Edna had told him, his second eldest son, Alistair, listened from the doorway and realised that what Edna had said probably made sense if you thought long enough about it. Alistair had an interest in carpentry, and so he'd watched with fascination as Edna and Joan had done the backbreaking work of building Edna's holiday home almost entirely on their own. They had dug into the rocky hill with nothing more than picks and crowbars. Whenever they struck a problem, they used it as an opportunity to innovate, such as the large immovable boulder that had stood where they had intended to put the living room. They decided to carve it into an armchair on which they could place cushions. All the materials for the house were recycled and Alistair had often seen the two women comb the beach for old planks of wood and fish boxes that had washed up on the sand, then lug their finds up the hill, the sound of their delighted voices carrying on the sea breeze. The end result was a beautifully curved structure with natural lines that fitted snuggly into the hill. The women had painted it the palest of pink, so it looked like a stone. But there was something else. On still summer nights he had listened to beautiful music wafting down from that intriguing house. The previous night, the music had been unlike anything he'd ever heard before. A choir had sung but not like the one that sang in the town's little church every Sunday morning. It had bewitched him, like Odysseus being called onto the rocks by the sirens. He couldn't stop thinking about it and decided to go and visit Edna to ask her what it was.

'That was *Lacrimosa* by Mozart you heard,' Edna told him. 'A requiem. It was the last piece of music he ever wrote. It's hauntingly beautiful, isn't it?'

Alistair nodded. The music was certainly different to the Bing Crosby tunes his father played at home. His eye fell to a pile of what looked like junk: twisted bits of wire and old wood. Were the women intending to burn it off? Edna watched the young man's puzzlement with amusement. She was good at recognising talent and sweeping people up into the whirlpool of her projects.

'We are building an add-on kitchen,' she told him. 'Want to help?'

And so, Alistair and Edna began to work side by side. The days passed in pleasant conversation about the deeper purpose of life. Every so often Edna would raise her hand to bring an end to the sawing or hammering, and would explain something to Alistair about the music that was coming from the record player.

'Beethoven's *Pathétique*,' Edna said one time. 'Listen to how this second movement is so different from the dark first one. So lyrical, so pretty, so divine.'

Alistair received both a musical and a building education from Edna. He was surprised at how that pile of junk had, under Edna's guidance and vivid imagination, started to turn into an attractive room. She was a magician. It was then he decided to confide something in her that had been weighing on his mind. He wanted to do something unique with his life, but his father had already lined up an interview with a bank for him.

Edna put down her hammer and looked Alistair straight in the eye. 'What you need is to get away from your father – at least for a while.

He's a good man to be sure, but his dreams are not your dreams. Why don't you go on an adventure? Go up north to Queensland and find your own feet.'

Alistair Smith would later give Edna credit for changing the trajectory of his life. He took her advice to explore Queensland, and later, when he returned to Lorne, he was filled with fresh ideas. Together with his brothers, Graham and Robin, he opened a cafe in the small township called 'The Arab'. With its ultra-modern design of bluestone, glass and canvas, it was only one of three Victorian cafes to have an expresso machine in 1956. While modelled on an Italian espresso bar, the brothers also added a Hawaiian surfie culture twist to it, with waitresses clad in bikinis. A feature of the cafe was its live music. The brothers are credited with turning the sleepy town of Lorne into a holiday destination for the ultra-hip. Young people from around the state were attracted to the atmosphere of bohemian cool, and although the activities there were quite innocent – students sprawling on cushions to discuss philosophy and debate world issues – the cafe was viewed by the more conversative locals as a hotbed of vice.

What Mr Smith thought of the cafe, or if he ever found out who was behind the idea of his son going to Queensland in the first place, I guess we will never know.

~

From the time I was young I had a tremendous need for personal freedom and to be independent. I've never been afraid to speak up about things I'm passionate about, even if everyone else in the room disagrees with me. I set out travelling on my own from the time I was eighteen, not because I couldn't have found other eighteen-year-olds to travel with me, but because I wanted to see everything through my own eyes. At the same time, I am social and love nothing more than an interesting conversation. I find the company of other creative people stimulating and I like to work in collaboration with others as well as on my own. I enjoy participating in group dance performances. But there are times, particularly when I'm involved in what I'm writing, that I like to tuck myself away and am perfectly content with my own company.

So when I regained my freedom and independence after an awful period of having lost it, I felt like I'd been given a second chance at life. At this point in my journey, I can't imagine under what circumstances I would consider giving up even an inch of it again. I'm not saying that things will never change in the future, but right now I can't even picture it.

My male friends seem to appreciate – and even admire – my fierce need for independence, but it's some of my female friends who are often uncomfortable with it. I can't help but think that they are projecting their own fears onto me, and their fears form into a question something like this: *Aren't you afraid of ending up a crazy cat lady or dying alone?*

Fear is sometimes given the acronym F.E.A.R. – False Evidence Appearing Real. All of us feel fears of some sort, but it's impossible to live an emboldened life if we are controlled by irrational ones. If we feel fear of any kind, we need to look it straight in the eye. So let's consider those examples in the above question.

Firstly, what's so wrong with being a cat lady? I happen to really like cats. If I could have twenty of them and maintain their welfare and keep my house clean, why not? It may not be everyone's cup of tea, but it sounds like a perfectly nice way to spend my life to me. That aside, let's examine the big one: the dying alone bit.

I hate to break it to anybody, but we are all going to die 'alone'. From the deaths I have witnessed, we don't take anybody from this side of life with us when we embark on that final journey. Most of the time, when people are transitioning from this life to the next, they aren't even aware of the people standing around their bedside. In fact, I'm not entirely sure they give a hoot about anything or anyone anymore. They are letting go and busy concentrating on the journey ahead. From that observation alone, it makes sense to spend a large part of this life truly getting to know ourselves, to love and value ourselves, and to be our own best friends. We won't be dying alone. It is our own self who will be the companion we travel with on the road out of here.

But most people already know this at a deep level. I think the fear of dying alone is more a fear of growing frail or sick and discovering that there is no one who really cares about us or who will come to our aid. It's a fear that has more rationale to it than the crazy cat lady or dying alone ones, and fortunately it's one that we can most likely avoid. But not by becoming so irrationally terrified by it that we create connections with the wrong people or give up on how we truly want to live.

Edna Walling didn't get old and frail alone. In her later years she moved to Queensland, chasing a warmer climate but also new adventures. Even after she had a series of strokes and accepted she was coming to the end of her life, she was still writing letters to politicians and newspapers about preserving the natural environment. She outlined books with the view that others might be willing to write them. She was performing her life's work until the very end, and making sure she left a meaningful legacy. The way her biographer Sara Hardy describes it, Edna had a whole group of people of varying ages, including her loyal friend Lorna Fielden, doing all sorts of things to help make Edna's life easier in her later years. The most touching thing I thought, as an animal lover, is that those friends even made a roster among themselves to ensure that Edna's remaining pets were fed.

A sad thing I witnessed when volunteering with an animal charity was a dying woman asking the charity's president to please rehome her beloved cat. 'I know none of my five daughters will care for him. They will just have him put down. They think I can't hear them. But I hear them all the time, arguing about the inheritance they will get.'

The woman had *five* daughters and not one of them was willing to look after their mother's loyal cat for the last few years of its life?

The biggest regret people seem to have when they come to the end of their lives is that they didn't really do what they wanted to do: they did what they thought they and everybody else thought they should do. They weren't true to themselves. And in not being true to themselves, they didn't love deeply enough the kinds of people who would really be there for them, and they wasted their lives trying to connect with and please people who wouldn't, and sometimes that later group, heartbreakingly I agree, included their spouse and their own children.

I have a friend I have known since childhood, Noelle. When we left school, Noelle knew what she most wanted to be was a mum and a homemaker. Not a 'yummy-mummy' or a 'soccer mum'. Just an ordinary mumsy-mum who enjoyed being with her children. She was a clever young woman with tremendous artistic talent and was shamed for her 'total lack of ambition'. Nonetheless, she stuck to her plan and was comfortable with who she was. I, on the other hand, knew that what Noelle desired was completely the opposite to what I did. I wanted to have adventures, see the world, live courageously and with boldness. I wanted to study and to keep studying, and wrestle with life's deeper questions. I was very focused on independence and a career. I was served quite a few negative platitudes myself, such as: 'If you don't get married, you'll end up bitter and alone.'

The interesting part of all this was that Noelle and I understood each other perfectly. We encouraged each other to go for what we really wanted out of life. Our friendship has lasted decades and has always felt very comfortable. She is a mother to four well-adjusted children, and I became what I most wanted to be ever since my mother put that copy of *Little Women* in my hands: a writer.

When we are connected to ourselves and know who we are and what we want, we will not only be truly emboldened but we can also connect with others at a very deep level, even when on the surface they seem to be completely different to us. And those people will be our greatest, and truest, supporters.

We can be alone but never lonely. We can be with others and be truly connected.

# FINAL WORDS

I hope that the stories I have shared with you have created a restless desire in you to find your own path to becoming emboldened. But on that path, it's important to remember that life is not a filtered Instagram picture or a digitally altered image. We are perfect in our imperfection. We are always changing, evolving and growing. There are times when we can be emboldened, and times when we need to rest and go within, so that we can be emboldened in the next season.

I'd like to leave you with one last story.

Carmen Maravillas, my flamenco teacher, had been my magical mentor. But I did end up being her last student. She beat her poor feet up so badly teaching me that she had to have surgery, and our lessons came to an end. Luckily, she is an artist as well as a dancer, and she continues to paint beautifully and passionately. Juan is still riding his racing bikes at eighty-eight years of age.

But in a way, the loss of Carmen as a teacher spoiled flamenco for me because I couldn't think of anyone else I wanted to learn it from. At the same time, I injured my foot in an accident, so the vigorous footwork required by flamenco dancing was out of the question until it fully healed.

But I yearned to dance, so I took a taster lesson in belly dance, more correctly termed *Raqs Sharqi* or *Danse Orientale*. The style requires strong and flexible feet to ground the movements and to travel, but the dance comes from elsewhere in the body and it is usually danced barefoot or in ballet slippers. So it is an activity that is kind to a dancer's feet. I loved that introductory lesson and wanted to learn more about the cultures and influences that created the dance style. Because its origins are in many ways gregarious and sometimes tribal in outlook, I decided to take group lessons rather than private ones.

I found a wonderful dance school that honoured and respected the origins of the dance. The head teacher, Rachel, explained that it was important for students to devote at least one full year to learning the fundamentals before trying more complicated movements. The belly dancer's stance is grounded, but the chest is also lifted, and the shoulder blades are drawn slightly backwards and downward. 'I want you to imagine that you have sunshine bursting from your heart,' Rachel instructed my class.

The image of sunshine bursting from the heart was a very powerful one for me, because trauma had left my heart feeling like a cold, hard rock in my chest.

I'd heard a TEDx Talk by the zesty Dilys Price OBE, who at eighty-one years of age became the oldest woman skydiver. She took up the sport at fifty-four years of age after a long period of feeling depressed and disconnected from life. She was a single mother, working long hours and living in a drab house in a drab neighbourhood. She knew she had to change something in her life and to find passion again. She took the advice of Goethe – to look at and think about something beautiful for five minutes every day. Because her house did not have an attractive outlook, she would close her eyes and imagine a glorious sunset with all its magnificent colours of pink, red and orange. After six months of this daily exercise, she realised that she felt more optimistic and excited about life. She had trained her brain to be happy.

I had developed the bad habit of lying in bed after waking up in the morning and thinking about all my problems. It was not a good way to prime my brain for the day. After hearing Dilys' talk, I was inspired to get out of bed as soon as the alarm went off and to stand in a belly-dancing pose while imagining sunshine bursting out from my heart. And sure enough, as Dilys had found, after a short while of daily practice I was feeling happier and lighter.

My belly-dance teacher, Rachel, also encouraged more advanced students to take beginners' classes again every so often to refresh their fundamental steps. This would ensure they were always keeping a solid foundation. After I had progressed in my lessons, I decided to take Rachel's advice and repeat a term of fundamentals lessons. In one of those classes, she was teaching a routine that wasn't difficult for me to follow, so I decided to perform an experiment on myself. I wondered if I could conjure up the spirit of *duende*. I surrendered myself to the movements and imagined that my heart was bursting with light. I don't know if I achieved *duende*, but I certainly felt wonderful and an incredible sense of bliss.

After class, a new student came up to me and said she had been moved by how much joy I expressed in my dancing. 'I really hope that I will grow to like the dance that much.'

When I reached my car, I thought about the class and what the student had said, and I realised that my journey with trauma was over. This was the end of that story. I was healed and it was time to go forward with my life.

But that doesn't mean that I will never experience challenges in my life again. Life does not work like that. It's more like a maths class – where the puzzles and exercises grow ever more complex with our life experience. But we can always keep coming back to the fundamentals and applying them again. We can remember that we are resilient, and we have navigated our way through difficult times before. Our sense of purpose can drive us forward and we can remember that challenges are often simply preparations for our purpose. Seeking out passion can enliven and motivate us. And connection – to nature and ourselves first, and then to other people – can bring us a sense of peace and wholeness that both grounds us and emboldens us.

No matter how broken and bruised you might be feeling at this point, no matter how much you believe that you can never recover, it is only the perspective of the moment you are standing in right now.

My grandmother Alexandra stood in that moment, my mother stood in it, and so did Virginia Hall, Carmen Amaya and Edna Walling. I've been there. Your ancestors had those moments too, and yet here you are still. For a reason, for a purpose, for a passion, for connection.

Up ahead of you on the path, perhaps hidden behind mists and trees or a bend in the road is another you. An emboldened you who is beckoning you forward. Like Virginia Hall climbing her mountain, all you have to do is put one foot in front of the other and keep going.

# ACKNOWLEDGEMENTS

I'd like to express my heartfelt thanks to my publisher, Kelly Doust, who approached me with the idea for this book and who, along with my agent, Catherine Drayton, patiently worked alongside me during the many attempts to figure out how to best tell the stories included. My gratitude also goes to my good friend and mentor, Maggie Hamilton, who first planted the seed several years ago that I might have something worthwhile to write about resilience. For this reason, Emboldened is dedicated to this exceptional trio of women.

Thank you also to the wonderful team at Affirm Press for all the care and enthusiasm they have shown throughout this project, with special mention to Martin Hughes, Keiran Rogers and Elizabeth Robinson-Griffith. Thank you also to editors and Anna Thwaites and Helen Cumberbatch.

Special thanks also goes to my brother, Paul, and father, Stan, for filling in the gaps in my knowledge of our family history, and to Roslyn McGechan for being my first reader and also for her attention to detail. Thank you to Carmen and Juan Maravillas for granting me permission to include them in my book, and to 'Paola' and 'Angela' who shared their stories with me in the hope that they might help people facing similar situations to their own. With love and gratitude,
Belinda Alexandra

# BIBLIOGRAPHY

**Resilience**
Alexandra, Belinda, *Sapphire Skies*, HarperCollins Publishers Australia, Sydney, 2014
Alexandra, Belinda, *Tuscan Rose*, HarperCollins Publishers Australia, Sydney, 2010
Alexandra, Belinda, *White Gardenia*, HarperCollins Publishers Australia, Sydney, 2022
Fitzpatrick, Sheila, *White Russians, Red Peril: A Cold War Migration to Australia,* La Trobe University Press in conjunction with Black Inc., Carlton, Victoria, 2021
Pushkin, Alexander, 'I lived to bury my desires', *The Poems, Prose and Plays of Alexander Pushkin*, Baring, Maurice (Translator), Yarmolinsky, Avrahm (Editor), Random House, New York, 1936
Russian Historical Society in Australia, *Tubabao – Russian Refugee Camp: Philippines 1949–1951*, Homebush, NSW, 1999

**Purpose**
Alexandra, Belinda, *Golden Earrings*, HarperCollins Publishers Australia, Sydney, 2011
Alexandra, Belinda, *Sapphire Skies*, HarperCollins Publishers Australia, Sydney, 2014
Alexandra, Belinda, *Southern Ruby*, HarperCollins Publishers Australia, Sydney, 2016
Alexandra, Belinda, *Tuscan Rose*, HarperCollins Publishers Australia, Sydney, 2010
Alexandra, Belinda, *The Invitation*, HarperCollins Publishers Australia, Sydney, 2018
Alexandra, Belinda, *The Mystery Woman*, HarperCollins Publishers Australia, Sydney, 2020
Alexandra, Belinda, *Wild Lavender*, HarperCollins Publishers Australia, Sydney, 2004

Cohan, Peter, 'Four Lessons Amazon Learned from Webvan's Failure', *Forbes.com*, 17 June 2013, www.forbes.com/sites/petercohan/2013/06/17/four-lessons-amazon-learned-from-webvans-flop

Moran, Victoria, *Creating a Charmed Life: Sensible, Spiritual Secrets Every Busy Woman Should Know*, HarperCollins Publishers, San Francisco, 1999

Pearson, Judith L., *The Wolves at the Door: The True Story of America's Greatest Female Spy*, Diversion Books, New York, 2005

Purnell, Sonia, *A Woman of No Importance: The Untold Story of Virginia Hall, WW2's Most Dangerous Spy*, Virago, London, 2019

Purnell, Sonia, 'Virginia Hall: America's Most Successful Female WWII Spy', *International Spy Museum Talk,* 18 November, 2019, www.youtube.com/watch?v=yQSCJNsRJMQ

Seligman, Martin EP, *Learned Optimism*, Alfred A. Knopf, Random House, New York, 1991

Stuhlmann, Gunter (Editor), *A Literate Passion: Letters of Anaïs Nin and Henry Miller, 1932–1953*, Harcourt Brace Jovanovich Publishers, San Diego, 1987

Winch, Guy (PhD), '10 Surprising Facts About Rejection', *Psychology Today*, 3 July 2013, www.psychologytoday.com/au/blog/the-squeaky-wheel/201307/10-surprising-facts-about-rejection

## Passion

Alexandra, Belinda, *Golden Earrings*, HarperCollins Publishers Australia, Sydney, 2011

Sevilla, Paco, *Queen of the Gypsies: The Life and Legend of Carmen Amaya*, Sevilla Press, San Diego, 1999

Totton, Robin, *Song of the Outcasts: An Introduction to Flamenco*, Amadeus Press, Portland, Oregon, 2003

## Connection

Alexandra, Belinda, *The French Agent*, HarperCollins Publishers Australia, Sydney, 2022

Gibbs, May, *Snugglepot and Cuddlepie*, HarperCollins Publishers Australia, Sydney, 1990

Hardy, Sara, *The Unusual Life of Edna Walling*, Allen & Unwin, Sydney, 2005

Kanazawa, Satoshi and Li, Norman P., 'Country roads, take me home ... to my friends: how intelligence, population density, and friendship affect modern happiness', *British Journal of Psychology*, Volume 107, Issue 4, pp. 675–697, bpspsychub.onlinelibrary.wiley.com/doi/10.1111/bjop.12181

O'Connell, Jan, '1956 The Arab coffee lounge opens in Lorne', *Australian Food Timeline* https://australianfoodtimeline.com.au/the-arab-cafe/

Walling, Edna, *Letters to Garden Lovers*, New Holland Publishers Australia, Sydney, 2000

## Final Words

Price, Dilys (OBE), 'It's Never Too Late', *TEDxCardiff Talk*, 9 June 2017, youtube.com/watch?v=zDy2gN4pu7c

# FURTHER RESOURCES

### Resilience

Nash, Gary, *The Tarasov Saga: From Russia Through China to Australia*, Rosenberg Publishing, Kenthurst, NSW, 2002

### Purpose

Gralley, Craig *Hall of Mirrors: Virginia Hall, America's Greatest Spy of World War II*, Chrysalis, Pisgah Forest, North Carolina, 2019

Linda and Tony Rubin Lecture, 'The Allies, Most Dangerous Spy Was a Woman: Virginia Hall', *United States Holocaust Memorial Museum*, 17 June 2021, www.youtube.com/watch?v=pq0UzaRJ520

Mitchell, Don, *The Lady is a Spy: Virginia Hall: World War II Hero of the French Resistance,* Scholastic Focus, New York, 2019

'Virginia Hall: The Most Feared Spy of World War II', *Biographics*, 8 July 2019, www.youtube.com/watch?v=G-n39E8dF_M

### Connection

Barrett, Margaret (Editor), *The Edna Walling Book of Australian Garden Design*, Anne O'Donovan Pty Ltd, Richmond, Victoria, 1980

Bickleigh Vale Village: Edna Walling's Vision for an English Cottage Garden (website), www.bickleighvalevillage.com.au

Dixon, Trisha and Churchill, Jennie, *The Vision of Edna Walling: Garden Plans 1920–1951*, Bloomings Books, Hawthorn, Victoria, 1998

Edmandson, Jane, 'Gardening Australia: Bickleigh Vale', ABC Television, 29 July 2018, www.youtube.com/watch?v=iXi1oaEJ064

'Edna Walling – A Big Hill Experience', *Otway Journal*, 2 February 2016, otwaylifemagazine.wordpress.com/2016/02/02/edna-walling-a-big-hill-experience/

Hitchener, Peter, 'Gardens in Australia, Bickleigh Vale & Edna Walling', Nine Network, 1996, www.youtube.com/watch?v=xpPuoGdv6hQ

Walling, Edna, *Gardens in Australia: Their Design and Care*, Bloomings Books, Hawthorn, Victoria, 1999

Walling, Edna, *The Australian Roadside*, Oxford University Press, Sydney, 1952

Walling, Edna, *A Gardener's Log*, Viking, Sydney, 2003